The Secret Kingdom for Educators

By the Dean and Faculty of
Regent University School of Education

Edited by Alan Arroyo, Ed.D.
and Hope Jordan, Ph.D.

Adapted from:
The Secret Kingdom:
Your Path to Peace, Love,
and Financial Security
By Pat Robertson

Learning Solutions

New York   Boston   San Francisco
London   Toronto   Sydney   Tokyo   Singapore   Madrid
Mexico City   Munich   Paris   Cape Town   Hong Kong   Montreal

Pearson Learning Solutions, 501 Boylston Street, Suite 900, Boston, MA 02116
A Pearson Education Company
www.pearsoned.com

Printed in the United States of America

1 2 3 4 5 6 7 8 9 10 V0CR 16 15 14 13 12 11

000200010270646226

CG

ISBN 10: 0-558-81397-6
ISBN 13: 978-0-558-81397-0

CONTENTS

FOREWORD

L ate in the 1970s, I found myself involved increasingly in the policies of our nation at home and abroad. More than anything, I wanted to know how the world works and what programs would make it better. I spent at least five years praying for wisdom and clear answers.

Then one day a simple thought revolutionized my thinking, and this is what it is. As Christians, we believe that Jesus Christ is God. That is precisely what He said when He claimed, "I and the Father are One."[1] The next stage in that realization was equally clear. If Jesus is God, then His clear statements that are not limited in regard to time, place, or recipient are actually universal truths which have the same force in the metaphysical world that the law of gravity or the law of thermodynamics would have in the physical world. In other words, the principles that Jesus enunciated are not just for Christians and Jews, but they apply to all men, in all cultures . . . everywhere!

Armed with this clear premise, my study of the Bible became incredibly dynamic. Suddenly, like nuggets of gold, fundamental, life-changing principles came into view. I outlined ten of these principles and they became the foundation of my national best-selling book *The Secret Kingdom*.

One such principle is what I have chosen to call "The Law of Use." It is taken from the well-known teaching of Jesus we call the parable of the talents.[2] Jesus said, "He who uses what is given him will have more, and he who does not use it will lose what little he has."[3] When I coupled this simple principle with the well-known financial law of compounding and what is known as the "exponential curve," I was astounded at what came forth. Here was a principle that was applicable in government, finance, in business, in marketing, in athletic performance, in art, in church growth and evangelism—in fact, in every single human endeavor. This key principle is foundational to the understanding of all human growth and development.

Likewise, another principle that Jesus taught is what I've called "The Law of Reciprocity." Most of us know it as "The Golden Rule"—or "Do unto others as you would have them do unto you."

Interestingly enough, reciprocity is the physical principle that drives our jet airplanes and sends rocket ships into space. For every action, there is an equal and opposite reaction. Just think how that principle could revolutionize society. If we would not like to have people pollute our air, then we should not pollute their air. If we would not like to be employed as slave labor, then we should not patronize goods that are made by slave labor. If we would not like to be overrun by hostile armies, then we should ensure that our armies don't overrun other countries.

---

[1] John 10:30 NIV.
[2] See Matthew 25:14-28.
[3] See Matthew 25:29.

I deliberately pushed that theory as far as I could possibly make it go. I thought of every conceivable situation that human beings encounter, whether it's in a marriage, whether it has to do with parenting, whether it has to do with the work environment, whether it has to do with politics, etc. The law of reciprocity applies in all of them. This is indeed the fundamental law of human relationships, in every situation, in every country, at all times . . . everywhere.

I was delighted when my good friend, Dr. Alan Arroyo, the dean of the School of Education at Regent University, asked me for permission to adapt the laws of *The Secret Kingdom* to his chosen field of education. Dr. Arroyo is a brilliant educator. In a short period of time, his school has produced the National Middle School Principal of the Year, the Virginia Teacher of the Year, three hundred other Teachers of the Year, and many others whose contributions to public and private education are astounding. I knew that Dr. Arroyo and his colleagues would bring forth applications of the laws of *The Secret Kingdom* which would enrich the educational milieu and bless countless teachers and administrators seeking to uplift educational curricula and the lives of their students.

I hope that this work entitled *The Secret Kingdom for Educators* will prove a blessing to those who read it and that you will find in it a fruitful place of study.

Pat Robertson
December, 2010

INTRODUCTION

By Alan Arroyo, Ed.D.
Dean
Regent University School of Education

"The world is in crisis. We are moving rapidly into a state of social, intellectual, economic, and moral decline. Anywhere you look today you can see evidence of looming disaster; you can hear urgent cries for change. Where can we turn for stability?"[4]

PAT ROBERTSON, *THE SECRET KINGDOM*

Dr. Herman Clark, Jr., was principal of an inner city elementary school in a crisis-riddled neighborhood of low income housing projects where the vast majority of the students were living in poverty. Their academic achievement, as measured by standardized tests, was way below city, state, and national averages. Parents were almost nonexistent at school events and parent/teacher conferences. The crime rate was one of the highest in the city.

Things could have looked bleak for Dr. Clark, except for one thing: he was a strong Christian who had been taught by his pastor-father that prayer and the application of biblical principles can turn any situation around from bad to good. He refused to let the visible world he could see around him dominate his thinking and destroy his faith in the invisible realm of God's Secret Kingdom.

Dr. Clark went to work to make his school a success. He changed the curriculum and hired teachers who were dedicated and skilled. He reached out to parents through home visits and GED preparation sessions. He ran parent workshops and invited the community to become involved in school events. He held extended tutoring sessions for students that included summers and some Saturdays. He obtained grant money to support teacher development, brought in nationally known experts to consult with the staff and parents, and closely monitored the achievement of students.

Most of all, Dr. Clark built a prayer network of churches in the community. He knew someone could do all of the visible, earthly things possible to improve a situation, but until he took hold of the spiritual realm, he would never see deep, sustainable change.

In time, it was obvious that progress was being made. Students were attending school at higher rates. Teachers were seeing improvements in reading and math. Parents were present during the school day and at sponsored events.

Within two years, Dr. Clark believed that the students had a good chance of performing well on achievement tests. Everyone worked hard in preparation for the big testing day. What a joy it was when the results came back that more than 80 percent of the students tested at or above grade level!

---

[4] Pat Robertson, *The Secret Kingdom: Your Path to Peace, Love, and Financial Security* (Dallas: Word Publishing, 1992), 19. Note: All subsequent footnotes referencing this book will be noted as "SK."

However, the celebration had barely begun when the central office contacted Dr. Clark. "Something must be wrong." said the central office personnel. "Students from this type of neighborhood never do well on tests. There must be testing irregularities."

Testing irregularities was a code name for cheating. The test results were nullified and a new testing date was set. The students, teachers, parents, and supportive community members were devastated. Dr. Clark heard them say, "All of that hard work! And for what? We can't do this again."

While temporarily disappointed, Dr. Clark went right back to work. Parents, teachers, and students came to school every Saturday to review the skills and materials of the curriculum. Teachers stayed late and labored well into the evening to plan and evaluate every day what they could do to advance achievement. Parents were taught how to work with their children at home. The network of pastors and churches stormed the heavens with prayer.

When the big testing day arrived, central office officials asked the parents and teachers to leave the premises. Outside proctors were used to avoid any semblance of cheating by students, teachers, or parents.

Nervously, Dr. Clark and the whole school community waited for the test results. Joy and jubilation erupted when they were notified: The test scores were higher the second time than they were the first! No "testing irregularities," just high test scores affirming all of the hard work as a result of tapping into the kingdom principles.

Power of the Secret Kingdom

How did the invisible become visible in that community? They practiced the laws of the Kingdom of God. The Law of Use says that the more you use something, the more it will increase in fruitfulness. The students regularly and diligently practiced their math, read their books, and worked on writing skills. Their skills grew exponentially.

Just as one kernel of corn produces not only one or two more kernels but hundreds, the Law of Use applied to education works the same way. When a student uses what he knows, he multiplies what he can do. He begins to read more fluently. He performs math problems and recalls facts. Students who can read 10 words a minute increase to 15, then 25, then 50. Before they know it, they are reading hundreds of words per minute.

If you practice running consistently, you will run further each time—two blocks, two miles, five miles, a half marathon, and maybe even a marathon. Now there are super marathon runners who cover 50 miles or more in one race.

The same principle works for learning, lifting weights, earning compound interest, or getting an education. It's a law of the kingdom of God.

Dr. Clark's neighborhood experienced a dramatic and lasting decrease in crime. Students and their parents went on to college. His story is just one out of thousands of examples where educators who believed in the invisible Kingdom realized success beyond their wildest dreams.

THE KINGDOM OF GOD AT WORK IN OUR SCHOOLS

In *The Secret Kingdom for Educators,* you will read many more examples like the story of Dr. Clark that prove how the principles of the kingdom of God helped educators to achieve success, whether or not they knew those principles came from the Bible.

Dr. Pat Robertson has graciously allowed us to use excerpts from his best-selling book *The Secret Kingdom: Your Path to Peace, Love, and Financial Security*[5] to explain the reality of the invisible world and the authority of believers to tap into it. When he wrote about the world in crisis in the quote at the beginning of this chapter, he predicted a bleak future unless people would take hold of the principles of the kingdom of God.

We are not the first people in history to face the discouraging secularization of religion, widespread poverty and violence, and intrusive governmental intervention—including in education—which is the subject of this book. Jesus faced the same conditions in His day. Times were tough, but He said in the first message He preached, "The time is fulfilled, and the kingdom of God is at hand."[6]

When Jesus spoke of the kingdom of God, He was referring to a group of laws or principles that operate in both the visible and invisible realms.

The visible realm is the only reality we see if we view the crisis conditions in the world and man's solutions as hopeless. However, people of faith see another, invisible realm—the Secret Kingdom in the invisible world.

Tapping into the Power of the Invisible Secret Kingdom

As educators become spiritually mature and tap into the kingdom of God, they will realize greater success in their profession. Highly successful educators are often people of faith. They know that prayer helps them to achieve educational results even when their students experience hardship and live in poor socio-economic conditions. When teachers tap into the invisible realm with all of its power, students reap the benefits. Educators that grow in their faith seem to humbly accept challenges others avoid, work well in a team because of their mandate to love one another, and persevere in the skills they need to facilitate the highest level of learning in their students. Even if the teachers never talk about their faith openly or pray in the classroom, God is at work in them and through His eternal principles.

Dr. Robertson said he came to understand this Secret Kingdom after "I mused over this for many weeks and months, tracking through Scriptures, praying for wisdom, and talking with one or two friends. As I badgered the Lord for wisdom, I began to realize that there are principles in the kingdom as enunciated by Jesus Christ and that they are as valid for our lives as the laws of thermodynamics or the law of gravity. The physical laws are immutable, and I soon saw the kingdom laws are equally so."[7]

The purpose of this book is to empower you as an educator to tap into the immutable laws of the kingdom of God so that you can understand how they can operate

---

[5] SK
[6] Mark 1:15 NKJV.
[7] SK, 47.

for you and those whose lives you touch. We will describe every law as it applies to education and give you models to help you understand the concepts. We will give you some specific examples to apply the laws to your educational setting. We trust that this book will assist you in using these laws and also inspire you to seek the Lord and the kingdom of God for yourself in all areas of your life.

REGENT UNIVERSITY'S CONTRIBUTION—UNITY WITH DIVERSITY

One of the unique and positive features of *The Secret Kingdom for Educators* is that all of the contributors are members of the faculty of the Regent University School of Education in Virginia Beach, Virginia, founded by Dr. Pat Robertson. We have unity in our faith in Jesus Christ, but we also come from a diverse array of cultures, experiences, and educational orientations.

Collectively, the team represents several major Christian denominations, independent churches, and predominately Black American congregations. We may not agree on certain historical, political, and educational perspectives, but we agree on most of the information in this book. Although the opinion of one contributor may not reflect the opinion of all of the contributors, we have such freedom in Christ that we still have unity in our basic, core Christian beliefs! We are also professional educators with hundreds of combined years of experience in public and Christian schools. We acknowledge that there are many social, economic, and political forces impacting education today and seriously consider them in our teaching and scholarship endeavors. In this book, however, we focus on a force not usually discussed in professional education circles, the force of the unseen and how that may affect teaching and learning relationships.

We believe that the unique range of educational orientations, writing styles, and approaches that we bring to this book will make it a worthwhile experience for a diverse group of readers because we know that educators come from a wide range of educational and faith perspectives. There is a long and wide table in God's kingdom. Even if you do not agree with one or more authors, we trust that you will keep reading because the whole is greater than the sum of its parts.

HOW WE HAVE ORGANIZED THIS BOOK

Here is a brief overview of how we have organized the book for you.

Section I (Chapters 1-3) begins with a broad historical view of how American education developed to its current state, including the spiritual underpinnings. You will also find a framework and overview that will help you to understand how the laws presented by Dr. Robertson in *The Secret Kingdom* apply to education. We make no apologies for the fact that we see the underlying problems and potential solutions for education as spiritual in nature. As you read, you will be able to understand why and see how much the spiritual realm affects the visible world.

Section I will set the stage for Section II where you will find more specific educational applications of Dr. Robertson's 10 laws of the spiritual world.

Section II (Chapters 4-13) will address the 10 laws of the Secret Kingdom. Each contributor will draw upon Dr. Robertson's original description of the law and integrate his or her educational experience, perspective, and broad application. The main purpose of this section is to give the reader more specific uses of the laws related to various educational settings. We know, for example, that some of the laws may be applied in a direct fashion and taught openly to students in some settings but not others. For example, the law of miracles may be explicitly explained in a biblical context in a Christian school or home school setting, but the teacher must be careful that references to miracles in a public school venue are appropriate to the curriculum. We have attempted to alert you to these differences in applications, but we trust that you will use your discretion as to the appropriateness of your respective situation.

Section III (Chapter 14) includes specific recommendations for teachers for the application of each law. We learned early in our exploration that secular research and evidence-based information support the application recommendations in Chapter 14. In the vast majority of cases, these practical ideas can be used in any setting, secular or Christian. Forms and surveys connected to the information in Chapter 14 will also appear in the Appendices.

The Appendices are special sections that we are making available for those who want to venture deeper into the concepts we have touched on in this book.

Appendix A. The Beatitude Journey—Personal Applications for Christian Educators embarking on a more personal spiritual journey of faith
Appendix B. Multiple Intelligences and Learning Styles Inventories
Appendix C. Understanding Reciprocal Relationships
Appendix D. Qualities of Industriousness
Appendix E. A Culture of Unity
Appendix F. Fidelity Self-Assessment
Appendix G. Embracing Change Inventory
Appendix H. Assessment of Caring Teacher Behaviors
Appendix I. Responsibility for 21st Century Instructional Proficiency
Appendix J. Innovations for Success
Appendix K. Moral Authority Case Study
Appendix L. Post Assessment: Ten Professional Standards for Practicing the Secret Kingdom Principles

We suggest that you read the book sequentially and then return to the chapters most pertinent to your individual interests and needs.

WE HAVE PREPARED THIS BOOK WITH YOU IN MIND

We believe the majority of the readers will be pre-service and in-service teachers in Pre-Kindergarten to Grade 12 settings. Homeschooling parents and persons assisting them in that pursuit may also greatly benefit from this book.

We would expect you to have some familiarity, if not belief, in the Christian faith. However, faith in Jesus Christ is not a prerequisite for reading this book. If you are not a believer in Christ, we pray that you will find that some of this material is practically useful and may even draw you to a better understanding of how the spiritual world impacts the physical reality.

Other readers whom we would expect to find this book useful are Christian education leaders in churches and parachurch ministries. Furthermore, we expect that school administrators, teacher educators, and staff developers may find *The Secret Kingdom for Educators* to be both a spiritual and educational resource for overcoming some of the most critical challenges in education that we face today. We do, however, encourage all readers to apply the principles and methods we recommend within the existing laws and policies that govern your respective schools. As you will see by the numerous success stories in several chapters in this book, educators can apply the principles without crossing the line in terms of "church and state issues."

Since the Regent University School of Education began 30 years ago, many of our graduates have received awards and recognition at the local, state, and national levels for their outstanding achievements. They have been able to perform with excellence in public and Christian school settings because their personal commitment to Christ and application of Secret Kingdom principles is matched by their integrity, their commitment to their students, and their respect for authority. It is our prayer that this book will pass along some of our passion for Christ and our love for all people that have made this institution a standard-bearer for excellence in the world of education today.

Part I
The Two Domains

CHAPTER 1
THE DOWNTURN OF AMERICAN EDUCATION

By Alan Arroyo, Ed.D.
Dean
Regent University School of Education

"The federal budget deficit is out of control, and the world wide debate over ecology and the environment is escalating as never before. Anyone can see that the problems are getting worse and the people of America and the entire world are reaching a point of desperation. Some people are apparently willing to try solutions that are not well thought out or well reasoned, just to make a change."[8]

PAT ROBERTSON, *THE SECRET KINGDOM*

In 1983, the same year that Pat Robertson published the first edition of *The Secret Kingdom*, educational bureaucrats in Washington released a shocking report called *A Nation At Risk*. It was such a severe indictment of the American education system that the public was astonished and America's top educators were thrown into a panic.
It said:

"If an unfriendly foreign power had attempted to impose on America the mediocre educational performance that exists today, we might well have viewed it as an act of war."[9]

U. S. DEPT. OF EDUCATION, *A NATION AT RISK* (1983)

Achievement scores were down. Approximately 13 percent of America's 17-year-olds were functionally illiterate, and the functional illiteracy rate among minorities was a staggering 40 percent. The performance of high school students on math and science tests paled in comparison to other developed countries, and "on 19 academic tests American students were never first or second and, in comparison with other industrialized nations, were last seven times."[10] The experts issued a clarion call for academically rigorous standards and regular measurements of student performance to determine compliance with those standards.
What happened as a result? Did educators rescue this sinking ship and sail on into a future filled with promise for the greatest nation in the world? In many cases, that was

---

[8] SK, 19.
[9] National Commission on Excellence in Education, *A Nation At Risk: The Imperative for Educational Reform* (Washington, DC: U.S. Government Printing Office, April 1983), accessed 2010, http://www2.ed.gov/pubs/NatAtRisk/risk.html.
[10] *A Nation At Risk.*

simply not the case. While some progress was made, the single most important issue was never identified or addressed, so the problem was never solved.

WHAT AMERICAN EDUCATORS NEED

When Dr. Robertson published the next edition of *The Secret Kingdom* in 1992, which we have used as the foundation for this book, many of the educators' recommendations still had not been uniformly implemented.

Now it is almost three decades later, but today's news still gives us relentless reports of economic crises, crime in government, environmental disasters, and yes, failure of our educational system. In a report called *A Nation Accountable*, the U.S. Department of Education gave an update on progress since *A Nation At Risk* that included this discouraging assessment:

> "American education outcomes on international comparisons have not improved significantly since the 1970s. International tests show that the United States is, at best, running in place, while other nations are passing us by. Many countries now match or exceed us, not only in the number of years their children attend school but also in how much those children learn. The United States was once the world leader in high school completion, but among our 25–34 year olds, it has now slipped to 10th place, falling behind such countries as Canada, Switzerland, and South Korea. It may fall farther behind yet. The same is true for achievement. On most international tests, the United States is standing still while others are gaining ground. With performance like this, it's no wonder that most foreign children studying in the United States find our schools easier than the ones they left back home—despite the fact that Americans spend more money per student than almost any other country in the world."[11]

U. S. DEPARTMENT OF EDUCATION, A NATION ACCOUNTABLE (2008)

As if that were not enough, experts included statistics that painted a bleak picture of what we can expect from future citizens raised in the environment of our public schools:

- "If we were 'at risk' in 1983, we are at even greater risk now. The rising demands of our global economy, together with demographic shifts, require that we educate more students to higher levels than ever before. Yet, our education system is not keeping pace with these growing demands."[12]

- "Of 20 children born in 1983, six did not graduate from high school on time in 2001. Of the 14 who did, 10 started college that fall, but only five earned a bachelor's degree by spring 2007."[12]

---

[11] U.S. Department of Education, *A Nation Accountable: Twenty-five Years After A Nation at Risk* (Washington, DC, 2008), 9, accessed 2010,
http://www2.ed.gov/rschstat/research/pubs/accountable/accountable.pdf.
[12] *A Nation Accountable*, 1.

- "Although the overall graduation rate for the class of 2000 was nearly 70 percent, for most minority students the likelihood of getting a high school diploma is about 50-50."[13]

Politicians and government officials propose policies and implement solutions that they are sure will fix the problems, only to repeatedly experience the same dilemmas. The warnings given by Dr. Robertson are still true today because we are not addressing the core issue: a lack of balance between an acknowledgement of God's principles at work, the value of the parental role in education, and an organized, accountable system in which to educate children. American schools are struggling to respond successfully to the recommendations of *A Nation At Risk* and other school reform reports. In too many areas education has continued its downward course because we live in a society that has lost its moral bearings that are required to meet the high standards of American formal education across various student populations. We are not seeing the original vision of our Founders for an educated, moral society based on the Bible.[14]

WHAT EDUCATORS WILL FIND IN THE SECRET KINGDOM

No discipline has more influence today than education. Negative forces that oppose Christ and His kingdom know that the best way to penetrate and change society is through education. That is why forward-thinking policy makers, decision makers, and educators must tap into the source of true knowledge, wisdom, and truth in the invisible realm where they can unlock the abundant resources of the Secret Kingdom.

Why was America's education system of the past a global leader, dating to colonial times? Why did we once dominate the world with our literate population and standards of excellence?

In order to understand the state of education in America today and how to restore excellence, we need to reflect on the visible education standards and practices that were in place in the days when we led the world in education. Many of these practices can be observed and defined, like standard core curriculum and rigorous school discipline. We also need to examine what has been happening in the invisible realm of education that can only be seen and understood from the spiritual perspective of the Secret Kingdom.

Whether or not you consider yourself a Christian, we hope that you will read on to see how the standards of Christ and the principles of the Secret Kingdom lay the

---

[13] *A Nation Accountable*, 11. See Figure 6.

[14] Primary sources demonstrating that America's Founders openly referenced Jesus Christ, God, and the Bible in public documents is readily available online. Some sources are the Library of Congress, state and federal government websites, and state historical societies. Look for colonial charters, state constitutions, and other official documents. One useful collection of primary source documents is the Avalon Project of Yale University, http://avalon.law.yale.edu/subject_menus/statech.asp.

foundation for an education system second to none. Educators who use these principles and strategies will be amazed by their ability to foster learning and development in their students. We hope that if educators tap into God's kingdom principles in the execution of their duties that education will be improved to the point of meeting the challenges of the 21st century.

America's Founders Stood Firmly on the Christian Faith

Several historical events have had a negative impact on society in general and on education specifically. We need to look at those events from the kingdom perspective.

Education in the United States was pioneered by Christians. That is an historical fact. Christian schools like Harvard and Princeton produced educated graduates who met the standards of the church and the standards of the world. Students studied not only English, Greek, math, science, and history but also the Bible and theology. They developed godly character through biblical standards under the instruction and example of their teachers.

In early America, every educated young man or woman was expected to carry Judeo-Christian values and moral character and strive to be a leader and steward of a better society for God's honor and glory. They were expected to become recognized both as citizens of the kingdom of God and citizens of the world.

Secular 'Faith' Has Failed Us

Our founders understood that the way to success in the visible world included a firm stand of faith in the invisible world. However, when educators abandoned Christ and became fixated on problem-solving only at the visible level, relying solely on human ingenuity and "secular humanism,"[15] ruling out God, America lost ground in education that has never been recovered. By every measure, it is clear that education's blind adherence to a "neutral" religion and schools that exclude God failed us.

What will "fix" America's education system so that we can once again lead the world? We will stop falling behind when we restore to educators the opportunity to place their firm reliance on the Author and Finisher of our faith.[16] As you will discover in this book, it will not be necessary for educators to march, strike, and crusade for religion to be put back in schools. Indeed, we encourage educators to practice the recommendations in this book within the confines of the existing laws. But the more educators tap into the principles of the Secret Kingdom where they can live, and move, and have their being[17] the more they will be personally ready to meet the challenges facing our field today..

---

[15] Secular humanism will be defined in more detail throughout the chapter and this book.
[16] See Hebrews 12:2.
[17] See Acts 17:28.

DECLINING ACHIEVEMENT IN THE FACE OF GLOBAL COMPETITION

While society continues the unfortunate, enduring commitment to visible solutions over invisible ones, presidential commissions have come and gone, laws have been proposed, and policies have been enacted to close the achievement gap, raise academic standards, and resume America's place as one of the most educated countries in the world. However, many of these efforts have failed. Some have been haphazard and confusing. Conflicting proposals have recommended 50 separate state standards while others have called for one set of national goals. There seems to be little progress through it all.

No Child Left Behind

It all came to a head when the "No Child Left Behind Act" was passed in 2001 with the encouragement of President George W. Bush. Surely, many thought, a federal mandate to drastically improve our schools would be the answer. Goals were set for every child to achieve at grade level. Testing was mandated. Billions of dollars were spent at the federal, state, and local levels. Penalties were imposed if regulations were not met. While there were some success stories and modest gains were made in reading and math in the early grades, overall the country was "under-whelmed" by the results. A 2009 Gallup Poll reported, "Of those familiar with the act, 21% say it has made the education received by public school students in the United States better, while almost half, 45%, say it has made no difference and 29% say it has made public school students' education worse."[18]

Why We Haven't Solved This Problem

We still face many of the same challenges set forth in shocking detail in *A Nation At Risk*. No doubt, laws will continue to be changed or replaced by new silver bullets—solutions with new sponsors, different names, and the same results. However, without God the country that harnessed nuclear energy, found cures for diseases, and put a man on the moon is basically impotent in overcoming the challenges identified in 1983.

Why can't the most powerful and prosperous country in the world successfully address its educational problems? The answer is both complex and simple.

The answer is complex because of a combination of historical events that have negatively affected society in general and education specifically.

The answer is simple because policy makers, decision makers, and educators can still tap into the source of true knowledge, wisdom, and truth in the invisible realm to unlock the abundant resources of the Secret Kingdom.

---

[18] Frank Newport, "Americans Doubt Effectiveness of 'No Child Left Behind,' " accessed 2010, http://www.gallup.com/poll/122375/americans-doubt-effectiveness-no-child-left-behind.aspx.

That is why this book is dedicated to tackling challenges in education by grabbing hold of the kingdom of God.

Basic Questions We Must Answer

Educators passionate for change need to ask these questions:

- What is the historical foundation of formal education?
- Was our country always in an educational crisis?
- How did we get where we are today?
- Where can we find solutions to the most pressing education problems in our history?

JUDEO-CHRISTIAN ROOTS OF AMERICAN EDUCATION

Since the beginning of human existence, there has been some form of education. In antiquity, parents taught children how to hunt and gather food as well as other survival skills. Adults taught stories, mores, and values of the culture to their children that were passed down from generation to generation.

The formal education process and structure as we know it today began more than 3,000 years ago within the Judeo-Christian tradition. Parents are admonished in scripture, "Train up a child in the way he should go: and when he is old, he will not depart from it."[19] Formal education was a long-standing, valued tradition in Jewish culture. Moses told the Israelites, "These commandments that I give you today are to be put upon your hearts. Impress them on your children. Talk about them when you sit at home and when you walk along the road, when you lie down and when you get up."[20] Later, Jewish scholars operated formal temple schools. Jesus actually dialogued with learned teachers in such a school at the age of 12, to everyone's amazement.[21]

Jesus, the World's Greatest Educator

Jesus himself is considered by believers and non-believers alike to be the greatest teacher the world has ever known. One commentator noted that even if Christ had not left provision for carrying on His teaching, "His life and example would have influenced profoundly the whole development of educational theory."[22]

Jesus' apostles followed the Lord's command to go and teach even with the likelihood of persecution and death. After the death of the apostles, the early Church

---

[19] Proverbs 22:6 KJV.

[20] Deuteronomy 6: 6-7 NIV.

[21] See Luke 2:41-47.

[22] Lynn Hartley Millar, *Christian Education in the First Four Centuries* (London: Faith Press, 1946), 10-11.

continued the command to teach people all things that Jesus had commanded.[23] They instructed new believers in basic Christian doctrine for two or three years after their conversion, often in teachers' homes.

---

[23] See Matthew 28:19-20.

SOME ACCOMPLISHMENTS OF JUDEO-CHRISTIAN EDUCATORS

Judeo-Christian Educator	Actions and Accomplishments
Moses (c. 1200 B.C.)	Told parents to teach the commandments at home[24]
Jewish temple scholars	Schools operated for children
Jesus	Commandment to go and teach[25]
Justin Martyr (103–165 A.D.)	First formal Christian schools
Pantaenus (died c.200 A.D.) succeeded by Clement (150-c.215)	Established school in Alexandria based on premise that education requires Bible doctrine as well as literacy, math, and grammar. Inclusive education with boys and girls, all races—unique in Western culture of the day.
Martin Luther (1483-1546)	All children need a Christian education in addition to academic and intellectual concepts.
Philipp Melanchthon (1497-1560) and Johannes Bugenhagen (1485–1558)	Protégés of Luther founded first public schools in Germany.
John Calvin (1509-1564)	Called for "elementary education that taught reading, writing, religion, and mathematics as well as secondary schools for the purpose of training citizens for civil and ecclesiastical leadership."[26]
Friedrich Froebel (1782-1802)	Christian who invented kindergarten said in his *Autobiography* that "you can see at once the reason why my system of education feels itself to be, and in fact claims to be, an education after the true spirit, and following the precepts of Jesus Christ."[27]
Thomas Hopkins Gallaudet (1787-1851)	Christian who pioneered education for the deaf wrote, "For were the kingdom of God fully come; that is, did it embrace and govern all men; then would his will indeed be done in earth as it is in heaven."[28]
Louis Braille (1809-1852)	Lost his vision at the age of three. At age 15 he invented a system of raised dots so that the blind could read and write. He started a school for the blind. As he lay dying from tuberculosis at the age of 43 he said, "God was pleased to hold before my eyes the dazzling splendors of eternal hope. After that, doesn't it seem that nothing more could keep me bound to the earth?"[29]
Black Churches, Julius Rosenwald, and the American Missionary Association	During and after the Civil War the funding to educate the freed slaves came primarily from Black churches, the American Missionary Association, and a Jew, Julius Rosenwald, leader of Sears and Roebuck. In the first 50 years after the war, Blacks went from nearly 100% illiterate to an astonishing 75% literate.

---

[24] See Deuteronomy 6: 6-7.

[25] "Go ye therefore, and teach all nations" (Matthew 28:19 KJV).

[26] Lars Qualban, *A History of the Christian Church*, New York: Thomas Nelson and Sons, 1958, 250.

[27] Friedrich Froebel, *Autobiography of Friedrich Froebel*, translated and annotated by Emilie Michaelis and H. Keatley Moore, "Come, let us live for our children" (Syracuse, NY: C. W. Barden, Publisher, 1889, available online through Google Books), 120.

[28] Thomas Hopkins Gallaudet, *Discourses on various points of Christian faith and practice. most of which were delivered in the Chapel of the Oratoire in Paris in the Spring of M.DCCC.XVI* [1816], (available online at Google Books), 80.

[29] "Christian History Timeline," accessed 2010, http://www.christianhistorytimeline.com/DAILYF/2003/01/daily-01-04-2003.shtml.

Universal Education—A Christian Innovation

The first formal Christian schools were established by Justin Martyr followed by Pantaenus, Clement, and others in the third and fourth centuries. While most instruction was focused on learning biblical doctrine, mathematics and grammar were also taught in many schools. As these schools spread, the doors were opened to boys and girls, often of various ethnic backgrounds. Inclusive education for both sexes and all racial origins was unique in the culture at the time. How surprised many of the educational elite would be if they knew that "universal education" was a Christian innovation!

Many educators today would probably express disbelief if told about the Christian origins of inclusive formal education. How shocked they would be to know that publicly funded, compulsory education was espoused by Reformation giants such as Martin Luther and John Calvin. Indeed, Luther believed that children needed both Christian instruction and academic and intellectual abilities to be successful, contributing citizens.

Luther's protégés, Philipp Melanchthon and Johannes Bugenhagen, founded the first public schools in Germany. Around the same time, John Calvin called "for elementary education that taught reading, writing, religion, and mathematics as well as secondary schools for the purpose of training citizens for civil and ecclesiastical leadership."[30] Alvin Schmidt, a Christian historian, noted that Luther and Calvin championed formal education open to the public based upon the biblical tenets that "'God is no respecter of persons' (Acts 10:34) and that every individual is responsible for his or her salvation (John 3:16)."[31]

In other words, God desires that all people work out their salvation through faith in Jesus Christ. A formal education from a Christ-informed perspective is pivotal in such a process. The foundation of formal, publicly supported education that was brought to the New World was therefore built on the Rock, Jesus Christ!

The desire of Christians to affect every age group and educational need spawned the growth of well-established education systems that still exist today. Christians were the first to establish Kindergartens (Friedrich Froebel). They created schools and instructional methods for students with disabilities—Thomas Gallaudet for the deaf and Louis Braille for the blind, respectively. They designed and operated libraries (St. Benedict of Nursia) and championed formal higher education (Peter Abelard, who laid the foundation for the University of Paris).[32]

During and after the Civil War, the American Missionary Association sent teachers to the South to found schools and educate the freed slaves. Many of the more than 100 Historically Black Colleges and Universities in existence today were founded by Christians. Funding for elementary schools was often raised by the Black churches, and a Jew, Julius Rosenwald, leader of Sears and Roebuck, donated millions in matching gifts.

Most educators would be surprised that as late as 1932, 92 percent of the colleges and universities in America had been founded by Christian denominations.[33] Harvard,

---

[30] Qualban, 250.

[31] Alvin Schmidt, *Under the Influence: How Christianity Transformed Education* (Grand Rapids, Michigan: Zondervan, 2001), 177.

[32] Schmidt, *Under the Influence*, 186-187.

[33] Donald G. Tewksbury, *The Founding of American Colleges and Universities Before the Civil War, With Particular Reference to the Religious Influences Bearing Upon the College Movement* (1932).

Yale, Princeton, William and Mary, Duke, and Columbia were all established for the sake of propagating the Christian faith. Even well-known institutions that are now public, such as the University of Kentucky, University of California at Berkeley, and the University of Tennessee, have faith-based roots.

LOSS OF FAITH IN THE INVISIBLE AND FIXATION ON THE VISIBLE WORLD

The original vision of Christian educational pioneers was not only to produce educated graduates by the world's standards but also to develop young men and women with the Judeo-Christian values and moral character to be leaders and stewards of a better society for God's honor and glory.

What happened? Judging from the current state of the mainstream culture and a society that has lost its moral bearings, the formal education system has yet to be successful in seeing the original vision become reality. Although universal, formal education from kindergarten to higher education was originally motivated by the desire to develop an educated citizenry with the morals and values of the Judeo-Christian perspective, these goals slowly changed to eliminate the Christian aspects. Instead of seeking first God's invisible kingdom, most educators began relying only on visible realities. Reliance on the Author and Finisher of our faith was replaced by the religion of secular humanism. Eventually, even the mention of God became a forbidden act in many public schools across the nation.

Unbalancing Education

The old analogy of the frog and the boiling water is alive and well in the saga of American education: A frog will obviously avoid a pot of rolling, boiling water. However, if he is placed in a pot of water at room temperature and the heat is slowly increased to boiling, the frog is soup before he knows it. The balance in temperature was disrupted by the gradual introduction of heat eventually creating an untenable situation for the frog.

In like manner, little by little the balance of acknowledging God's principles, valuing positive parental involvement, and operating effective education systems was upset. Did the unbalancing of actions that made American education so strong cause it to decline? Changes crept up slowly, but steadily, as you will see in the coming sections of this chapter.

HOW AMERICAN EDUCATION BECAME WORLD-RENOWNED

The early explorers and settlers who came from Europe to America were not only motivated by the visible or tangible wealth that the New World might bring them; they were also excited by the prospect of being able to live, worship and educate their children according to their particular Christian beliefs. They desired to exchange their visible kingdom where they only knew repression and religious bigotry to a place where they could experience the kingdom of God. This fact is especially evident when we study the early English settlers in Virginia and New England.

Spiritual Growth Fostered Academic Increase

From the settling of Jamestown (1608) and Plymouth (1620) through the mid 1600s, parents and clergy emphasized these two goals of education:

1. Spiritual growth through the study of the Bible
2. Development of an educated citizenry through reading, writing, and civics

However, in the 1640s it was noted that second and third generations were spending more time on establishing settlements than on educating their young in literacy and citizenship skills. Historian Edward Eggleston observed that the conquering of the land made for good settlers but poor spellers and writers.[34]

Colonists in both Virginia and New York reacted to the fears that a brave but uneducated population was soon to govern this new world and passed laws that required parents to ensure that their children read and understood the principles of religion and the laws of their respective settlements. Massachusetts, Connecticut, and other colonies went a step further. They passed laws requiring towns to assure reading and writing instruction by 12 years of age followed by the learning of a trade or useful skill. The reading of Scripture was of paramount importance in these laws:

> "Forasmuch as the good education of children is of singular behoof and benefit to any Common-wealth . . . to learn some short orthodox catechism without book, that they may be able to answer unto the questions that shall be propounded to them out of such catechism by their parents or masters or any of the Select men [local government leaders]. . . . And further that all parents and masters do breed & bring up their children & apprentices in some honest lawful calling, labour or imployment, either in husbandry, or some other trade profitable for themselves."[35]
>
> MASSACHUSETTS BAY SCHOOL LAW (1642)

Tax-supported schools began in Virginia, Maryland, and New York by 1689.[36] Eventually, most of the other colonies required governments to assure that the children were being educated.

The early colonial account on the establishment of formal, tax supported education systems that emphasized biblical Christian teaching appears to be in keeping

---

[34] Edward Eggleston, *The Transit of Civilization* (New York: Appleton & Co., 1961), 233.

[35] *Massachusetts Bay School Law* (1642), accessed 2010,

http://www.constitution.org/primarysources/schoollaw1642.html.

[36] Lawrence Cremin, *American Education: The Colonial Experience 1607-1783* (Harper & Row, 1970), 125 and 183.

with Luther's and Calvin's ideas on education. Indeed, what would be wrong with a government-supported system that mandated the teaching of Scripture with literacy and civic education? The fledgling colonies needed an educated citizenry from a Judeo-Christian perspective.

Some may argue that government support and mandates were needed for the establishment of an education system to generate a citizenry with the academic training and skills to build a just and moral society. Indeed, there was a seemingly productive combination of an abiding faith in God, formal schooling, and local government responsibility at one point in early American history. Others may counter that shifting the ultimate responsibility for formal education from the family and the church to the government took the pressure off of parents to "train up their children", setting the stage for parents to take a secondary role in the education process. Still others may assert that well-intentioned government involvement actually increased the probability of taking God out of the schools. You may form one of the above positions or draw other conclusions after reading the remainder of this chapter. Did something affect the balance that eventually impacted the entire education system?

COMMON SCHOOL MOVEMENT

As time went on, the movement for government-supported schools—and even government-mandated schools—increased into a national movement. By the mid-19th century, the abolition of slavery and the influx of immigrants created the need to educate as many children as possible to perpetuate American values of "a sense of justice, a love of mankind, and a devotion to duty."[37]

No one championed the movement more than Horace Mann, first secretary of education in Massachusetts. Most scholars credit Mann with transforming a hodgepodge of schools into a state-run school system where every child was entitled to a free education and where a literate and moral society could be shaped.[38]

Mann later published his ideas on the Common School Movement, as it came to be called, in his *Annual Reports on Education*. His ideas swept the nation and shaped the development of American public education for the next half century. A well-intentioned person saw a visible need. However, did he seek the invisible faith world first to solve problems as earlier progenitors of education had done?

Mann has been described as a "religious" person who often referred to God in phrases such as - the all wise Author of the universe.[39] He desired to create an education system that would instill Christian values in youth without promoting any one denomination. Mann's proposition sounds reasonable. Indeed, Mann promoted the reading of the Bible in schools and exhorted educators to "train them [students] up to the love of God and the love of man; to make the perfect example of Jesus Christ lovely in their eyes."[40]

---

[37] William F. Cox, Jr., *Tyranny through Public Education* (Longwood, FL: Xulon Press, 2003), 279.

[38] Cremin.

[39] Horace Mann, *Life and Works of Horace Mann*, Vol. II (Boston: Lee and Shepard Publishers, 1891; available online at Google Books), 227.

[40] Mann, *Life and Works*, 19-20.

Human Goodness Replaces Voice of God

However, by delving into Mann's past and his "theology" we can better understand the limits of his "religion." Horace Mann was born into a Calvinist family but became a Unitarian at the age of 23. Unitarianism was born out of the Enlightenment period in history where the belief only in the natural, visible order of things replaced faith in an unseen spirit and reality.

Mann believed in the basic goodness of humans who had it in themselves to create a just, compassionate society. He believed that "natural religion,"[41] as opposed to "revealed religion,"[42] was needed in the schools. He called educators to teach so that "the human intellect, under a course of judicious culture, can be made to grow brighter and brighter, like the rising sun, until it shall shed its light over the dark problems of humanity."[43] According to Mann's Enlightenment tradition, the power to transform the world comes more from the human heart than it does from the voice of God.

Mann proposed that scriptures could be read in school but he limited readings to certain passages. Passages dealing with moral behavior, the joys of heaven, and a loving God could be read in schools but not directly taught and discussed with students. Portions of Scripture that referred to ultimate judgment and the need for repentance and salvation were to be avoided.[44]

Mann's shift away from his Calvinist upbringing seemed to move him to an adherence to a natural religion where the whole spirit and truth of the Gospel was not overtly taught and practiced. Instead of building on the kingdom of God, as early Christian proponents of formal education had done, he developed a hybrid, camouflaged version of the humanistic Enlightenment philosophy as the foundation for the Common School Movement. Mann became a legend in his own time and his principles and practices spread across the nation like wildfire.

One could argue that a state government supported system that still acknowledged God produced a strong nation. If the American education system stayed the course with the Common School movement according to Mann, would our schools be better today? Would Mann's brand of religion be strong enough to maintain a balanced education system in the face of the many future challenges? We may never know the answers to those questions since the heat was gradually raised in the education pot to weaken its Judeo-Christian influence.

Humanism—the New Religion

The goals of formal education from Luther and Calvin were just what a nation "under God" needed. Children were to be literate and trained in the ways of God under the authority of their parents with the Bible as the spiritual road map. However, the water

---

[41] Mann, *Life and Works,* 424.
[42] Mann, *Life and Works,* 423 and 560.
[43] Mann, *Life and Works,* 244.
[44] Cox, *Tyranny Through Public Education,* 283.

warmed with the flame of enlightened humanism under Horace Mann's philosophy. Self-esteem and the goodness of the human soul became moral imperatives in the schools at the expense of a relationship with an active God who is the source of all truth and goodness. The gradual warming of the educational waters brought the pot to a low simmer under the influence of John Dewey and other secular humanists in the late 19th and early 20th centuries.

JOHN DEWEY AND SECULAR HUMANISM

Secular humanism is a logical offshoot of the Enlightenment concept that humans alone have the innate potential capacity to bring a utopian heaven to earth. While Mann's concept of natural religion at least acknowledged God and promoted selected Judeo-Christian precepts, secular humanism denied the existence of any supernatural being or any associated invisible world or secret kingdom. The term secular refers to visible, temporal realities as opposed to the unseen, spiritual realm of faith in Christ. Secular humanists deal with the here and now. There is no eternity. Only human wisdom and ingenuity can save the world. If any entity is to be worshipped, it is humanity, not God. According to secular humanist beliefs, man created God and religion.

> "Religious humanists regard the universe as self-existing and not created. . . .
> "We are convinced that the time has passed for theism."[45]
>
> *HUMANIST MANIFESTO I* (1933), SIGNED BY JOHN DEWEY

Champion of Secular Humanism

No person championed the secular humanist movement in America more than John Dewey. Dewey is often known by educators as the father of a movement called "progressive education", which was most popular in the 1960's and 70's. We will see, however, how Dewey's underlying philosophy of secular humanism still impacts education today.

Formation of John Dewey's Philosophy of Progressive Education

- Secular environment at Johns Hopkins where he earned his Ph.D.
- Charles Darwin's theory of evolution
- Scientific method, not the Bible, as the way to truth
- Personal experience better than teacher-directed curriculum
- Children best prepared for life not by adult authorities but by doing their own projects

---

[45] Kurtz, Paul, ed., *The Humanist Manifesto I and II* (New York: Prometheus Books, 1973). Also available online at the website of the American Humanist Association, http://www.americanhumanist.org/Who_We_Are/About_Humanism/Humanist_Manifesto_I.

> - Government a better judge of education decisions than parents
> - Communist education system in Soviet Union a good model for America
> - Progression away from God to secular humanism
> - Use of education to change beliefs of society

Dewey was heavily influenced by Charles Darwin's theory of evolution. He believed that the scientific method was the only way to truth—not divine revelation or biblical teaching. While he taught philosophy at a number of institutions, including the University of Chicago, his most prolific work came during his tenure at Columbia Teachers College from 1904-1930.

Dewey's basic educational philosophy said that the school is not a place where children are prepared for life by adult authority figures but a place where they should "learn by doing." Problem-solving and experiential learning were the keys to success at the expense of teacher-directed curriculum, content, and academic competency.

Did progressive education develop great thinkers and world leaders in America? *A Nation At Risk* concluded in 1983:

"Many 17-year-olds do not possess the 'higher order' intellectual skills we should expect of them. Nearly 40 percent cannot draw inferences from written material; only one-fifth can write a persuasive essay; and only one-third can solve a mathematics problem requiring several steps."[46]

U. S. DEPT. OF EDUCATION, *A NATION AT RISK* (1983)

Dewey's model had failed. Generations of teacher educators, pre-service teachers, were led to believe that students would pick up the academic content they needed primarily by trial and error, experimentation and problem solving. While some educators believe that Dewey was misunderstood on the issue of the need for an organized curriculum, it remains that progressive education spawned many failed initiatives such as the open classroom concept where there were literally no interior classroom walls in school adopting the system. The students would learn in "centers" individually or in small groups, and choose many of their own learning experiences. They would conference with the teacher every day to monitor the achievement of learning goals, which the students helped determine. The concepts had intuitive appeal to progressive educators but a successful track record was not established as exemplified in the above quote from *A Nation at Risk* report.

Influence of Soviet Education

Most educators agree that students need to become motivated and should actively participate in the instructional process. Certainly problem solving and experimentation are valuable skills for success in school and beyond but Dewey went further. His progressive education philosophy had many features in common with the Party

---

[46] *A Nation At Risk.*

philosophy in the Soviet Union. Education historian Diane Ravitch chronicled Dewey's socialist ideas that became obvious when nationally recognized Columbia Teachers College faculty members, including Dewey, visited the Soviet Union in the 1920s and were indelibly impressed by its education system.

"Dewey saw what he wanted to see, particularly the things that confirmed his vision for his own society. He believed that the gains of the revolution were being secured by educators in the nation's classrooms, that its leaders were animated by a spirit of community, and that it aimed to raise the aesthetic cultivation of the people. Propaganda was everywhere, but he justified it because it was employed not for private gain but for the good of humanity."[47]

In the Soviet schools, everyday life experiences such as removing dead animals from the village road and disposing of the remains were utilized as science lessons instead of taking children through a well-designed, sequenced science curriculum. Experience over content was emphasized in the Soviet schools. The emphasis on student experiences over adult constructed curriculum and instructional practices became the core of progressive education movement in this country.

While science teachers found some of Dewey's problem-solving methods to be beneficial, they also noted that Dewey's philosophy minimized the importance of a solid core of basic scientific knowledge. The teacher's role was to set up a student-centered environment whereby the child could choose how, when, and what they would learn. However, when adherence to a core curriculum with clear standards was lost, the results were dismal.

Again, quoting from *A Nation Accountable*:

"Yet, while we have come a long way, it is a national shame that nearly a third of our high school students still do not take the rigorous program of study recommended in 1983 for all students, regardless of whether they intend to enter the workforce and college after high school." [48]

U. S. DEPARTMENT OF EDUCATION, *A NATION ACCOUNTABLE* (2008)

Secular Humanism—an Insidious Legacy

The most insidious legacy Dewey left in American society was his strict and ardent allegiance to secular humanism, the godless philosophy that still permeates the halls of schools and universities today. As a former president and active member of the American Humanist Association, John Dewey was a major contributor to a document outlining secular humanism tenets and philosophy, *Humanist Manifesto I* (1933).[49]

---

[47] Diane Ravitch, *Left Back: A Century of Failed School Reforms* (New York: Simon & Schuster, 2000), 206.
[48] *A Nation Accountable*, 3.
[49] *Humanist Manifesto I.*

Dewey commented a year later, "Here are all the elements for a religious faith that shall not be confined to sect, class, or race. Such a faith has always been implicitly the common faith of mankind. It remains to make it explicit and militant."[50]

Humanist Manifesto I was written to further the establishment of religion that can be "shaped for the needs of this age."[51] The vast majority of educators apparently never saw the connection between this godless philosophy and the failed educational system.

Dewey set in motion a religion where humans are gods and little humans are little gods. These little gods (our students) determine their own path to education and life since the true power to change the world is within them. He favored the authority of the government over parents when making educational decisions affecting children. Under his system, belief in a supernatural God and recognition of the authority of parents and the church inhibits child-centered education.

The term "progressive" not only referred to Dewey's innovative education methods. Dewey actually wanted to see "progress" away from faith in God to the new religion of humanism, not only in formal education but in all of society. He knew that the best way to penetrate and change society is through education. Seeds of atheism, implanted in the humanistic philosophy, would eventually remove any formal prayer, Bible reading, or Christian references from the publicly supported schools Luther, Calvin and America's founders had envisioned to propagate the Judeo-Christian tradition.

Dewey's beliefs have impacted generations of teacher educators who in turn have inculcated legions of teachers in the core beliefs that God has no place in the learning environment, parents and teachers do not know what is best for students because children learn independently, and content knowledge could be readily acquired, organized, and remembered through experiential learning. Some of our Regent University graduate students report that as undergraduates at many secular institutions they were mocked and ridiculed if they mentioned Judeo-Christian beliefs and its importance in the educational process as well as the critical role parents and adult authority figures play in the learning and development of students. These attitudes and actions can easily be traced to Dewey's philosophy.

TEMPORARY TRIUMPH OF ATHEISM

The infusion of Dewey's humanism into society that began in the early 1900s opened doors for increasingly destructive forces. Events occurred in the 1960s that brought the pot of formal education to the boiling point. In 1963, atheistic humanism raised the heat on education one more notch when the U.S. Supreme Court ruled in

---

[50] John Dewey, *A Common Faith*, based on the Terry Lectures delivered at Yale University (Yale University Press, 1934; copyright renewed 1962 by Roberta L. Dewey; available online on Google Books), 87.
[51] *Humanist Manifesto I.*

Abington Township School District v. Schempp (consolidated with *Murray v. Curlett*)[52] to ban Bible reading and prayer as school-sanctioned activities.

Edward Schempp and his wife had filed suit against a law requiring Bible reading in Abington Township, Pennsylvania, where their children were students.

Madalyn Murray O'Hair, a devoted and outspoken atheist, had also filed suit on behalf of her son, William Murray, to ban the required Bible reading in Baltimore City, Maryland, public schools.

The two cases were consolidated and the U.S. Supreme Court agreed 8-1 that such practices violated the Establishment Clause of the First Amendment in the U.S. Constitution.[53]

> "Because of the prohibition of the First Amendment against the enactment by Congress of any law 'respecting an establishment of religion,' which is made applicable to the States by the Fourteenth Amendment, no state law or school board may require that passages from the Bible be read or that the Lord's Prayer be recited in the public schools of a State at the beginning of each school day— even if individual students may be excused from attending or participating in such exercises upon written request of their parents."[54]
>
> U.S. SUPREME COURT, *ABINGTON TOWNSHIP SCHOOL DISTRICT V. SCHEMPP* (1963)

Overnight, prayer and Bible reading were prohibited in public schools. Twenty years later, in 1983, *A Nation At Risk* gave the tragic evaluation of the first generation to grow up under the shadow of that decision.

CONCLUSION

During a period of 400 years, American education moved from reliance on the secret, invisible kingdom to an obsession with visible "realities," from a vehicle to instill kingdom-of-God principles into school children who would be our future citizens, to a place where the only "religion" allowed to be taught in schools is secular humanism.

The change did not happen quickly but in stages or steps that relied less on God's kingdom and more on the pride and arrogance of humans. Well-intentioned leaders gradually opened the gates to the next level of decline by institutionalizing atheistic, secular humanism in schools instead of relying on Jesus' promise, "But seek ye first the kingdom of God, and his righteousness; and all these things shall be added unto you."[55]

---

[52] *Abington Township School District v. Schempp*, 374 U.S. 203 (1963), accessed 2010, http://caselaw.lp.findlaw.com/scripts/getcase.pl?court=us&vol=374&invol=203.

[53] The First Amendment to the U.S. Constitution states in part, "Congress shall make no law respecting an establishment of religion, or prohibiting the free exercise thereof," accessed September 12, 2010, http://www.archives.gov/exhibits/charters/bill_of_rights_transcript.html.

[54] *Abington Township School District v. Schempp.*

[55] Matthew 6:33 KJV.

Jesus was referring to food and clothing, but this passage could easily be interpreted to include the invisible realm where the secrets of a quality education for our children and society can be found in the Secret Kingdom.

Despite abundant visible resources, good intentions, and hard work, the reality of a literate, educated, moral, and God-loving culture is currently a distant dream. Is all lost? No, not yet anyway. We have seen glimmers of hope in recent history when leaders have used God's principles to tap into the invisible secret wealth of His kingdom with surprising outcomes. For example, after centuries of crushing slavery and discrimination, young Martin Luther King, Jr., relied upon precepts of the invisible kingdom to build the highly successful Civil Rights Movement of the 1950s and 1960s. Much of this change featured brave actions by students and was focused on the schools.

We hope that we have provided a vision for educators to find the power and authority for change in the Secret Kingdom. Instead of relying solely on the limited, visible world and man's intellect to solve educational problems, they will discover a realm where they can find the creativity, guidance, wisdom, and power needed to fulfill the original vision for American education. That is the topic of the next chapter and the rest of the book.

RESOURCES

Robertson, Pat. *The Secret Kingdom: Your Path to Peace, Love, and Financial Security.* Dallas: Word Publishing, 1992.

CHAPTER 2

TAPPING INTO THE POWER OF GOD'S INVISIBLE WORLD

By Alan Arroyo, Ed.D.
Dean
Regent University School of Education

The invisible realm is that "which we do not see now but which will be fully revealed at the close of the age. From the beginning to the end, the Bible teaches that these two dimensions are real and very powerful."[56]

PAT ROBERTSON, *THE SECRET KINGDOM*

I have experienced the power of God's invisible kingdom frequently over my long career as an educator. The most vivid example I can recall occurred when I was principal of an alternative high school for students who were at risk of failure because of learning or behavioral problems. The school was in an old building with dim lighting in the hallway. The doors were locked and could only be opened from the inside.

We were in a tough neighborhood with gang activity alive and well in the streets of that part of town. There was an unusual amount of gang warfare during this time. My staff and I were very aware that we had students involved in gang activities after school. However, we were committed to keeping the streets out of the classroom and protecting every student in our care during the school day.

Seeing Beyond the Visible to the Unseen Realm

One day we had a field trip for students who were performing well in school. Most of the teachers, security staff, and students went on the trip. I stayed behind with a handful of teachers and the students who did not earn the right to go off campus.

The day was going well until around 11 AM when I was doing my usual patrol down the halls. The students were in the classrooms and everyone was accounted for, but up ahead I could see three large figures coming out of the darkness halfway down the long hallway. A knot formed in my stomach because no one else was supposed to be in the building.

As the three gang members came closer, I had two thoughts: these were the toughest looking humans I had ever seen and I was a dead man. Shootings and muggings of school personnel in this city were not unheard of. Principals and teachers were often threatened in my school and others. Unfortunately, sometimes the threats were acted

---

[56] SK, 37.

upon by students, fellow gang members, and even family members. These three intruders could easily have harmed me with no one around as witnesses. I had a good idea what Elisha's servant must have felt when he saw the ruthless Syrian army.[57]

The Bible says that when the prophet Elisha exited his tent to find that the Syrian army had surrounded the camp, his terrified servant yelled, "We are surrounded!" However, Elisha didn't feel fear and trepidation. He stayed calm. He prayed that the Lord would open the eyes of the servant to the invisible world. Suddenly he saw the heavenly host everywhere surrounding the Syrians. Elisha's words rang true when he said, "Don't be afraid. . . . Those who are with us are more than those who are with them."[58] Imagining the worse I could not yet see God's kingdom at work.

When Your Life Is in Danger, "Thy Kingdom Come"

As I walked toward the men, I assumed they were looking for a rival gang member who attended my school. They wanted him, not me, but if I got in the way, too bad. I had a duty to protect the young man they were after from a sure beating or maybe worse.

About 20 paces away from them, I heard myself say, "Thy kingdom come. Thy will be done, in earth, as it is in heaven."[59] Suddenly, the threesome stopped. Their cocky attitude and strutting gait suddenly turned into a nervousness that astounded me.

The leader took a half a step forward and stammered out the words, "Is Robert Planto here?"

I took a step toward them and they took a step back. I said serenely, "I'm sorry but outside visitors are not allowed in the building." Then I added calmly but firmly, "I'm afraid you will have to leave the building.

Surprisingly, the leader said, "All right." The trio turned around and exited the premises. I was amazed but thankful. Was it my overbearing presence that stopped them? I am barely 5 foot 7. Was it my persuasive speech that convinced them to leave? I was so nervous I could hardly talk.

I am convinced that when I asked for the kingdom to come, it did. Just as angels obviously protected Elisha, I strongly believe the three thugs sensed a protection and power around me.

We later discovered that one of the students who went on the field trip purposefully left the outside door ajar so the three gang members could enter. It was all part of a plan to wreak harm upon Robert and anyone who tried to interfere. Their plan was thwarted and one or more of us avoided injury due to a presence that was peaceful to me but unnerving to the intruders. It was the kingdom of God affecting a very real and potentially dangerous situation.

---

[57] See 2 Kings 6.
[58] 2 Kings 6:16 NIV.
[59] Matthew 6:10 KJV.

ABUNDANT LIFE ON EARTH, NOT JUST HEAVEN

The Bible gives us glimpses into the power of the invisible world and how to bring that secret power to bear on events in the visible world. Few people doubt the reality of a visible world. However, Jesus said He brought the invisible reality to earth—with power. We can access this kingdom reality with all of its benefits and affect this present world and eternity at the same time. This message is part of the Good News. Yes, those who believe and confess the Lord Jesus Christ as their Savior are saved into eternal life, but Jesus wanted us to know that salvation is not only a passage to heaven but also brings abundant life on earth.

The Lord wants His followers to lay hold of the invisible kingdom, to seek it constantly, and to make it our primary focus in everything we do. Jesus made this clear when He said:

> "Therefore do not worry, saying, 'What shall we eat?' or 'What shall we drink?' or 'What shall we wear?' For after these things the Gentiles seek. For your heavenly Father knows that you need all these things. But seek first the kingdom of God and His righteousness, and all these things shall be added to you. Therefore do not worry about tomorrow, for tomorrow will worry about its own things. Sufficient for the day is its own trouble."[60]

Jesus is telling Christians to seek, pursue, and avail ourselves of God's eternal principles and set in motion the invisible world that controls the visible reality. It is a promise and a law of enormous proportions. Keep your mind on things above and the things below will fall into place.

This Power Is Within Your Reach

The provisions that we need to solve problems and meet needs in education are within our reach. As Dr. Robertson says:

> "I firmly believe that the principles of the kingdom are God's answers for the world . . . Their insights into the workings of the kingdom can offer powerful solutions to the problems of this or any other time."[61]

Jesus grabbed hold of the kingdom when He healed the sick, calmed the storm, fed thousands with a few loaves and fishes, and raised the dead. When He prayed and spoke aloud, incredible, unbelievable, powerful things happened seemingly out of thin air. Through His death, resurrection, and Holy Spirit we can take the kingdom—this invisible, rich reality—into our own hands, as well, and we can do it right now.

---

[60] Matthew 6:31-34 NKJV.
[61] SK, 38.

KINGDOM POWER TO CHANGE EDUCATION

Teachers are expected to be miracle workers, especially in our current educational environment. Ask teachers about what roles they play in school and you are likely to hear terms such as disciplinarian, student advocate, advisor to peers, nurse, counselor, playground and lunch room monitor, bus patrol monitor, content expert, parent advisor, special education team member, fundraiser, and oh, yes, teacher. The fact that students learn at the rates they do, given the expectations of teachers and administrators, is truly remarkable. Exceptional educators find ways to facilitate the learning of their students in ways that are beyond expectations.

The Kingdom in Action—Whether You're a Believer or Not

Success stories like Principal Herman Clark of Norfolk, Virginia, whom you read about in the Introduction, are big news in the media and education journals. You might ask, "Are there other reasons that Dr. Clark succeeded besides his Christian faith? Surely other teachers who do not have spiritual ties have turned around schools." Yes, since these laws are absolute and unchangeable, the laws of the kingdom work even for those who inadvertently tap into the laws without believing in the One Who created the laws.

For example, you probably saw the national headlines about a principal with a strong personality who turned around a school from failure to high achievement. He practiced some of the same educational practices and parental supports that Dr. Clark utilized. However, instead of praying for the unseen power and resources to change his school, this principal relied on the power he could access in the visible realm. He used his overpowering will and at times his intimidating persona. For a few years, the school did well. The principal was on all the TV talk shows touting his accomplishments. Unfortunately, the celebrity status went to his head and he started neglecting his duties as principal. His great efforts began to deteriorate and he was eventually fired.

Finding the Secret Power to Sustain Change

Anyone can practice the laws of the kingdom and be successful to a point. However, the kingdom is available to you permanently if you are born again, mature, and growing in your faith, exercising principles found in Scripture.

Dr. Clark knew he was putting his hope in the Lord. He also knew about things he could do under the power and influence of the Holy Spirit to apply the invisible principles to the visible world and get amazingly tangible and measurable results, so his results were sustained and long lasting. Teachers, students, parents, and community members were deeply affected—spiritually, mentally, and emotionally for the rest of their lives.

Lord, I want this (handwritten margin note)

38

As Dr. Robertson says, "The Bible, quite bluntly, is a workable guidebook for politics, government, business, families, and all of the affairs of mankind."[62] As Dr. Clark demonstrated, when you put biblical principles into practice with the wisdom that comes from God, the remarkable happens and no one is ever the same.

PRINCIPLES OF KINGDOM ABUNDANCE

Pat Robertson defines two principles of kingdom abundance that will help educators to understand the power available to them in the Secret Kingdom:

"*First*, there is absolute abundance in the kingdom of God.

"*Second*, it is possible to have total favor with the ruler of that abundance."[63]

The principle of absolute abundance is illustrated by God's creation. God brought abundance out of nowhere when He provided manna in the desert for the children of Israel. Jesus multiplied the loaves and fishes from just a few morsels and fed thousands. God's abundance of plant, marine, and bird life is profuse throughout the planet. It is a fact—almost a miracle—that this abundance is daily multiplied three, ten, thirty, or a thousand fold. A kernel of corn can produce hundreds of seeds and each seed produces hundreds more.

The principle of total favor is illustrated by God's grace bestowed on us in Jesus. The Bible says, "And Jesus grew in wisdom and stature, and in favor with God and men."[64] God pronounced His favor over His Son as He emerged from the water after being immersed by John the Baptist. God said, "You are my beloved Son, in whom I am well pleased."[65] Jesus pleased the Father and Jesus passed on that gift to us. The Bible says, "For it is by grace you have been saved, through faith—and this not from yourselves, it is the gift of God—not by works, so that no one can boast." [66]

Taking these two principles together, Dr. Robertson says, "God the Father . . . was going to pour out His grace and blessing on His only begotten Son and on those who belong to Him."[67]

---

[62] SK, 48.
[63] SK, 69.
[64] Luke 2:52 NIV.
[65] Mark 1:11 NKJV.
[66] Ephesians 2:8-9 NIV.
[67] SK, 70.

CONCLUSION

As an educator, you will receive power and authority from the unseen realm when you visualize what you can achieve if you access the resources of the Secret Kingdom. Dr. Robertson says:

"By visualizing the perfect shot, they [golfers] set the pattern in the mind, and then they simply follow through with the body. Clearly, their success with this technique has been spectacular.

"The same has been true with runners and jumpers. God has given us minds and bodies that work that way. Our bodies will obey our minds, for the most part. Added to that is the fact that our spirits can be in touch with God. Now if our spirits govern our minds and our minds govern our bodies, then God in the invisible world governs us in the visible world."[68]

What can you envision for yourself and your students that will take you beyond the limitations relying solely on the visible world that John Dewey and others imposed on American education? What resources can you access in the invisible world of power in the kingdom of God?

In the next chapter, we will give you a Framework for accessing this power source and introduce you to laws of the Secret Kingdom that will empower you in every aspect of your personal and professional life. In subsequent chapters we will describe how the Laws of the kingdom can be translated into effective education practices for public, private, and home school settings.

When you get in touch with God and let Him govern your world, you will learn how to tap into His abundance. Your needs will be supplied and the people around you will be blessed. It will be only a matter of time before your impact on education will be multiplied as others take up the challenge and become exemplary educators who tap into the Secret Kingdom. Then we could see a tidal wave of change that will affect the nation and ultimately, the world.

---

[68] SK, 80.

RESOURCES

Robertson, Pat. *The Secret Kingdom: Your Path to Peace, Love, and Financial Security.* Dallas: Word Publishing, 1992.

CHAPTER 3

THE FRAMEWORK

By John Hanes, Ph.D.
Assistant Professor
Regent University School of Education

" 'You are the light that gives light to the world,' Jesus said.
In darkness, the man or woman who carries the light does not follow;
he or she leads the way."[69]

PAT ROBERTSON, *THE SECRET KINGDOM*

What is this Secret Kingdom? What are the Laws and how do they operate? How can educators use these kingdom resources to bring positive change to their world?

In this final chapter of Section I, these logical questions and others will be addressed as we provide a conceptual framework from which to understand the laws of the kingdom in the context of education.

You will not find this framework directly in the Bible, but it is a legitimate and defensible way to organize the laws so that they will be more easily remembered when you read an entire chapter on every law in Section II. The order of the laws is not prescriptive. Individual educators will approach it with different interests, strengths, and capacities. No one is compelled to begin at a certain point (for instance, with the Law of Use) and then work through the other laws in order. However, these ten laws, when understood and mastered as a whole, will provide a synergistic force with great power.

Pat Robertson's 10 Laws of the Secret Kingdom

In *The Secret Kingdom*, Dr. Pat Robertson promulgates 10 laws of the kingdom[70] in the order shown below.

1. Law of Reciprocity
2. Law of Use
3. Law of Perseverance
4. Law of Responsibility
5. Law of Greatness
6. Law of Unity
7. Law of Fidelity
8. Law of Change

---

[69] SK, 252-253 and chapter sequence.
[70] The initial 1982 version of *The Secret Kingdom* had eight laws, and the revised, expanded 1992 edition added the Laws of Fidelity and Change.

9. Law of Miracles
10. Law of Dominion

Educators' Framework for Understanding the Laws—DO, BE, SPEAK

We have rearranged the order of these laws in a new visual framework for purposes of this book.

1. Law of Use
2. Law of Reciprocity
3. Law of Perseverance
4. Law of Fidelity
5. Law of Unity
6. Law of Change
7. Law of Greatness
8. Law of Responsibility
9. Law of Miracles
10. Law of Dominion

Although the laws could fall into a number of possible logical groupings, in this chapter we shall focus on these three groupings:

DO—What you do (actions)

1. Law of Use
2. Law of Reciprocity
3. Law of Perseverance
4. Law of Fidelity
5. Law of Unity
6. Law of Change

BE—Who you are inside (your inner being)

7. Law of Greatness
8. Law of Responsibility

SPEAK—What you say when you are a person who is in contact with God (praying or proclaiming the truth).

9. Law of Miracles
10. Law of Dominion

Such a framework helps with both memorization of the laws and understanding relationships that exist among them. Here is a summary of each of the three categories:

(1) **DO.** Six of the laws we call sacred-secular laws of the visible and invisible kingdoms. They can be treated as both kingdom principles in the invisible realm and secular directives to action in the natural or visible realm. They are actions you take. They are something you "DO."

These laws can produce somewhat similar results for believer and non-believer alike. We see these operating every day in terms of earthly accomplishment, particularly in business, the academy, sports, and politics.

This helps explain the marketplace success of Dr. Robertson's book *The Secret Kingdom*. Even though he wrote it from a clearly biblical perspective as a Christian author, others outside of the Christian worldview could see the practical application of his laws and principles to their lives and use them to their advantage. As you will see in later chapters, an understanding of these laws empowers Christians to be outstanding educators even if they work in the secular environment of the public schools.

(2) **BE.** Two of the laws require an inner biblical orientation before true power can flow through them. They describe something you are, labeled "BE."

(3) **SPEAK.** The final two laws must be spoken, either out loud or in silent prayer. They are labeled "SPEAK."

WHERE THE LAWS FIT IN THE FRAMEWORK

Figure 1 shows the three component parts of the framework. Note that the sections are distinguished by the three words DO, BE, and SPEAK. The reader should also note that although this volume's chapter sequence orders the laws of Fidelity, Unity, and Change as expressed in the text of this chapter, the sequence for the third row in Figures 1, 2, and 5, reading left to right, reverses the positions of the Laws of Change and Fidelity for the sake of the overall graphic relationships of all ten laws.

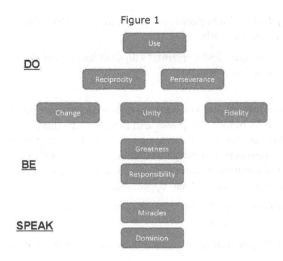

Figure 1

"DO" signifies what you do that stems from the application of the six natural, sacred-secular laws. Each of the six laws involves some sort of intentional effort on the part of an individual who attempts to put these laws into practice.

"BE" goes beyond just doing. The Laws of Greatness and Responsibility involve action, but they also have properties that must become a natural part of the essence of the individual who claims them. If you think about humility as an essential part of the Law of Greatness, it is very hard to "fake" this attribute for any length of time. You are either a humble individual in contradistinction to what the world would have you to be, or you are not, and this will become clear to those who know you beyond a passing moment.

"SPEAK" characterizes the Laws of Miracles and Dominion because verbalization is necessary to execute them. God expects us to take the authority that He has granted us and exercise it through confident expression buttressed by faith in Him.

DO (action steps). The six sacred-secular laws are Use, Reciprocity, Perseverance, Fidelity, Unity, and Change. Great success may follow you regardless of your theological orientation if you work hard (Use) with a giving, sharing nature (Reciprocity) and with persistence over time (Perseverance) and if you manage Change, maintain Fidelity, and bring Unity to your surroundings.

The Law of Use. Using what you have, which includes exercising your God-given gifts and talents, is the key principle of success in life.

The Law of Reciprocity. The Golden Rule should be the foundation of all personal, national, and international relations.

The Law of Perseverance. Those who struggle through trials and persevere achieve the best in life.

The Law of Fidelity. True riches will only accrue to those who remain faithful to what God has entrusted to them.

The Law of Unity. When people share a common vision, they have exponential power to change the world.

The Law of Change. God's spiritual kingdom requires continuous change in the old structures of this world.[71]

BE (personal intent). Two of the laws deal with personal intent. They require an inner biblical orientation before true power can flow through them. These are the laws of Responsibility and Greatness. While these qualities may be seen partially in secular individuals and organizations, it is only through the grace of God that they become inherently invested in a natural manner that exudes true grace and care toward those at all stations of life, particularly the poor and oppressed.

The Law of Greatness. True greatness comes from loving others unconditionally and serving them selflessly.

The Law of Responsibility. Increased blessings require increased obligations to others.[72]

SPEAK (what you say based on your contact with God). The final two laws must be expressed verbally, either out loud or in silent prayer, before their God-ordained effects are manifested: Miracles and Dominion.

The Law of Miracles. In the Secret Kingdom, nothing is impossible.

The Law of Dominion. God expects man to reign over the earth as His steward.[73]

IMPACT OF WHAT YOU DO (ACTION STEPS)
(Laws of Use, Reciprocity, Perseverance, Fidelity, Unity, and Change)

---

[71] SK, 252-253.
[72] SK, 252.
[73] SK, 253.

Figure 2

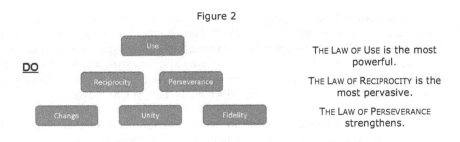

DO

THE LAW OF USE is the most powerful.

THE LAW OF RECIPROCITY is the most pervasive.

THE LAW OF PERSEVERANCE strengthens.

THE LAW OF FIDELITY brings faithfulness even in small things.

THE LAW OF UNITY is central to all the laws.

THE LAW OF CHANGE accommodates action steps.

The Law of Use is so powerful that we place it at the apex of our framework. Dr. Robertson calls the Law of Use "probably the most powerful of the principles in terms of day-to-day life,"[74] and he believes this to be "the most important principle for human growth and development to be found in our world."[75] Like the other "DO" Laws, this law operates so predictably and tangibly that secularists have tapped into and benefited from it without acknowledging or recognizing the Source. The employment of our talents yields mighty returns when harnessed with the exponential growth curve. Jesus presages this approach in the parable of the talents where two of the servants double their gifts, but one merely buries his in the ground.

The Law of Reciprocity, which Dr. Robertson calls the most pervasive[76] of the kingdom principles, occupies the left side of this second level. The Law of Reciprocity pervades both the physical and interpersonal world. Newton's Third Law of Motion (for every action there is an equal and opposite reaction) and the Golden Rule (do unto others as you would have them do unto you) concisely represent the physical and interpersonal realms, respectively.

The Law of Perseverance occupies the right side of the second level. This law is a concomitant of the Law of Use because industrious effort may not come to fruition unless you continue to persist until you prevail, even if it takes a long time. Giving up often short circuits what could have been a true triumph from either a sacred or secular perspective. Over time, if you develop the habit of perseverance, it accrues to provide strength for future endeavors, including the practice of the other nine kingdom laws.

The Law of Fidelity complements the Law of Perseverance just above it. Without being faithful in small things, a person cannot maintain a larger allegiance to greater matters. Perseverance and Fidelity interact over time to produce synergistic—and often extraordinary—results when employed together.

---

[74] SK, 150.
[75] SK, 135.
[76] SK, 114.

The Law of Unity properly occupies the center position of the third level because it also relates to the other nine laws. As Dr. Robertson notes,[77] unity must begin with the individual internally and then spread out to increasingly larger types of organizations (family, church, nation). Even the kingdom of Satan cannot experience small successes without unity. The Law of Unity, Dr. Robertson points out,[78] flows naturally through the concept of serving (which is demonstrated within the Law of Greatness).

The Law of Change is the first law on the third level of this initial section of the framework. It has a natural association with the Law of Reciprocity (just above it) because change is inherent in a reciprocal relationship. In a physical science or interpersonal relationship, if one initiates an action, then a response of some nature usually issues from the target of the action. Accommodation to the necessity for change propels both Christian and secular activities, but God-directed action aims for the most important aspect of change—transformation in Christ.

IMPACT OF WHO YOU ARE—BE
(Laws of Responsibility and Greatness)

With "BE" we initiate serious distinctions for Christians *vis-à-vis* the secular world. Although the Law of Greatness and the Law of Responsibility can be taken at face value by viewing them as imperatives to "be great" or "be responsible," God's kingdom defines greatness in a different manner. Even without a biblical interpretation, you can interpret these terms as you will and live them out.

For instance, many would consider Napoleon as a great man in history, but Jesus would not necessarily consider him great from the perspective of the kingdom of God. Napoleon's power was earthly, limited to what he could accomplish by force, not a result of responsibly following eternal principles.

Figure 3

BE — Greatness / Responsibility

THE LAW OF GREATNESS paradoxically emanates from being a servant. This is pure humility born of knowing exactly who I am (a miserable sinner) and Who God is (my perfect, holy, and only Savior). Because humility cannot be faked for long, it must stem from a genuine redemptive relationship with Jesus Christ.

THE LAW OF RESPONSIBILITY extends from blessing. The more blessed, the more the responsibility to those in need. This is an essential in Christ's Kingdom.

---

[77] SK, 196.
[78] SK, 191.

The Law of Greatness in God's kingdom, as Dr. Robertson indicates,[79] revolves around becoming like a child in terms of trust, openness, and humility. It also means becoming a servant of all. While these qualities may be seen partially in secular individuals and organizations, it is only through the grace of God that they become inherently invested in a natural manner that exudes true grace and care for those at all stations of life, particularly the poor and oppressed. We place the Law of Greatness just below the Law of Unity on our expanding framework (Figure 1).

The Law of Responsibility, like the Law of Greatness, has a special dimension within God's kingdom that far exceeds what the secular world might view as being a "responsible person." In the kingdom, it includes a kind of *noblesse oblige* (nobility obligates).[80] As one becomes more responsible (nurtured particularly by the Laws of Use, Reciprocity, and Perseverance), God holds the person to account to take a greater responsibility for others, particularly the aforementioned poor and oppressed.

IMPACT OF WHAT YOU SPEAK
(by faith, based on a relationship with God)
(Laws of Miracles and Dominion)

We distinguish the final two laws, **the Law of Miracles** and **the Law of Dominion**, in their mode of expression that represents intimate contact with the Lord of the universe. This contact requires submission to God's authority and faith in Him. In return, we obtain that authority ourselves and we exercise it via spoken expression, either in audible voice or silent prayer. As a result, we begin to tap into the spiritual energy that feeds the material world.

Figure 4

SPEAK THE LAW OF MIRACLES and THE LAW OF DOMINION are exercised by expression of the spoken word. Both require God's grace.

We place these two laws at the bottom of our framework (Figure 4) because some believers may exercise them after the other laws are deployed. One way or the other, the "speak" principles will constitute an additional supernatural driving force for the whole entity.

---

[79] SK, 182-183.
[80] SK, 169.

Again, we acknowledge that there are educational settings where the "speak" principles cannot be overtly exercised. However, praying for miracles, for example, can be done during private prayer time outside of your classroom or school.

ENERGY FLOW THROUGH THE FRAMEWORK

In the six laws of the upper part of the structure—DO—a possible secular emphasis may allow a focus on "me" or "we." That is, there may be a tendency to self more so than others. However, when we move down to BE—the Laws of Greatness and Responsibility—the focus shifts decidedly to "thee"— serving those who need our help and care, especially those who are poor and oppressed. The final move to SPEAK—the last two Laws of Miracles and Dominion—directs our attention to "Thee," that is, God, Who directs our execution of miracles and dominion through what we hear from Him and what we eventually speak to ourselves and others. (See placements in Figure 5.)

Figure 5 also presents a possible energy flow pattern through the diagram from the interaction of kinetic energy (energy of motion) and potential energy (energy of position).

The six natural, secular-sacred laws involve action or movement in a broader sense. These utilize primarily kinetic energy.

The Laws of Greatness and Responsibility tap into spiritual energy used on behalf of others. They are more position oriented and move toward a balance of kinetic and potential energy.

When you engage the Laws of Miracles and Dominion, you now move directly into the realm of God's mighty acts that extends beyond natural laws. The potential energy here is unlimited because the Creator has no constraints whatsoever, including the standard conservation laws of classical physics. He is the Lord of all things who spoke the universe into existence out of nothing or *ex nihilo*. As you begin to move in this realm, you will gain access to unlimited power to unleash the kinetic energy that serves God's perfect will.

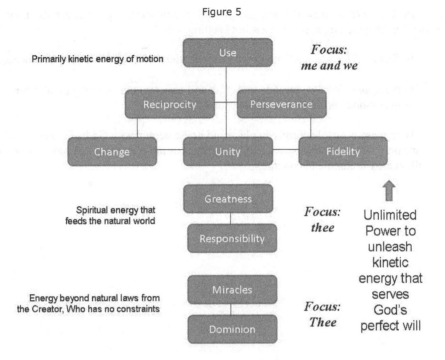

Figure 5

The Cross and an Arrow Pointing Upward

Note that the overall framework forms both a cross and an arrow depending on how you want to view it. From a Christian perspective, all power and salvation flows from the cross of Christ. His purchase of our redemption came at a ferocious and terrible cost and we must always keep this at the forefront of our thinking. This knowledge infuses the ten Laws of the Secret Kingdom and drives our proper use of them.

The arrow shape reflects the overall strength of the ten laws when taken together. The vertical orientation also points to Christ, the ultimate source of these laws.

CONCLUSION

We hope that these visual and conceptual models will assist you to organize and understand the interrelationships of the Secret Kingdom laws as we move into more specific explanations and applications in the remaining three sections.

In Section II, we describe how the laws affect educators in general but also how the laws can be generally applied in a school setting.

In Section III we expand into detailed applications of these principles for teachers.

In the Appendices, we provide tools that will assist you in applying all of these laws to your personal, professional, and spiritual life.

With these principles firmly in place and implemented with God's guidance and grace, we pray that you may approach the challenges of the classroom and school system with unbounded strength and courage.

RESOURCES

Robertson, Pat. *The Secret Kingdom: Your Path to Peace, Love, and Financial Security.* Dallas: Word Publishing, 1992.

Part II
Laws of the
Secret Kingdom for Educators

Part II
Laws of the
Secret Kingdom for Educators

CHAPTER 4

THE LAW OF USE

By James Swezey, Ed.D.
Assistant Professor, Christian School Program Chair
Regent University School of Education

*"The Law of Use...coupled with the exponential curve, is probably the
most powerful of the principles in terms of day-to-day life.
It is the fundamental law for the growth and development—or the
decline—of all organizations and societies in both the invisible and visible
worlds. Beginning with the cradle, it touches everything—child
development, intellectual development, professional development,
physical development, social development, and on and on."* [81]

PAT ROBERTSON, *THE SECRET KINGDOM*

"He who is faithful in a very little thing is faithful also in much." [82]

When I was a young teacher, I used to dream of the day when I would move on to greater responsibilities and increased opportunities. However, I discovered through my experiences that I would first have to demonstrate my willingness to make the most of whatever situation I was in by making full use of the talent, time, and treasure already entrusted to my care. I didn't realize it at the time, but I was learning about the power of the Law of Use.

I still clearly remember the first time I seriously considered becoming a principal. Based on my existing situation, this seemed like a distant dream. I had been hired as a high school teacher, and among my contracted duties was the unwelcome assignment of serving as student activities director and leading the student government program. I tried hard to get reassigned because I did not want to take on those unpopular responsibilities. The student government program was in a state of decline and activities were viewed with disinterest by the student body. In fact, during student elections my first year, many positions went uncontested and I worked the halls like a carnival barker, imploring students to run for offices.

Under my supervision, however, the program actually began to grow. School-sponsored activities became a hit and I had to begin a second leadership class for students interested in serving the school as informal, unelected leaders.

One day at the end of the school year, the principal dropped by my classroom. He said that based on his observations of my faithfulness in fulfilling these "small" responsibilities, he thought I should pursue a graduate degree so that I could become

---

[81] SK, 150.
[82] Luke 16:10 NASB.

principal after he retired. My least favorite duties became the very catalyst God used to eventually promote me to principal of a school! All too often, we are so busy looking at the greener pastures on the horizon that it inhibits us from serving faithfully today where God has placed us. The Bible lays out a clear path to follow: "Trust in the Lord and do good; Dwell in the land and cultivate faithfulness."[83]

The Most Important Principle for Your Development

Pat Robertson identifies the Law of Use as "the most important principle for human growth and development to be found in our world."[84] He explains that it encompasses every facet of personal and communal life, and I would include a professional educator's life as well. He writes, "We follow it to our benefit; we ignore it to our peril."[85]

God gives each person a unique measure and combination of gifts and talents, and He expects us to use them for His glory and our advancement. In fact, God endows every Christ-follower with special supernatural abilities (known as spiritual gifts) that we are to use to advance His kingdom. The Law of Use is God's principle of stewardship and accountability for everything that He has entrusted to us. This chapter explains how you can harness this powerful law to make the most of your life to the glory of God.

THE LAW OF USE IN JESUS' PARABLE OF THE TALENTS

The Law of Use is clearly brought to life in one of Jesus' most famous stories, the Parable of the Talents. As a Master Teacher, Jesus often communicated truth to His students through parables. A parable is basically a story "told to pose problems for the reader . . . It is told to address and capture the hearers, to bring them up short about their own actions, or to cause them to respond in some way to Jesus and His ministry."[86] Parables usually reflect real-life situations and offer a clear lesson when interpreted properly.

In Matthew chapters 22 and 23, we read that Jesus knew His ministry was drawing to an end. We observe Him in Jerusalem openly confronting the Pharisees and the religious leaders as the time for the Passover celebration approached. In Matthew 24, Jesus warned His disciples that the end of the age was approaching and that others would seek to deceive them, but that they were to prepare and remain faithful.

In the next chapter, Matthew 25, Jesus provided three illustrations to emphasize His message. First is the Parable of the Ten Virgins, which speaks of readiness. Third is the metaphor of the sheep and the goats, which refers to the coming judgment at the end of the age. Sandwiched in between these two is the Parable of the Talents.

---

[83] Psalm 37:3 NASB.

[84] SK, 135.

[85] SK, 135.

[86] Gordon D. Fee and Douglas Stuart, *How to Read the Bible for All Its Worth* (Grand Rapids, MI: Zondervan, 2003), 149, 152.

The Plot

According to author Max Lucado, a talent was the largest unit of money in Jesus' day.[87] Lucado explains that a talent represented a lifetime of earnings for a laborer, roughly what today would be $1.15 million for someone who earned $30,000 a year. The context of the parable is important because it provides us with a broader understanding of the response Jesus was trying to elicit from His followers. Here is the story as Jesus told it:

> "Again, it will be like a man going on a journey, who called his servants and entrusted his property to them. To one he gave five talents of money, to another two talents, and to another one talent, each according to his ability. Then he went on his journey. The man who had received the five talents went at once and put his money to work and gained five more. So also, the one with the two talents gained two more. But the man who had received the one talent went off, dug a hole in the ground and hid his master's money."[88]

The Characters

The story presents four main characters.

The first is the master of a household who had three servants. The man is obviously a person of some means as he possessed great wealth.

The next character is the first servant to whom the master entrusted a vast sum of money. By receiving five talents, the first servant was entrusted with an amount exceeding $5.75 million dollars!

The second servant received two talents, or roughly $2.3 million.

The third servant received one talent, or just over one million dollars.

The Challenge

We can clearly see that Jesus was working hard to gain the crowd's attention! I'm sure that those who gathered to hear Jesus teach were beginning to imagine what they would do with such large sums of money.

As Jesus wove the story, the first two servants immediately took their master's money and made wise investments on his behalf and, over time, doubled his money. But the third servant took the million dollars, dug a hole, and buried it in the ground.

Pat Robertson explains that the third servant "was afraid that if he went out and bought wool or oil or some such item, a depression would come and he would lose the

---

[87] Max Lucado, *The Cure for the Common Life: Living in Your Sweet Spot* (Nashville: Thomas Nelson, 2005), 54-55.
[88] Matthew 25:14-18 NIV.

money. Or maybe robbers would steal it. Or maybe someone would outsmart him or cheat him, say, at the weights and balances. Perhaps he would make a wrong decision. So, impotent with fear, he preserved his lord's investment by hiding it in a safe place."[89]

The Penalty

Then Jesus built up the tension. He told of the master's return after a long absence when he asked his servants to account for the money he had entrusted to them.

I'm sure the first servant was excited to share how he had taken his lord's money and doubled it. "His master replied, 'Well done, good and faithful servant! You have been faithful with a few things; I will put you in charge of many things. Come and share your master's happiness!' "[90]

The second servant stepped forward and reported that he, too, had doubled his master's money and this servant received the same enthusiastic response from his master.

The third servant must have grown a bit nervous by now, hearing of the great success of the other two, but maybe he comforted himself by thinking that everything would turn out fine for him, too, because at least he could return all the money he had received. Jesus provided what Paul Harvey used to call "the rest of the story" when He described what occurred next:

> " 'Then the man who had received the one talent came. "Master," he said, "I knew that you are a hard man, harvesting where you have not sown and gathering where you have not scattered seed. So I was afraid and went out and hid your talent in the ground. See, here is what belongs to you."
>
> " 'His master replied, "You wicked, lazy servant! So you knew that I harvest where I have not sown and gather where I have not scattered seed? Well then, you should have put my money on deposit with the bankers, so that when I returned I would have received it back with interest.
>
> " ' "Take the talent from him and give it to the one who has the ten talents. For everyone who has will be given more, and he will have an abundance. Whoever does not have, even what he has will be taken from him. And throw that worthless servant outside, into the darkness, where there will be weeping and gnashing of teeth." ' "[91]

The Moral of the Story and a Warning for Us

Pat Robertson explains why the master was so angry with the third servant:

> "The man was considered wicked and sinful, given to evil . . . because he refused to take what his lord had given him and put it to work, improving upon it.

---

[89] SK, 135.
[90] Matthew 25:21 NIV.
[91] Matthew 25:24-30 NIV.

"Note that quantity wasn't the key. Their use of what they had been given was what mattered. Proper use gave them entry into the place of joy. Improper use barred the third man."[92]

We need to remember that God will judge all mankind and ask us for an account of how we spent our lives and how we invested that which He entrusted to our care. Scripture makes it clear that we will be judged for every word and deed. Whatever we do for God in accordance with His will brings rewards. Whatever we do for our own glory will be burned in the fire like wood, hay, and straw.[93] As stewards of *all* that God entrusts to our care, we need to make the best use of our talents, time, and treasure!

SHE MADE THE MOST OF HER TALENTS

Making the most of what God has given you can take many paths. Roberta, known to her friends as "Bobbie," grew up on the Alaskan Frontier during the years of the Great Depression and World War II. Her alcoholic father often abandoned the family for months or even years at a time, leaving them destitute. She dropped out of high school at the age of 15 in order to go to work and married at the age of 19.

Her husband, who joined the Marines right out of high school, also grew up under difficult circumstances after his father died when he was only six months old. Together they raised six children and after the youngest started kindergarten, Bobbie went to work for two hours a day at a local elementary school, selling breakfast items to students.

Her faithful service as a humble cafeteria worker was soon rewarded and she worked her way up through the food service ranks from cashier to cook and eventually all the way up to district manager. She would also eventually earn her GED and travel throughout the San Francisco Bay Area, providing leadership to various school districts.

She retired after more than 25 years, leaving behind an enduring legacy of faithful service. Not bad for a high school dropout! She explained that God took her from an entry level job that required few skills to one that stretched her beyond her own abilities, causing her to always rely on Him.

You see, God honors the faithful development and use of the gifts He gives us. What may seem like a small talent can go a long way when He blesses our efforts.

AUTHORITY, WORDS, INFLUENCE, AND TOUCH

Pat Robertson describes a trend by the media, academia, and the political elite towards the subversion and undermining of "Christian principles and traditional family

---

[92] SK, 137.
[93] See 1 Corinthians 3:12-15.

values that have upheld this society from its beginnings."[94] He writes, "During the past fifty years these utopian dreamers have all but destroyed public education in America while they have fastened upon our nation a wasteful and profligate governmental system."[95] Increased federal government intrusion in public education at all levels during the Bush and now Obama administrations reinforces Dr. Robertson's claim that the role of government in all facets of our lives will continue to expand. Once again, as America finds itself in turmoil, those most affected by the crisis are the nation's school children.

The Law of Use and the other Secret Kingdom principles presented in this book will give educators hope for righting this ship. Consider the potential impact of the Law of Use at work in the following four areas that teachers deal with every day:

1. A teacher's use of authority
2. A teacher's use of words
3. A teacher's use of influence
4. A teacher's use of touch

1. A Teacher's Use of Authority

While the Law of Use is often applied to finances, the principle easily applies to anything that God entrusts to our stewardship. For instance, the students who enter our classrooms each morning are entrusted to our care by their parents.

In loco parentis is a Latin phrase used in education that means a teacher serves "in place of the parent." Historically based in English Common Law, this doctrine is often interpreted to mean that the teacher operates with the same responsibilities and authority as the parent, with their permission. While implementation of this doctrine has waned over the last century, it is still a widely accepted legal tenet.

Scripture clearly affirms the primacy of parental authority in the instruction of children,[96] although parents can delegate this duty to others, such as educators.[97] Whether in public, private, or Christian schools, as Christian educators we represent our Lord to the students and families we serve and we are responsible to represent Him well, lest we face His judgment. This premise is clearly supported by the familiar admonition to teachers found in the New Testament epistle of James:

"Not many of you should presume to be teachers, my brothers, because you know that we who teach will be judged more strictly."[98]

---

[94] SK, 133.

[95] SK, 133.

[96] See Deuteronomy 4 and 6; Psalm 78, Ephesians 6:4.

[97] See 1 Chronicles 27:32, Acts 22:3, 1 Corinthians 4:15.

[98] James 3:1 NIV.

2. A Teacher's Use of Words

While this warning from James to teachers that they will be more strictly judged is often repeated among Christian teachers, it is rarely discussed within its full biblical context. The warning is immediately followed by an expansive treatise by James on the treacherous power of words:

> "When we put bits into the mouths of horses to make them obey us, we can turn the whole animal. Or take ships as an example. Although they are so large and are driven by strong winds, they are steered by a very small rudder wherever the pilot wants to go. Likewise the tongue is a small part of the body, but it makes great boasts. Consider what a great forest is set on fire by a small spark. The tongue also is a fire, a world of evil among the parts of the body. It corrupts the whole person, sets the whole course of his life on fire, and is itself set on fire by hell.
>
> "All kinds of animals, birds, reptiles and creatures of the sea are being tamed and have been tamed by man, but no man can tame the tongue. It is a restless evil, full of deadly poison.
>
> "With the tongue we praise our Lord and Father, and with it we curse men, who have been made in God's likeness. Out of the same mouth come praise and cursing. My brothers, this should not be. Can both fresh water and salt water flow from the same spring? My brothers, can a fig tree bear olives, or a grapevine bear figs? Neither can a salt spring produce fresh water."[99]

It's no wonder that James cautioned teachers about words because that is how we earn our living. Our words are powerful! They can be a source of wondrous healing spoken into the lives of broken children or they can add to injuries already suffered.

Too many of us use our words carelessly. Some of the hurtful things that come out of our mouths are rationalized as jesting when they are actually biting sarcasm. You can know you are guilty of this if you regularly find yourself saying, "I was only joking."

We need to model Jesus' use of words to bless our students, not curse them. Jesus prayed for children and also spoke words of blessing over them. The Bible says, "And he took the children in his arms, put his hands on them and blessed them."[100] Blessing comes from the Greek compound word *eu-logos*, which literally means "good-word." Likewise, we are to speak good words over and pray for our students.

What a wonderful classroom environment we can create following Jesus' model by showing our love for the students entrusted to our care!

3. A Teacher's Use of Influence

Attention to the welfare of children was of foremost importance to Christ, even in the midst of a busy ministry schedule. Because of our highly influential position in the lives of children, this must be our philosophy of education, as well. One of the most striking

---

[99] James 3:3-12 NIV.
[100] Mark 10:16 NIV.

images in the New Testament, mentioned above, describes how much Jesus esteemed children. It is repeated in the synoptic Gospels of Matthew, Mark, and Luke:

> "Then some children were brought to Him so that He might lay His hands on them and pray; and the disciples rebuked them. But Jesus said, 'Let the children alone, and do not hinder them from coming to Me; for the kingdom of heaven belongs to such as these.' After laying His hands on them, He departed from there."[101]

Jesus' own disciples didn't understand their Master's heart for children. He had to rebuke them for turning them away from Him. Jesus didn't view the children as an intrusion on His ministry. They *were* His ministry.

4. A Teacher's Use of Touch

The need for human touch is one of the five primary expressions of love identified by family counselor Gary Chapman, Ph.D.[102] Jesus understood the impact of appropriate touch combined with the power of prayer. While teachers in all schools need to be aware of the regulations and laws in their region, as a nation we threw the proverbial baby out with the bathwater by often removing all physical contact with students. Because of the increasing sensitivity to adults touching children, your physical contact may be only a handshake, a high five, or a fist bump. But these gestures can be effective symbols of how you desire to touch the lives of your students and vice versa. You can also "touch" lives by lifting up your students in prayer during your private devotion time.

DEVELOPING YOUR TALENTS SO THAT YOU CAN DEVELOP OTHERS

Each of us begins our teaching careers with a certain measure of God-given ability to serve as educators. We each possess various levels of subject knowledge, pedagogical knowledge, and what Jacob Kounin described as "withitness."

For years now we have challenged our students to become life-long learners, but how many of us model this behavior for our students? What have you done lately to improve the talents that God gave you in order to increase the return on His investment?

Develop Your Hidden Creativity

You can experience the Law of Use in your life if you recognize your talents and use them to set new, challenging goals.

---

[101] Matthew 19:13-15 NASB.

[102] Gary D. Chapman, *The Five Love Languages: The Secret to Love that Lasts* (Chicago: Northfield Publishing, 2010).

Recognize your talents and use them in new ways. You need to quit being complacent towards the gifts that God has given you. You need to recognize that your talents will shrivel and wither, like muscles that atrophy from lack of use. It won't happen overnight, but it *will* happen. It's an immutable law! You need to work to hone your current gifts as a signal to God that you are ready to take on more.

Set challenging new goals for yourself. Secondly, you need to set new goals for your life. You need to dream new dreams and take on new challenges. Like the airplane at takeoff, it's important that your goals are not too low or too high. If your goals are too low, you might lack inspiration and never take off. If they are too high, you may grow discouraged, stall in your efforts, and come crashing back down to earth. Pat Robertson reminds us, "[God] wants us to have goals that are demanding enough to keep us occupied, but are not overtaxing, and to stick with them long enough for them to come to fruition."[103]

Develop Your Knowledge, Presentations, and "Withitness"

Consider devoting some time, energy, and financial resources into developing each of these three areas: subject knowledge, effective delivery of information, and "withitness."

Subject knowledge. First, in order to be faithful stewards of instruction, we must continually increase our mastery of subject knowledge. Whether you're a teacher in a self-contained elementary or preschool classroom, a special education or resource teacher, a content expert in a middle or secondary school, a homeschooling parent, or a tenured professor in an elite research university, you must continue to both broaden and deepen your subject expertise.

Effective delivery of information. Second, we must also improve our ability to not only know the information but also to deliver that information more effectively. While you may already know many time-tested methods of teaching that have been handed down over the decades, you and your students will also benefit if you acquire innovative practices that expand your pedagogical repertoire.

"Withitness." Finally, consider how you might improve your "withitness." Jere Brophy defined withitness as:

> ". . . remaining 'with it' (aware of what is happening in all parts of the classroom at all times), even when working with small groups or individuals. [It] is also demonstrating this withitness to students by intervening promptly and accurately when inappropriate behavior threatens to become disruptive."[104]

---

[103] SK, 143.
[104] Jere E. Brophy, *Teaching Problem Students* (New York: Guilford Press, 1996), 11.

The debate continues as to whether or not withitness is something that is inherent in teachers and is therefore static or if it is malleable and teachers can be taught to improve in this area by "growing eyes in the backs of their heads."[105]

Madeleine Kovarik believes that teachers can increase their withitness in seven ways. This is another example of how the Law of Use can be applied to improve your effectiveness as a teacher.

1. Build relationships with your students.
2. Create a visually open environment.
3. Separate yourself from your students' actions so that you can remain objective.
4. Move around the classroom.
5. Face students as much as possible.
6. Plan ahead for good transitions.
7. Stop misbehavior before it escalates.[106]

Be sure to keep practicing and using these skills! If the examples listed above are not second nature to you now, they soon will be.

EXPONENTIAL IMPACT WHEN YOU APPLY THE LAW OF USE[107]

Properly applied, the Law of Use will bear fruit in your students' lives and throughout your lifetime. When coupled with the principle of the exponential curve, it can potentially yield a harvest too large to measure!

Law of Use and Financial Increase

Pat Robertson describes the amazing financial implications of the exponential curve in the Law of Use when he tells how a person can turn $100 into more than $50 million. If someone were to double $100 annually for 20 years, that person would generate $52,428,800! He goes on to explain how in just five more years it would grow into $1.6 billion and after another ten years, $1.6 trillion! Of course even that amount would barely begin to address our national debt, but you get the picture.

Law of Use and Schools of Education

Another example of the exponential curve can be observed corporately through the impact of educational organizations. For instance, Regent University's School of Education was established in 1980 as a graduate school of education with three faculty members and a dean. The school's first graduation ceremony found only a single woman walking across

---

[105] Madeleine Kovarik, "Being a With-It Teacher," *New Teacher Advocate 16*, no. 2 (Winter 2008), 10.
[106] Kovarik, 10.
[107] SK, 139.

the school's steps to receive her diploma. Yet, just 30 short years later, the graduating class of 2010 mushroomed to 183, including 23 students with doctoral degrees.

By running a conservative statistical model to estimate how many students those teachers' lives have touched, Regent's faculty estimated that more than a million K-12 students have been impacted by the school's graduates over the past 30 years. And to demonstrate the amazing power of the exponential curve, assuming modest growth in school enrollment, over the *next* 30 years Regent School of Education graduates will reach more than 50 million students!

Law of Use for World Evangelization and Discipleship

If Christians were to apply the principle of the exponential curve and the Law of Use to the process of making disciples, in a matter of years we could win people to Christ worldwide and train them in biblical principles. Sadly, individually and corporately, Christians are failing at the task of Jesus' Great Commission. Jesus said:

> "All authority in heaven and on earth has been given to me. Therefore go and make disciples of all nations, baptizing them in the name of the Father and of the Son and of the Holy Spirit, and teaching them to obey everything I have commanded you. And surely I am with you always, to the very end of the age."[108]

Consider how different things could be if each believer brought just one other person to the Lord each year. Wendell Miller ran the mathematical equation and discovered an astonishing possibility:

> "If each believer won and discipled one person each year, and if each newly-discipled believer won and discipled one person per year, starting with one believer … at the end of one year there would be two believers, at the end of two years there would be four believers, at the end of three years there would be eight believers, and at the end of four years there would be sixteen believers. Assuming that this mathematical increase were continued for 36 years, the total number of Christians would exceed 6 billion. This mathematical example shows the power of God's plan for explosive reproduction."[109]

It is a staggering example of the potential of the Law of Use.

BEWARE THE POLITICS OF ENVY

One of the greatest barriers to successful implementation of the Law of Use is what Pat Robertson describes as the politics of envy[110] and the evil twin of lust. He wrote,

---

[108] Matthew 28:18-20 NIV.
[109] Wendell E. Miller, "Rethinking the Great Commission, Part V: Explosive Reproduction," accessed 2010, http://www.biblical-counsel.org/commiss5.htm.
[110] SK, 142.

"To want full accomplishment immediately is lust. It is a sin and calls for a violation of the pattern of God. It is wanting something for nothing."[111]

We often look at the lives of successful people and exclaim, "I wish I had her abilities!" but it is truly a sign of spiritual immaturity when we expect or even demand of God something for which we are not prepared.

Maybe you're a classroom teacher and you view those in administration and think to yourself, "I wish I had her salary" or "I wish I had his authority to implement new policies; then things would really change around here!"

The problem is that we want to jump from teacher to administrator or administrator to the district office in a single step without first demonstrating faithfulness with the talents and responsibilities God has already entrusted to our care.

Check Your Attitude

Pat Robertson writes, "God's way is the way of gradual, sure growth and maturity, moving towards perfection."[112] Your life may follow a pattern somewhat similar to someone else, but your flight plan will still be unique. You might be able to take off the runway like a fighter jet pulling several Gs, or you might be like the lumbering cargo plane that requires a 10,000-foot runway to gather speed and get off the ground. Whatever your potential trajectory, you'll never get off the ground unless you're willing to first leave the gate. Every day you have the opportunity to choose what attitude you'll take to the airport.

JAIME ESCALANTE'S DETERMINATION TO USE HIS GIFTS

Jaime Escalante (1930-2010) was an extraordinary teacher who determined in his mind that he would make the most of his talents and abilities. His can-do attitude provided him the opportunity to reach new heights with his students! He did not allow childhood poverty to keep him from success. From humble beginnings in Bolivia, he went on to become one of America's most successful and famous educators. His life story was captured in 1988 in the film *Stand and Deliver* and in Jay Matthews' book, *Escalante: The Best Teacher in America.*

Matthews' book provides an excellent portrait of Escalante's unlikely rise to national prominence. He was born in La Paz, Bolivia, on December 31, 1930, to parents who worked as school teachers. His father was an abusive drunk who often abandoned the family, leaving Escalante's mother to raise him and his four siblings. Somehow she managed to set aside enough money to send her promising son to a prominent Jesuit high school. As Matthews explains, "To Jaime [the new school] was heaven, a place where quick wits and passion for odd corners of human knowledge could charm the priests and

---

[111] SK, 142.
[112] SK, 143.

let them forgive his many transgressions."[113] Despite his difficult surroundings, Escalante used his gifts in mathematics and proved to be an exceptional student.

After he graduated from high school and served a brief stint in the military, a friend encouraged Escalante to become a teacher. With no other prospects, he enrolled in the Normal Superior (a teacher's college) and as a sophomore was asked to teach high school physics. Again Escalante diligently applied himself to his work and after a short period of time was offered two additional teaching jobs and opportunities to provide private tutoring.

> "After mornings at San Calixto and afternoons at National Bolivar, he taught a late class at the Commercial High School, or saw tutees or instructed at a military academy night school. . . . Escalante had become a minor legend, the teacher who was working at three different schools before he had even graduated from the Normal."[114]

Escalante's successes weren't just his own. His students benefited from his instruction and began to be recognized in their own right, winning academic awards annually. His achievements in the classroom also brought him a level of modest prosperity as well, but he was frustrated that he had to work three or four jobs to provide for his family.

In 1963 the 33-year-old physics teacher sold everything he owned to pursue his dream to teach in America. Arriving with his wife and children, unable to speak much English, this esteemed teacher accepted a job mopping floors in a Los Angeles restaurant. Since California would not recognize his Bolivian experience or education, it took him another *ten years* to earn a college degree and teaching credentials. When he finally graduated, Escalante took a teaching position in one of the lowest achieving schools in the country. However, he went right back to using his gifts as an unorthodox educator and would go on to achieve national acclaim for his ability to teach underprivileged minority students advanced mathematics.

With his help, they achieved outstanding scores in calculus Advanced Placement exams—an achievement that many of his fellow educators had thought impossible. Hundreds of students endured their own form of hardship to make it through his rigorous and often unorthodox teaching methods. Some of their AP scores were so high on the exams that the testing bureau accused them of cheating and they had to retake the exams. But ultimately they benefited from his hard work and faithful dedication.

Jaime Escalante's story is one of exceptional determination and the Law of Use. Against overwhelming odds, he determined to use his gifts in the service of others. Instead of pursuing a career in engineering or the emerging computer industries that could have brought him wealth, he poured out his life in the halls of some of America's toughest schools. He inspired a generation of students to identify and foster their own gifts and by so doing, he changed the lives of hundreds of students.

---

[113] Jay Matthews, *Escalante: The Best Teacher in America*, (New York: Henry Holt and Company, 1988), 25.
[114] Matthews, 45.

HELPING YOUR STUDENTS DISCOVER AND USE THEIR TALENTS

The students who enter our classrooms every year are created in God's image and His image is reflected in the unique gifts or talents that He gives to each child. One of the most sacred duties of a teacher is to help identify the talents inherent in each student and then draw them out. As you know, the first step is taking the time to get to know your students well. In these days of tight district, state, and federal budgets, class sizes mushroom and we are assigned more students and less time to get to know them as individuals. Therefore, we must be strategic in our efforts to identify their gifts and provide them with opportunities for development.

Using a Classroom Survey

One way that you can apply the Law of Use in the classroom to develop your students' gifts and talents is to take a classroom survey. One particularly helpful website provides an article by B. Danesco with four hints as to how teachers can effectively survey their students to help them discover more about themselves: know your goal, know your students, encourage honesty, and allow for extra comments.[115]

Know your goal. The author encourages teachers to first "know your goal." By establishing clear goals through questions that align with your desired results, you are more likely to elicit the information you need. Your questions might be broad: "The three things I do best in school are . . . ." Or they may be specific: "Studying fractions makes me feel happy or sad." From these questions and others you can begin to ascertain your students' interests and talents so that you can help them use them most effectively.

Know your students. The second step is to "know your students." For example, when asking questions it is important to word them in such a way that the students understand what you are asking them to answer. Questions designed for younger children will need to be reworded for older students so they won't feel you are talking down to them. A question asking a fourth grader whether or not fractions make them happy or sad would need to be reworded for sophomores taking geometry.

Encourage honesty. Third, teachers need to encourage students to take the survey seriously and provide responses that honestly reflect their true thoughts, attitudes, and feelings. To encourage frank answers to sensitive questions, you may need to consider offering students anonymity.

Allow for extra comments. Teachers need to design the surveys in such a way that allows open comments. It may be helpful to ask students questions that require more than yes or no answers. Or you could ask them to respond using a numbered scale of 1-5. This

---

[115] B. Danesco, "Implementing Student Interest Surveys: Tips for Survey Methods" (2009), accessed 2010, http://www.howtodothings.com/education/a2751-how-to-implement-a-student-interest-survey.html.

affords them the opportunity to freely express themselves and may provide you with unexpectedly rich information.

Differentiated Instruction

Recognizing that each of our students is uniquely gifted by God and possesses talents that need to be fostered begs the question, "What do I do about it?" Carol Ann Tomlinson asks the question this way: "How do I divide time, resources, and myself so that I am an effective catalyst for maximizing talent in all my students?"[116]

Students come into our classrooms with personal histories and varying developmental differences and needs that affect how they learn. These factors must impact how we teach. "Developmental differences refer to differences in students' thinking, memory, emotions, and social relationships that result from maturation and different kinds of experiences"[117] and "developmentally appropriate practice refers to instructional practices that match teacher actions to the capabilities and needs of learners at different developmental levels."[118]

The pedagogical practice of meeting students' differing needs and abilities is called differentiated instruction, and teachers who are committed to helping all students develop their gifts work to create differentiated classrooms. Tomlinson explains:

> "In differentiated classrooms, the teacher is well aware that human beings share the same basic needs for nourishment, shelter, safety, belonging, achievement, contribution, and fulfillment. She also knows that human beings find those things in different fields of endeavor, according to different timetables, and through different paths. She understands that by attending to human differences she can best help individuals address their common needs. Our experiences, culture, gender, genetic codes, and neurological wiring all affect how and what we learn. In a differentiated classroom, the teacher unconditionally accepts students as they are, and she expects them to become all they can be."[119]

Tomlinson identifies and describes several pertinent characteristics of the teacher who is able to create a healthy classroom environment for a diverse group of students. Among those attributes are five that are critical to unleashing the talents in our students:

1. The teacher appreciates each child as an individual.
2. The teacher remembers to teach whole children.
3. The teacher strives for joyful learning.
4. The teacher offers high expectations—and lots of ladders.
5. The teacher uses positive energy and humor.[120]

---

[116] Carol Ann Tomlinson, *The Differentiated Classroom: Responding to the Needs of all Learners*, (Alexandria, VA: Association for Supervision and Curriculum Development, 1999), 1.

[117] Paul Eggen and Don Kauchak, *Educational Psychology: Windows on Classrooms* (8th ed.), (Upper Saddle River, NJ: Pearson Education, Inc., 2010), 12.

[118] Eggen and Kauchak, *Educational Psychology*, 12.

[119] Tomlinson, *The Differentiated Classroom*, 10.

[120] Tomlinson, *The Differentiated Classroom*, 31-34.

When you are a teacher, you model for students your own gifts and demonstrate how you have identified and fostered your personal talents over the years by employing the Law of Use. This must obviously be done in a spirit of humility, but how else can students learn unless others model it for them?

Recognizing Talents the Size of a Mustard Seed

If you recall Jesus' parable of the talents, you'll remember that it wasn't important if the servant received one, two, or five talents. What mattered most was whether or not he took those talents and put them to use. So, it's not the number of talents or even the degree or size of the ability that counts most. Even a small, seemingly unimportant talent in the eyes of others can be used of God to accomplish great things! Another parable Jesus told clearly illustrates this point:

> "[Jesus] presented another parable to them, saying, 'The kingdom of heaven is like a mustard seed, which a man took and sowed in his field; and this is smaller than all other seeds, but when it is full grown, it is larger than the garden plants and becomes a tree, so that the birds of the air come and nest in its branches.' "[121]

Too many of us become stagnant in our lives as professional educators. We get complacent, doing the same things the same way, year in and year out. It's critical that we challenge one another to take even what we may consider small seeds and plant them so that they can grow and become shade trees under which others can find refuge and refreshment.

As an educator at any level, you can encourage people to identify, develop, and employ their talents in service to others. A memorable example is a woman in her early thirties who worked for years as a teacher's aide in a kindergarten classroom. She was content to serve in that capacity and exhibited no inclination to take on greater responsibility. She felt her talent was only the size of a mustard seed and was insignificant. She secretly dreamed of teaching in her own classroom, but didn't think she was capable of returning to college and earning her degree.

However, as others observed her with the children and saw the love she displayed for them, they envisioned her teaching in a classroom of her own. Although she lacked the confidence needed to stretch on her own and make the most of her talents, with some encouragement from other educators she began to slowly increase her responsibilities by assisting with instruction and eventually creating entire lessons of her own. People came alongside her and encouraged her to consider returning to school to finish her undergraduate degree and attain her teaching certificate.

At first she was resistant to the idea because it all seemed so overwhelming, but their consistent support began to germinate and like a small seed began to take root and grow. It took her a few years to complete her degree, but what a day of celebration it was when she was hired to teach in her own kindergarten classroom. She quickly became one of the school's most creative and dedicated teachers! Her small mustard seed grew into a tree under whose branches five-year-olds now gather to learn and to grow.

---

[121] Matthew 13:31-32 NASB.

DEVELOPING THE LEADERS YOU INFLUENCE

Those who encouraged this woman to develop were applying the Law of Use on behalf of someone else. Educators carry an added responsibility to maximize not only our own talents, but the talents of those who are within our spheres of influence. Campus principals, in particular, are in an extraordinary position to elicit astonishing results in our schools. If you will harness the collective creative abilities of others, schools could once again become places of transformation for all!

This responsibility is multifaceted and complex. Not every principal will fulfill this responsibility in the same way. Marzano, Waters, and McNulty identify 21 responsibilities of the school leader in their book, *School Leadership that Works: From Research to Results.*[122]

Maximizing Your Investment in Others' Lives

For our purposes, the authors identify three responsibilities in particular that will allow you as a principal to maximize your investment in the lives of others and, in turn, allow them to capitalize on their own talents.

Become an agent of change. The first is to act as a change agent. The change-agent principal must be willing to actively challenge the status quo.

Open doors for input. The second is to allow input from others by involving them "in the design and implementation of important decisions and policies."[123]

Lead the way to innovation. The third is to act as an optimizer. In this capacity, the principal "inspires and leads new and challenging innovations."[124]

LAW OF USE APPLICATIONS BEYOND THE CLASSROOM

As an educator, you might not make a great deal of money and you might not feel wealthy, but remember—it's not how much you possess, it's how you use it that counts. God calls us to be cheerful givers[125] and we need to be willing to use our time, talents, and money to support local charitable causes.

---

[122] Robert Marzano, Timothy Waters, and Brian McNulty, *School Leadership that Works: From Research to Results* (Alexandria, VA: Association for Supervision and Curriculum Development, 2005), 42-43.
[123] Marzano, Waters, and McNulty, *School Leadership*, 42.
[124] Marzano, Waters, and McNulty, *School Leadership*, 43.
[125] See 2 Corinthians 9:7.

Giving Yourself to Your Church and Community

The investment of your God-given talents is needed in your local church and community. God entrusts you with wealth, work, and wisdom so that you can serve others in His name. If you have more time than you do money, you can invest your work in support of those in need. The Apostle Paul specifically instructed believers "to be rich in good works."[126] You might consider investing time through your church or you might work with an organization like Habitat for Humanity, Big Brothers and Sisters, or the local Rescue Mission.

Also, consider the significance of investing your wisdom. When you became a Christian, you received the mind of Christ.[127] Think of it! You have so much to offer through the use of your mind and creativity. You could serve on the board of a non-profit organization and use your discernment to provide leadership, helping them make the best decisions about how to distribute resources in order to serve others.

Using Your Supernatural Spiritual Gifts

The topic of spiritual gifts is too often neglected, even in our churches. "A spiritual gift is a special attribute given by the Holy Spirit to every member of the Body of Christ according to God's grace for use within the context of the Body."[128] It seems unfathomable that special, supernatural gifts are given by God to every believer and yet many churches leave these gifts of His grace ignored, unattended, and unopened. Unused!

What a tragedy! Christian education in our churches and Christian schools must address this egregious deficiency if the Christian community is ever going to operate in power. As educators, we need to take the lead in not only identifying and fostering our own spiritual gifts but also teaching others how to discover, develop, and use their own.

CONCLUSION

The keys to the Kingdom of God are no longer a secret. You can unlock the door to a successful life by employing the Law of Use and the other laws described in subsequent chapters in this book. In fact, when different laws and principles are linked together, the potential for impacting your life and the lives of others is limitless!

---

[126] 1 Timothy 6:18 NASB.

[127] See 1 Corinthians 2:16.

[128] C. Peter Wagner, *Your Spiritual Gifts Can Help Your Church Grow* (Ventura, CA: Regal Books, 1979), 42.

Exponential Power of Use

Physically, we know that the more our muscles are used, the stronger we become. *Mentally*, the same principle is true. The more we use our minds, the better we can learn. *Socially*, the more we exercise Christian love through acts of service, the more we are able to engage effectively with others. *Emotionally*, as we extend forgiveness to those who hurt us, we can move beyond past hurts just as Christ forgives us.[129] *Spiritually*, we can soar to new heights as we identify, develop, and employ the supernatural and spiritual gifts granted to us by the power of the Holy Spirit. As mentioned above, Pat Robertson describes the exponential power of the Law of Use:

> "The Law of Use . . . coupled with the exponential curve, is probably the most powerful of the principles in terms of day-to-day life. It is the fundamental law for the growth and development—or the decline—of all organizations and societies in both the invisible and the visible worlds. Beginning with the cradle, it touches everything—child development, intellectual development, professional development, physical development, social development, and on and on."[130]

Final Applications

As you have read, the Law of Use is highly practical and can apply to almost every imaginable aspect of your life. The Law of Use can transform you both as a Christ-follower and as a professional educator if you will take those things God entrusts to your care and work to see them multiplied.

First, invest time and energy in your own spiritual growth so that you can reach new levels of maturity, power, and authority in Christ.

Then, invest in your professional development as an educator and watch by faith as God opens new doors of opportunity for service.

Finally, invest yourself more deeply in the lives of your students. Prayerfully consider that God ordains all of the students who sit in your classroom in order that you can pour the love of Christ into their lives. Pat Robertson draws his chapter on the Law of Use to a close by writing:

> "I am convinced that this law—put to work with the commitment, the virtues, and the accompanying subprinciples—can produce giant steps toward easing and ultimately removing the crises that grip the world. It will touch world hunger, the economic quagmire, energy depletion, Third World needs, educational and social injustice, church evangelism, moral decadence, disease, and inadequate health care."[131]

Collectively, we can invest in one another and generate a return on God's investment in us that will change our world!

---

[129] See Colossians 3:13.
[130] SK, 150.
[131] SK, 151.

RESOURCES

Brophy, Jere E. *Teaching Problem Students*. New York: Guilford Press, 1996.

Chapman, Gary D. *The Five Love Languages: The Secret to Love that Lasts*. Chicago: Northfield Publishing, 2010.

Danesco, B. "Implementing Student Interest Surveys: Tips for Survey Methods." *Howtodothings.com* (2009): http://www.howtodothings.com/education/a2751-how-to-implement-a-student-interest-survey.html (accessed September 9, 2010).

Eggen, Paul, and Don Kauchak. *Educational Psychology: Windows on Classrooms*. 8th ed. Upper Saddle River, NJ: Pearson Education, Inc., 2010.

Fee, Gordon D., and Douglas Stuart. *How to Read the Bible for All Its Worth*. Grand Rapids, MI: Zondervan, 2003.

Kovarik, Madeleine. "Being a With-It Teacher." *New Teacher Advocate* 16, no. 2 (Winter 2008).

Lucado, Max. *The Cure for the Common Life: Living in Your Sweet Spot*. Nashville: Thomas Nelson, 2005.

Marzano, Robert, Timothy Waters, and Brian McNulty. *School Leadership that Works: From Research to Results*. Alexandria, VA: Association for Supervision and Curriculum Development, 2005.

Matthews, Jay. *Escalante: The Best Teacher in America*. New York: Henry Holt and Company, 1988.

Miller, Wendell E. "Rethinking the Great Commission Part V: Explosive Reproduction." *Biblical-counsel.org* (1997): http://www.biblical-counsel.org/commiss5.htm (accessed September 9, 2010).

Robertson, Pat. *The Secret Kingdom: Your Path to Peace, Love, and Financial Security*. Dallas: Word Publishing, 1992.

Tomlinson, Carol Ann. *The Differentiated Classroom: Responding to the Needs of all Learners*. Alexandria, VA: Association for Supervision and Curriculum Development, 1999.

Wagner, C. Peter. *Your Spiritual Gifts Can Help Your Church Grow*. Ventura, CA: Regal Books, 1979.

CHAPTER 5
THE LAW OF RECIPROCITY

By William F. Cox, Jr. Ph.D.
Professor, Founder—Christian Education Programs
Regent University School of Education

" 'Do not judge lest you be judged,'[132] the Lord said, which drives directly at attitudes. Anyone who is critical, constantly faulting others and cutting associates, will not rise to the top. He will get back what he gives. The one who makes his department look good, including his boss, is the one who will get the salary increase he needs. 'The way you give to others is the way God will give to you.'[133] That's a law."[134]

PAT ROBERTSON, *THE SECRET KINGDOM*

Young Johnny wanted to do his best in class but regularly seemed to be sidetracked by personal issues. He had a negative self-concept that his teacher believed most likely resulted from living all his life in an emotionally abusive home. In class Johnny was easily frustrated and his attention seemed to drift in and out. He unpredictably shifted between daydreaming, sullenness, and outbursts of anger. In the early grades, most of Johnny's teachers held little hope for him because of their own frustrations with dealing with all of his peculiarities. Johnny projected negativity toward his teachers and they unconsciously reciprocated in their attitudes toward him.

Positive Perspective of a Christian Teacher

However, when Johnny entered Mrs. Smith's class, she had a positive vision for him in spite of how he acted and regardless of what his former teachers had to say about him. Mrs. Smith was a Christian. She carried the love of Jesus in her heart for all of the children under her tutelage. While there were times when she really had to work at loving Johnny, most of the time she could love him very naturally.

For instance, one morning Mrs. Smith sat with Johnny and gently reviewed his assignment for the day in nice easy steps. She slowly coached him through each step separately. She decided that she would give Johnny credit for any part of a particular assignment that he did correctly rather than deduct points for everything he did wrong.

As Johnny began to experience these moments of affirmation and success, she had less and less reason to reinforce the small successes and instead was able to

---

[132] Matthew 7:1 NASB.
[133] Luke 6:38 NCV.
[134] SK, 117.

commend him for larger victories without necessarily ignoring the small accomplishments.

In addition, Mrs. Smith regularly gave Johnny handwritten notes that affirmed who he was as a person, especially his gifts and talents. These notes did not necessarily relate to his school performance. Additionally, Mrs. Smith encouraged Johnny's interests. He began to gain confidence in doing something that he was naturally good at doing without consciously realizing it.

Finally, as Johnny began to experience regular classroom success, Mrs. Smith would occasionally ask him to help a transfer student who had some of the same disadvantages that Johnny had now overcome.

As you can imagine, thanks to Mrs. Smith Johnny graduated successfully and over the years periodically wrote to his former teacher to share his life accomplishments, giving her due honor. She had brought the Kingdom of God into his life in a tangible way even when he was not aware of it.

Don't be mistaken. Not everything was trouble-free for both Johnny and Mrs. Smith, but no matter what Johnny did, she found some way to affirm him. Yes, he still had to pay the penalty for violating classroom rules, but Mrs. Smith never chastised him with hurtful words that would make him feel as if he were inherently bad. She never dishonored him in front of others. In addition, she invested the time to teach Johnny the academic and behavioral skills he needed to become a successful student.

In summary, Mrs. Smith demonstrated love qualities found in 1 Corinthians 13 and Beatitude qualities found in Matthew 5. She was an intercessor and peacemaker in Johnny's life. She gave love and received love. As a result of the Law of Reciprocity operating in the Secret Kingdom, she enjoyed reciprocated blessings from Johnny over a good portion of her life.

DEFINING THE LAW OF RECIPROCITY

In simple terms, the Law of Reciprocity is receiving back in kind that which was given.

It has its counterpart in physics in the scientific principle of Sir Isaac Newton's third law: "For every action, there is an equal and opposite reaction."

It is clearly affirmed in biblical statements such as Jesus' words, "Give, and it will be given to you." [135]

In the area of the tithe, it is affirmed in the Old Testament verse that God will reciprocate the tithe with blessings in abundance (Malachi 3:10), and the New Testament teaching that we reap what we sow (Galatians 6:7).

It is foundational to statements like "What goes around comes around" and The Golden Rule: "Do unto others as you would have them do unto you" (Matthew 7:12).

Obviously this principle has many applications in the natural and spiritual realms. As many of us have experienced and as explained in *The Secret Kingdom*, interpersonal human relationships regularly reflect this principle in the way, for instance, people

---

[135] Luke 6:38 NIV.

typically return smiles and pleasant greetings. But as also explained in *The Secret Kingdom*, the Law of Reciprocity works both ways. It is the same whether our actions are for good or evil.

Maintaining the Right Motives

When your primary motive for activating the Law of Reciprocity is not personal gain—even though you know that good deeds and even favors are returned to those who give—you can keep the proper focus. This law demonstrates God's reality—the realm where you want to live.

The Law of Reciprocity applies to education in a straightforward matter. That is, whatever good you want to receive, you first need to give. And since this Law is primarily about interpersonal matters, what you give should essentially conform to the Golden Rule—do to/for others as you would like to be treated. And for that truly to be "golden," what you do should conform to Kingdom values. These values include treating people in a kind, loving, edifying, dignifying, honoring, selfless manner.

People will naturally reciprocate when you demonstrate a firm commitment to their good and they see that your actions are the right thing to do and are not done in a manipulative fashion. Overall, it should be obvious that anything done in the spirit of reflecting godly, Kingdom values brings God's Kingdom into that environment.

Let's see how this law works in specific ways.

Equal and Opposite Reactions Bringing about Good

Now that we have covered both the definition and a classroom-based example of how love is reciprocated, we move to a more intricate understanding of the Law of Reciprocity. Specifically, building on the "equal and opposite reaction" analogy in physics, we focus now on the so-called "opposite" force to demonstrate the effectiveness of the Law of Reciprocity. In essence, the Law of Reciprocity can effectively overpower an "opposite" or resisting force of a negative nature to change the environment to positive. Following is a simple illustration of this spiritual dynamic.

In a certain work environment, an upper-level administrator would stare right through anyone he passed in the hallways. This invariably left most employees feeling intimidated and insecure whenever they were around him, even beyond the hallways. One employee decided to counteract that negativity with the graciousness of Jesus Christ. Every time this particular Christian encountered the off-putting supervisor, he greeted him with a warm eye-to-eye greeting and a cordial question about his welfare, his health, or some other gesture of goodwill. After some period of time, the off-putting supervisor gradually warmed-up to return the pleasant greetings.

I personally took the above illustration seriously to conduct what I call an edifying experiment with a certain other off-putting person. In my former neighborhood there was a man who walked the block almost always at the same time in the morning that I was driving to work. He had anger written all over his demeanor and posture. The lady occasionally with him (who presumably was his wife) invariably stayed several paces behind him. Whenever I passed him in my car he never looked anywhere other than straight ahead as if my car and I were not even in the universe. I conducted my "experiment" by smiling, waving, and even occasionally, tapping my horn as I drew near to him. Over time, I began to notice his eyes shift toward me and then sometime later I could see the corners of his mouth turn upward. My experiment is still in process but it looks like the "force" of bringing God's Kingdom nature into that situation is powerful enough to effect the beginnings of reciprocity in my hard-as-nails neighbor.

This transforming power inherent in promoting Kingdom ways via the Law of Reciprocity has a long historical record. For instance, there are recorded accounts of prisoners of war reciprocally receiving kindness from their captors as a result of prisoner kindness. Sometimes the kindness will be returned but through other sources. A classical case in this regard is seen in the Old Testament biblical account of how Joseph enjoyed favor in prison even though the charge (false as it was) of attempting to seduce Potiphar's wife could have easily resulted in his death. Though punished in the short run, Joseph's desire to not dishonor Potiphar was eventually and amply reciprocated by the way he received back great honor from Pharaoh when Joseph was put in charge of Egypt's resources.

CONCLUSION

In conclusion, there are a number of important understandings to garner from the above explanations. For one, the Law of Reciprocity is a basic law of the universe that actions tend to have in-kind, reciprocating consequences. An example of this simple yet profound truth of the Law of Reciprocity is illustrated by Pat Robertson in *The Secret Kingdom*. He says, for instance, that "you will find nice people anywhere you go if you're nice to them"[136] and a smile given is typically reciprocated.

In these instances, we see the "natural" use of the Law of Reciprocity but there is much more to the Law of Reciprocity when applied with Kingdom anointing. When the spiritual force of the love of Christ is brought into seemingly intractable situations like the example of Johnny or accompanied by the express favor of God (as with Joseph), overtly negative forces can be turned positive.

Herein is the wonder of the Law of Reciprocity. Spiritually negative forces can be displaced and replaced with positive qualities when empowered by Kingdom ways. It's not just the triggering of the humanly natural tendency to reciprocate pleasing actions. The Law of Reciprocity also diminishes inappropriate reactions and draws forth the locked-up potential of edifying, in-kind reciprocations.

When you think about it, this is the essence of the Kingdom. New Testament teachings such as the Beatitudes (Matthew 5:3-12), admonitions to turn the other cheek (Matthew 5:39), to love unconditionally (1 Corinthians 2:4-7), or to feed your enemy (Romans 12:20) reflect the same reality and spiritual warfare potency that Jesus engaged in on the cross. They depict spiritually empowered ways that God's Kingdom takes you beyond superficial reciprocations to combat evil and negativity at the deepest levels.

---

[136] SK, 114.

They set you in place to receive heavenly rewards as reciprocation for your heavenly actions here on earth.

You will see in Chapter 14 how the Law of Reciprocity can be further applied in the academic setting. Several practical, research based practices will be described in terms of how reciprocity is evident in algebra, for example, and how it can be used to encourage reading comprehension with your students. It is an amazing law that can generate many fruitful applications to any educational setting.

RESOURCES

Robertson, Pat. *The Secret Kingdom: Your Path to Peace, Love, and Financial Security.* Dallas: Word Publishing, 1992.

CHAPTER 6

THE LAW OF PERSEVERANCE

By John Hanes, Ph.D.
Assistant Professor
Regent University School of Education

*"God slowly yields the good things of the
kingdom and the world to those who struggle."*[137]

PAT ROBERTSON, *THE SECRET KINGDOM*

*"If you can force your heart and nerve and sinew
To serve your turn long after they are gone,
And so hold on when there is nothing in you
Except the Will which says to them: 'Hold on!' "*[138]

RUDYARD KIPLING, "IF"

The quote above from *The Secret Kingdom* by Dr. Pat Robertson and those lines from Rudyard Kipling's poem "If" express the forceful nature of perseverance. The impact of the Law of Perseverance goes beyond the exercise of patience or an occasional struggle. One source defines *perseverance* as "steady persistence in a course of action, a purpose, a state, etc., esp. in spite of difficulties, obstacles, or discouragement."[139]

Per in the prefix of persistence means "through, thoroughly, utterly, very."[140]

Severe has a number of definitions including: "harsh; unnecessarily extreme," and "difficult to endure, perform, fulfill, etc."[141]

You might say that *perseverance* is "thoroughly difficult endurance"!

In *The Secret Kingdom* Dr. Robertson includes a personal experience with perseverance as he traces the history of the Christian Broadcasting Network (CBN) from

---

[137] SK, 158.
[138] Rudyard Kipling, "If," in Roy J. Cook, compiler, *One Hundred and One Famous Poems With a Prose Supplement* (Chicago: The Cable Company, 1929), 108.
[139] Dictionary.com Unabridged (based on the Random House Dictionary, © Random House, 2010), s.v. "perseverance," accessed: July 3, 2010, http://dictionary.reference.com/browse/perseverance.
[140] Dictionary.com Unabridged, s.v. "per-," accessed July 3, 2010, http://dictionary.reference.com/browse/per- .
[141]. Dictionary.com Unabridged s.v. "severe," accessed: July 3, 2010, http://dictionary.reference.com/browse/severe.

the arrival of his family in the Tidewater area of Virginia with only 70 dollars to the major institution of God's grace that it has become today. He points out how God brought his ministry along through a series of struggles, each one designed to position the institution for the next challenge to come, all the while growing in service to Him.[142]

JAIME ESCALANTE AND THE MATH STUDENTS AT GARFIELD HIGH SCHOOL

As mentioned in Chapter 4, the popular 1988 movie *Stand and Deliver* featured the late Jaime Escalante,[143] an incredible teacher. However, the film left the impression that he pretty much took a group of poor, mostly Hispanic math students who struggled with fractions and built them into outstanding calculus scholars over the course of a single school year. Escalante did, indeed, teach at Garfield High School in East Los Angeles, but his calculus program was built over a number of years.

Escalante persevered mightily as an individual both in the short and the long term. As an immigrant teacher from Bolivia, he had to study English in the evenings for a number of years before acquiring his teaching credentials in California. He worked for Burroughs Corporation during the day and after only two hours in his first Garfield math classrooms he called his former employer asking for his old job back. However, he never had to return because he came up with a plan that he knew would work if he followed the principles of perseverance.

Escalante found a handful of basic math students in junior high school who were willing to take Algebra I before they reached high school. In this way he built a pipeline for students coming from junior high schools who were introduced to Algebra before they reached Garfield. In high school they would take necessary feeder courses before they encountered calculus as juniors and seniors. Once the momentum began, the district's open enrollment policy wildly increased his class sizes so he offered before and after school tutoring to students in each of the courses that he taught.

In 1979, after five years of development, Escalante taught calculus for the first time at Garfield High School. From that time forward, the Advanced Placement (AP) calculus exam attempts and the number passing increased rapidly through 1987 when 73 Garfield students passed the regular AB version of the AP examination and another 12 students passed the more advanced BC test. Each class and each tutoring session constituted a short term trial of perseverance and the many additional sessions over time became a long term endurance contest for Escalante.

Likewise, each class of students taught by Escalante exhibited a corporate endurance, both in the day-to-day engagement with intellectually challenging concepts and also over time as the mass of material to be mastered continued to expand.

The first group of 12 students in 1982 who took the AP examination were initially disqualified because the Educational Testing Service did not believe that these at-risk students could achieve at such a high level. However, Escalante and the students

---

[142] SK, 162-163.
[143] Jerry Jesness, "Stand and Deliver Revisited," *Reason.com* (July 2010), accessed July 27, 2010, http://reason.com/archives/2002/07/01/stand-and-deliver-revisited.

persevered and took a second examination and all of them passed. The power of their perseverance was affirmed.

Core Attributes of Perseverance

The example above of Garfield High School students and their teacher is a positive example of the rewards for scholastic perseverance. While *tenacity* generally has implications of positive value, *persistence* may not always be viewed with favor,[144] such as when a child persistently interrupts his mother's personal conversation. However, the application of the Law of Perseverance carries a positive connotation when compared with its synonyms.

A POWERFUL TRIO—LAWS OF USE, RECIPROCITY, AND PERSEVERANCE

As you read this book, you will encounter the ten laws from Pat Robertson's book *The Secret Kingdom* that we have applied to the realm of education. The description of these laws is included in Section II of this book.

The first three laws that we cover are Use, Reciprocity, and Perseverance. These three are intimately related and of themselves form a powerful trio sufficient to accomplish great value for God's kingdom.[145]

Applying the Law of Use loses effectiveness if the Law of Perseverance is neglected. For example, you might begin an exercise program with good intentions and an initial investment of sincere effort, but if you fail to persevere in the face of various temptations you may doom the enterprise to failure. Likewise, you might initiate a relationship with another person and achieve a positive response, but without a sustaining effort on your part to persevere in your relationship with that person you could become discouraged when reciprocation does not occur in a visible and immediate manner.

HARNESSING THE POSITIVE POWER AND ACHIEVING THE POSITIVE RESPONSE

Dr. Robertson points out the importance of positive thinking in maintaining perseverance.[146] Because God is Spirit, His Spirit represents the ultimate positive power in the universe. God speaks with the power to create and perform miracles and it is our portion to act in the same positive manner, because when we revert to negative thoughts they contribute to self-fulfilling prophecies of failure.[147]

---

[144] Synonyms, Dictionary.com Unabridged, s.v. "perseverance," accessed July 3, 2010, http://dictionary.reference.com/browse/perseverance.

[145] SK, 161.

[146] SK, 154-156.

[147] SK, 156.

Our greatest source of positive power is Jesus Christ Who enables us to have new life in Him. When His new life replaces negative thoughts in our life with positive ones, this new life is enthusiastically contagious and opens up the existence of unlimited possibilities.[148] However, Dr. Robertson issues this warning and challenge:

> "But certain risks go with new life and growth—the risks of freedom, we might say—but God prepares us for those risks, through perseverance and struggle, building our muscles, as it were, for each new phase. To refuse to struggle is to stand still, to stagnate."[149]

God wants us to ask Him for our needs, but as Jesus said, the nature of this asking is to *keep asking* (and *keep seeking, keep knocking*). Jesus said, "Ask and it will be given to you; seek and you will find; knock and the door will be opened to you."[150]

You need faith in a positive future outcome to persevere for the long haul. Each of us must be prepared to emulate the importunate widow in the Bible.

> "Then Jesus told his disciples a parable to show them that they should always pray and not give up. He said: 'In a certain town there was a judge who neither feared God nor cared about men. And there was a widow in that town who kept coming to him with the plea, "Grant me justice against my adversary."
>
> " 'For some time he refused. But finally he said to himself, "Even though I don't fear God or care about men, yet because this widow keeps bothering me, I will see that she gets justice, so that she won't eventually wear me out with her coming!" ' "
>
> "And the Lord said, 'Listen to what the unjust judge says. And will not God bring about justice for his chosen ones, who cry out to him day and night? Will he keep putting them off? I tell you, he will see that they get justice, and quickly. However, when the Son of Man comes, will he find faith on the earth?' "[151]

Dr. Robertson says, "Don't be afraid even to make a ruckus. God prefers persistence much more than slothfulness and indolence. He wants people who will travail and perhaps stumble a bit, but keep on going forward, just like the toddler who's trying to learn to walk. The child builds muscles and learns. One day he will run."[152]

We gain strength through testing, and this testing demands perseverance for successful completion. The adversary, Satan, attempts to disrupt the kingdom of God by continually fostering "discouragement and depression."[153] Armed with this knowledge, we must stand with perseverance, and God will make a way of victory for us.

---

[148] SK, 156-157.
[149] SK, 158.
[150] Luke 11:9.
[151] Luke 18:1-8.
[152] SK, 159.
[153] SK, 160.

TIME AND TYPE OF PERSEVERANCE

In treating the Law of Perseverance, we shall look at four possible aspects derived from a framework of time and type separation.

Long-term and short-term perseverance. Although perseverance is usually associated with lengthy endurance, we'll try to distinguish both a short-term (less than several days) and long-term view.

Individual and corporate perseverance. For type, both individuals and groups of individuals (a "corporate" function is defined as two or more persons working together) may exhibit perseverance under challenging pressures.

Figure 1. Time and Type of Perseverance

	Short Term	**Long Term**
	Jesus' Passion	Jesus in the wilderness
	Jacob wrestling with the angel	Moses over his adult lifetime
Individual	Jaime Escalante in tutoring sessions	Jaime Escalante building math program
	Col. John Ripley at the Dong Ha bridge	Bonhoeffer in prison
	Paul and Silas beaten and in jail	The Christian Church in the Book of Acts
	Shadrack, Meschack, and Abednago in fiery furnace	Jewish people throughout the Old Testament
Corporate	Garfield High School students taking the AP Calculus exam	Garfield students mastering mathematics
	Torpedo Squadrons at Midway	Christians in Rome during the plagues
	Perpetua and Felicity in the arena	The Back to Jerusalem Movement

We shall explore the examples in Figure 1 through several of the sections that follow.

GREAT STORIES OF PERSEVERANCE

Several lessons from history serve to confirm the validity of perseverance in the lives of people and institutions. Abraham Lincoln, Thomas Edison, and the Wright Brothers all had to struggle against failure, defeat, and ridicule before achieving accomplishment in the fields of politics, invention, and flight, respectively. Initially, these examples and stories that we employ here may seem unrelated to education, but we need to remember that we are educating for a lifetime of challenge, both vocationally and spiritually. What we do in school builds habits of perseverance for these later struggles.

Perseverance in the *Bible*

Within the aforementioned time and type framework, the Bible provides a large number of illustrations for perseverance, and we shall mention a few here.

In the Old Testament, Moses struggled for a large part of his life in his efforts to obey God, lead the children of Israel out of Egypt, and guide the nascent nation to the Promised Land. This is an example of a long term individual endeavor, as is Noah's dedication to the task of constructing the Ark.

In the shorter term, Jacob persevered through his wrestling match with God's angel.

Throughout the Old Testament and historically to the present day, the Jewish people have corporately persevered through seemingly uncountable trials of faith and persecution.

Shadrach, Meshach, and Abednego offer a dramatic example of corporate short term perseverance when they refuse to bow before the gold statue built by King Nebuchadnezzar. Under threat of burning in the fiery furnace, they make a classic response for those who intend to persevere: "Your Majesty, we don't need to defend ourselves. The God we worship can save us from you and your flaming furnace. But even if he doesn't, we still won't worship your gods and the gold statue you have set up."[154]

Jesus suffered 40 days of temptation in the desert at the hands of Satan and a briefer, more intense period during the Passion. These are examples of long-term and short term individual perseverance from the New Testament.

The on-going growth of the Church following Pentecost reflects a long term corporate test of endurance inspired by the Holy Spirit.

In the shorter term, Paul and Silas persevere together through beating and jailing.[155]

Individual Perseverance in Military Action—Viet Nam

Modern military operations provide us with examples of short term individual and corporate perseverance that are dramatic and providential. The extreme nature of these

---

[154] Daniel 3:16-18 CEV.
[155] See Acts 16:19-40.

particular situations reminds us as educators that we are preparing students not only for the next examination but also for possible life and death challenges that may define who they are in relation to themselves, others, their nation, and ultimately to God Himself.

The exploits of U.S. Marine Col. John W. Ripley[156] in destroying Viet Nam's Dong Ha Bridge on Easter Sunday of 1972 seem miraculous in the telling. Although American participation in the Vietnam War was winding down at that time, a number of American combat advisors, known as "covans" or trusted friends, remained with the South Vietnamese forces to help guide their increasingly difficult resistance to North Vietnamese advances.

In the largest of these Northern intrusions, the Easter Offensive, the North Vietnamese attempted to use the Dong Ha Bridge across the Cam Lo-Cua Viet River. It was the only span capable of supporting their 200 Soviet-made T-54 heavy tanks. This invasion represented almost certain defeat for the South if they were successful.

Col. Ripley received orders to destroy the 200 meter heavily reinforced Dong Ha Bridge. He had only 500 lbs. of explosives available to accomplish the task. With little or no rest following a three-day firefight with no food and only water to drink, Ripley - proceeded to move the ordinance 100 feet under the bridge going hand-over hand, dangling beneath the span while exposed to rifle and artillery fire from 20,000 troops on the northern shore of the river. For three hours, Ripley persevered. He made some 12 such hand-over-hand passages, each time with 40 lbs. of explosives strapped to his back and his legs bleeding from the razor wire that he had to negotiate at the shore line.

After Ripley placed the last charge and returned safely to the southern end of the span, he helped detonate the explosives and brought down the bridge. Ripley certainly had tremendous "corporate support" from the brave South Vietnamese Marines who essentially lost the bulk of a battalion. Only 52 of approximately 700 returned from almost a week of steady engagement. However, Ripley alone had carried out what was considered to be a certain death assignment that was doomed to failure before it even began. Notably, as Ripley, a devout Catholic, relates in his YouTube narratives (recorded before his death in October of 2008), it was his rhythmic chanting of "Jesus, Mary, get me there" that enabled him to move from one hand grasp to another, even when he was convinced that he had no strength remaining. For Col. Ripley, perseverance was a defining character trait that enabled him to succeed in the face of the impossible.

Corporate Perseverance in Military Action—Midway (World War II)

For the true corporate military example, the battle of Midway[157] at the start of June, 1942, offers three torpedo plane squadrons that persevered for only a few minutes but set the stage for victory at a time when America was still reeling from Japan's successful bombing of Pearl Harbor and subject to losing even more of its decimated naval forces to a Japanese Fleet that included four of that nation's top fleet aircraft carriers and a premier

---

[156] Debbie Thurman, "Hangin' Tough," *The Virginian Pilot*, April 4, 2010, 11.

[157] Herman Wouk, *War and Remembrance* (Boston: Little, Brown and Company, 1978), 276-344. Although many historical volumes on Midway are referenced through Wikipedia and similar websites, I have chosen a novel with sound historical footings because of the focus on the torpedo squadrons (pp. 311-313) for a listing of all crew members and their birthplaces.

selection of aviators. Although completely uncoordinated, several unsuccessful air strikes from Midway Island preceded the American carrier launched torpedo plane assault aimed at the Japanese carriers. Unfortunately, the torpedo bombers had to attack low on the water with relatively slow aircraft. This made them extremely vulnerable to anti-aircraft and fighter plane gunfire, and, again, no Japanese ship suffered damage; however, several of the torpedo bombers were shot down (only 14 of 82 crew members survived). The perseverance built throughout the attack (think of being in one of the last few planes in the last squadron to begin the approach with, perhaps, strong knowledge that death awaited and that any kind of success was really impossible).

It may have been Divine providence, but the seemingly wasteful loss of the torpedo squadrons set the table for triumph by forcing the Japanese commanders to delay launching their rearmed aircraft for a naval engagement with American carriers rather than another bombing of Midway Island and by drawing their fighter cover down to deck level for the destruction of the torpedo planes. With their decks strewn with ordinance and fuel lines and relatively little fighter defense at altitude, the Japanese carriers offered an inviting target. This is when American dive bombers coincidentally arrived for an assault that destroyed three of the carriers (the fourth was sunk the following day). This battle became the hinge point for the naval war in the Pacific theater, and much of the credit for the outcome belongs to the torpedo squadron crews whose perseverance birthed victory.

Perseverance in Christian History and Missions

Over the past 2,000 years, the Church has bloomed with stories of perseverance in service to Christ. The confessors, martyrs, missionaries, and simple servants throughout history have endured torture, deprivation, and death via sudden encounters, long term imprisonment, or protracted struggle to care for those in need. Whether suffering has been short term (Perpetua and Felicity in the Arena) or long (Dietrich Bonhoeffer in prison), individual (John Bunyan) or corporate (early Christians staying in the city of Rome to treat those dying of the plague, both Christian and non-Christian), these Christians very often presented an enigma to observers in their cultures. They gladly persevered with grace, forgiveness, and love despite harsh treatment and ridicule. Because this charitable, self-sacrificing perseverance is counter to the understanding of most cultures, their behavior challenged many to consider seriously the source of such kindly endurance.

Today, the Back to Jerusalem[158] movement of the Chinese Underground Church represents a long-term corporate instantiation of Christian perseverance in the face of sometimes fierce opposition. The Underground Church in China has sent and continues to mobilize thousands of missionaries back down the old Silk Roads that had formerly connected China to the Middle East for commercial purposes. Knowing that the countries involved do not welcome Christians, the Underground Church continues to follow the Great Commission with trust and perseverance.

---

[158] Paul Hattaway, Brother Yun, Peter Xu Yongze, and Enoch Wong, *Back to Jerusalem: Three Chinese House Church Leaders Share Their Vision to Complete the Great Commission* (Waynesboro, GA: Authentic Media, 2003).

INTENTIONALITY IN THE SCHOOL ENVIRONMENT

As educators we need to fully understand that our motivation for developing perseverance extends far beyond the mere academic realm, as important as that may be. We seek to inculcate the habit of perseverance using primarily scholarly vehicles, but we realize that the application extends to realms of adventure as the preceding examples have emphasized.

We must be intentional in our efforts to insert perseverance into all aspects of our school environment. We begin by inviting Christ and the Holy Spirit to build perseverance in us. We also need to pray for our students and their parents/guardians that they too demonstrate the level of perseverance needed for success.

Next we inform these key stakeholders along with others in the school community that we shall be including a perseverance component in our courses and activities during the new academic year. We plan the process and gradually introduce its components in each course and activity on a gradual basis. Both parents and students need to be aware that specific challenges will be built into many aspects of the school experience, and that we feel perseverance is an essential character trait that needs attention and development.

Along the way to full implementation of perseverance components, all stakeholders should intentionally participate in mutual exhortation and encouragement, because for many students the idea of completing extended, challenging tasks may be something new in their lives (as it may be for some parents and teachers as well).

Motivating Students to Study Perseverance

We want to address the concept of conation, a uniting of motivation and volition, with special emphasis on the volitional aspects.

Understanding extrinsic and intrinsic motivations. Motivation for both individuals and groups usually involves a mix that is both extrinsic and intrinsic. Extrinsic motivation comes from either the carrot or the stick. Grades, awards, and approval serve as examples of carrots just as the inner feelings of satisfaction and excitement following the completion of a difficult task represent intrinsic motivators.

Watching films about heroes of perseverance. Ideally, we are trying to develop, as much as possible, an "iron will" within each student. The 1994 movie, *Iron Will*, is loosely based on a true story of an early 20th century dogsled race from Winnipeg, Manitoba, to St. Paul, Minnesota. Showing this and similar movies may help students and other stakeholders better understand the character trait of perseverance. Often quest type films, like *The Lord of the Rings* trilogy, present individual and group examples of perseverance, both in short action sequences and over the course of an entire movie or even a series of videos. It is helpful to bring the vignettes and themes of perseverance to the attention of the students as they view the films.

Engaging in challenging activities. While success in an academic task that requires a persistent effort may denote a student's or group's improving perseverance, another characteristic of interest is the attitude toward challenging activities. Aleksandr Solzhenitsyn once remarked that the difference between Christians in the West and those in the East could be discerned by their reactions to a severe burden. Those in the West prayed to God that the burden might be eased, but those in the East prayed for stronger backs to bear the burden. There is a parallel here for the shifting attitudes that we hope to observe in our students over time. Hopefully, they will move from a posture of complaint and frustration to one of welcoming (or at least accepting) the challenges presented by tasks that they know will require extensive effort on their part. The previously mentioned experience of Paul and Silas in jail offers a fine example of what seems pleasing to the Lord in times of challenge and extreme difficulty: not complaining but rather "praying and singing praises to God."[159]

At some point, each student may have reached a kind of critical mass in terms of effort expended on a particular project, and we must be assiduously sensitive to this point for every student in a differentiated manner (the point will be different for every student). We need to tell the student that we are pleased with the progress, and it is time to move on to another project where perseverance will be further enhanced.

PERSEVERANCE AS CURRICULUM

Purposefully, we would like the curriculum to reflect an increasing emphasis on perseverance over the course of a school year, especially if this is the first year for such a focus at a particular school. Cognitive dissonance and delayed closure are consistent with current thinking on the development of creativity in terms of the reciprocal nature of divergent and convergent thinking,[160] and we can use these concepts to help shape the persevering attitude that we seek for our students in each academic discipline.

We should keep in mind that more than obvious benefits may accrue to those students who persevere in the face of difficulties. According to recent cognitive research, even unsuccessful attempts to answer questions on challenging tests may provide a key to effective learning.[161] There is a level of "desirable difficulty" that is consistent with the idea that "the harder it is to remember something, the harder it is to later forget."[162]

We often use scaffolding and differentiation as pedagogical tools of the educational professions, and they apply equally well to our injection of perseverance into various curricular elements. Some students, for whatever reasons, enter our classrooms

---

[159] Acts 16:25 CEV.

[160] Po Bronson and Ashley Merryman, "The Creativity Crisis," *Newsweek*, July 10, 2010, accessed July 16, 2010, http://www.newsweek.com/2010/07/10/the-creativity-crisis.print.html.

[161] Nate Kornell, Matthew Jensen Hayes, and Robert A. Bjork, "Unsuccessful Retrieval Attempts Enhance Subsequent Learning," *Journal of Experimental Psychology: Learning, Memory, and Cognition* 35 (2009), 989-98.

[162] Benedict Carey, "Forget What You Know about Good Study Habits," *New York Times*, September 6, 2010, accessed September 7, 2010, http://www.nytimes/2010/09/07/health/07mind.html.

seeking challenges, and they need much fewer support structures for persevering to the completion of a complex project than others, such as special needs individuals, many of whom struggle to get through relatively simple acts like eating breakfast and brushing their teeth. All of these students are precious gifts from God and deserve our best efforts to afford them appropriate development of the habit of perseverance.

Figure 2. Planning a Curriculum on Perseverance

Subject	Short Term Individual	Long Term Individual	Short Term Corporate	Long Term Corporate	Literature	Film
English/Language Arts						
Mathematics						
Science						
Social Studies						
The Arts						
Special Education						
Technology/ 21st Century Skills						
Vocational Education						
Physical Education						
Sports/Extra Curricular						
Community Service						

Figure 2 illustrates a planning table that elaborates the whole potential curriculum with application to a particular student or grade level. The structure here follows the time and type approach to perseverance presented in Figure 1 (with additional columns for specific literature and film considerations). Not all of the cells need content, but a planning team could seek to cover all four perseverance time-types within the course of a year via various curricular infusions.

The sciences offer us fields that are rich in examples of perseverance where we can note the long term persistence of individuals like Newton, Galileo, Pasteur, and Edison along with the solid teamwork required by NASA for the initial lunar landing mission. The measurement precision and strict protocol provisions of laboratory assignments give students the opportunity to experience first-hand what real world scientists do to enable a truer understanding of God's beautiful creation. As students move higher in grade level, the laboratory experiments should help nurture perseverance through more challenging and longer term endeavors, such as plant growth studies and automated physical measurements executed over more than a single lab session.

Science class projects. Science labs allow for the introduction of 21st century skills in a natural manner as students have the opportunity to operate as both individuals and teams of two or more students for different assignments. Here, we hope to engender creative problem solving, critical thinking, communication, and collaboration. An all-class term project aimed at solving a scientific problem of importance, either locally or globally, is another way to elicit 21st Century skills enhancement.

All-school science fairs. In most parts of the country, all-school science fairs present deadline-defined events that demand participation by every student enrolled in a science course. Schools can initially sponsor their own science fairs as gateways to local, district, regional, state, and international fairs. Making participation at the school level a graded event for each course helps to guarantee that students will submit an entry. We hope that this extrinsic motivator will move to the intrinsic and volitional phases as positive feedback rewards those whose efforts reflect both insight and hard work.

As an additional motivator, a particular instructor may want to make the course grade contribution increase according to a student's success at the various possible levels of attainment. For instance, an instructor could offer a grade of "A" for the course if the student's investigation wins at the state level. Such a reward may be warranted because the science fair provides a venue that is a real-world scientific experience, and the qualified judges at the higher levels of competition visit the top exhibits to question students in detail about their work (thus removing, to some degree, dependence on others, like mom or dad).

BARRIERS TO PERSEVERANCE

Two great sins against God are presumption and despair, and both of these also hamper perseverance. If a student presumes that all is well from the beginning of an academic project, then the necessary effort to complete the task will be compromised. Likewise, despair means that the student has given up and nothing more can be accomplished. Pascal noted in the *Pensées* that diversion and indifference[163] burden the modern society and these seemingly opposite twins steal the attention of students from academic tasks, particularly those that require persistent focus over time. Our present society brims with digital diversions of all kinds and nonchalant indifference has always had the appeal of looking "cool."

As educators, we have the responsibility of mentoring our students as they learn and practice perseverance. At a minimum, this means that we should point out to individuals and groups of students that these threats are constantly in play, and that all of us need to be on guard lest we knowingly or unknowingly surrender our ability to move forward in the tasks that God has committed to our attention. We especially need to come alongside those students who live with despair, pray with them for Christ's inspiration,

---

[163] Peter Kreeft, *Christianity for Modern Pagans: Pascal's* Pensées *Edited, Outlined and Explained* (San Francisco: Ignatius Press, 1993), 167-206.

and celebrate each small step that they make in terms of academic progress, enhanced understanding, and dogged determination.

CONCLUSION

Jaime Escalante presents an excellent example of two actions that the Christian educators must keep in mind as they interact with their students on a day-to-day basis.

First they must *model* those characteristics of perseverance that they want their students to emulate. Escalante made the on-going effort to be available for tutoring beginning well before and running long after official school hours (to the extent that a janitor's complaints nearly got him fired early in his American teaching career).[164]

Second, they must *mold* the students in terms of the perseverance that they wish to inculcate. Not only did Escalante make himself available to his students, but he demanded that they share his extra time slots in order to accomplish the exceptionally high goals that they had collaboratively set.

In order for students to succeed in school and in life, they will need to persevere through many challenges, large and small, short term and long term, and individually and corporately. This is particularly true of those who are Christ's followers, especially to those who, by following the Laws of the Secret Kingdom, are marked with a fragrance that invites either appreciation or offense.[165]

While these special Christians should take joy in the persecution that indicates that they have obtained the Kingdom of God, they must also maintain perseverance in the face of significant difficulties.

An old hymn, *He Who Would Valiant Be* (modified by Percy Dearmer from lines in Bunyan's *Pilgrim's Progress*) suggests the attitude and outcome that we seek for our students:

"He would valiant be 'gainst all disaster,
Let him in constancy follow the Master.
There's no discouragement shall make him once relent
His first avowed intent to be a pilgrim.

"Who so beset him round with dismal stories
Do but themselves confound – his strength the more is.
No foes shall stay his might; though he with giants fight,
He will make good his right to be a pilgrim.

---

[164] Jerry Jesness, "Stand and Deliver Revisited," *Reason.com*, July, 2010, accessed July 27, 2010. http://reason.com/archives/2002/07/01/stand-and-deliver-revisited.
[165] SK, 99-100.

"Since, Lord, Thou doth defend us with Thy Spirit,
We know we at the end, shall life inherit.
Then fancies flee away! I'll fear not what men say,
I'll labor night and day to be a pilgrim."[166]

---

[166] "He Who Would Valiant Be," accessed July 26, 2010.
http://www.cyberhymnal.org/htm/h/w/hwhowvbe.htm.

RESOURCES

Robertson, Pat. *The Secret Kingdom: Your Path to Peace, Love, and Financial Security.* Dallas: Word Publishing, 1992.

CHAPTER 7
THE LAW OF FIDELITY

By George Selig, Ed.D.
Distinguished Professor of Educational Leadership
Regent University School of Education

"When the final judgment comes, those surprised by the outcome will comprise a multitude beyond reckoning. Many who have regularly been excused by society for 'little sins' will find heaven's doors slammed in their faces. . . . The Law of Fidelity is at once a solemn warning and a promise of eternal blessing. Even as I write these words I am solemnly praying, 'Lord, when it's over, will you say to me, "Well done, good and faithful servant. . . . Enter into the joy of your Master"?' "

PAT ROBERTSON, *THE SECRET KINGDOM*

Jesus expressed the essence of the Law of Fidelity when He said, "Whoever can be trusted with very little can also be trusted with much, and whoever is dishonest with very little will also be dishonest with much."[167] The Law of Fidelity encompasses the essence of moral behavior. It includes what is commonly known today as character development. Fidelity is a common quality that is essential to every aspect of the lives of individuals and nations. When fidelity begins to break down or becomes thought of as quaint or outdated, the evil consequences threaten the very fabric of our existence.

Unfortunately, in today's society, we see all too many examples of a loss of fidelity, such as elected leaders who break trust with their constituents and become involved in immoral actions that compromise their personal integrity and involve them in criminal acts. Society has become so immune to these actions that we hardly give these news reports a second glance. Teachers have an opportunity to turn that situation around and restore the virtue of fidelity to society through our students.

Loss of Fidelity in the Gulf of Mexico

In 2010 a large and esteemed oil and gas corporation experienced a catastrophic explosion on one of its rigs in the Gulf of Mexico. Millions of gallons of crude oil spewed from the well a mile under the surface causing devastation of the fishing industry, the recreation industry and the wetlands along the Gulf Coast. The damage has yet to be fully comprehended, but we know that its effects will linger for decades. An official government report gave this summary:

---

[167] Luke 16:10 NIV.

"The BP Deepwater Horizon drilling rig, situated about 50 miles off the coast of southern Louisiana, exploded on April 20, 2010, resulting in 11 deaths, 17 injuries, and one of the worst environmental disasters in U.S. history. This disaster happened after the oil and gas industry had repeatedly assured the American public that such a disaster was not possible."[168]

While the cause is still under investigation, some reports indicate that corners were cut during the construction and operation of the well. It appears that one or more of the companies involved failed to follow standards recommended by the oil and gas industry for drilling at extreme depths and in some instances used sub-standard materials, ignoring the protests of their own engineers. The results have been catastrophic, not only to the Gulf but also to the standing and reputation of the company itself.

This catastrophe might be explained in a number of ways such as greed, lack of oversight, and arrogance, but one trait that probably explains what happened most concisely is lack of FIDELITY. Perhaps if this company had been faithful to industry standards and to its shareholders, this terrible event might never have occurred.

EVERYDAY EXAMPLES OF FIDELITY

When you are a person of fidelity, you can be trusted to follow through on your promises and pledges. You remain committed to your principles.

Soldiers show fidelity to their country by serving with sacrificial, total commitment, even in the face of death.

Scientists show fidelity to their discipline when they are faithful to follow proper research methods and procedures. However, when fidelity is compromised in the field of pharmaceutical science, for example, researchers manipulate their data to get favorable results so they can rush their products to market. In so doing, they violate their consciences and their own personal ethics. Their abandonment of fidelity just to make huge profits puts their fellow citizens at risk of life-threatening drug reactions and death.

Business people show fidelity when they keep your trust and treat their customers in an honest and straightforward manner.

Teachers demonstrate fidelity when they use teaching and classroom management methods that have been proven to be the most fair and effective, even when those methods are not the ones the teacher might find the most enjoyable to use.

Students show fidelity when they are devoted to their studies, committed to their relationships, and honorable in their intentions and actions.

Millions of men and women—married couples—remain faithful to each other in spite of exposure to opportunities to violate their wedding vows.

---

[168] "Estimating the Economic Effects of the Deepwater Drilling Moratorium on the Gulf Coast Economy," Inter-Agency Economic Report (September 16, 2010), accessed 2010, https://www.piersystem.com/external/content/document/2931/899311/1/Drilling_moratorium_official_repo rt_0915.pdf.

Store clerks return money to a customer who was accidentally overcharged and customers return items that did not ring up on the cash register.

A youngster goes to the door of a house to confess that he accidentally threw a snowball through the glass window while engaging in a snowball fight.

A citizen fills out his income tax honestly, refusing to take unwarranted deductions such as padding the amount given to charitable causes.

These seemingly small acts are big examples of fidelity that confirm again what Jesus observed, "You have been faithful with a few things; I will put you in charge of many things."[169]

HEROES OF FIDELITY IN HISTORY

We can still find heroes throughout history whose names ring valiantly down through the annals of time.

Schoolteacher Hero of the American Revolution

One story that has always resonated with the American public is the story of Nathan Hale, a Connecticut schoolteacher at the time of the American Revolution who joined the Continental Army. By 1776 he had become a captain.

When the British seized control of Long Island and were threatening New York City, General George Washington realized that he could not defend the entire area without more reconnaissance. He was hard pressed to know where the British would attack next so that he could properly defend that area. He knew that civilian spies were often unreliable so he asked for volunteers from the army.

In those days, spying was considered too demeaning for gentlemen and most of his men wanted no part of this effort. However, Nathan Hale rejected the words of discouragement from his friends and other officers and agreed to be a spy for Washington. He told his friends that this task was necessary for the public good and therefore an honorable thing to do.

Unfortunately, while on his mission Captain Hale was captured and brought in for questioning before General William Howe, commander of the British Army. Because Captain Hale was out of uniform, war custom required that he be hanged.

Captain Hale remained loyal and steadfast in the face of his imminent execution. As they placed the noose around his neck, he uttered these immortal words that ring down through history as an example of ultimate fidelity: *"I regret that I have but one life to give for my country."*

This man who never wrote anything important, never owned property, never married or had children, went down in history as one of our greatest patriots, a true American hero and an example for all of us because he was faithful to the very end. He was a model of fidelity!

---

[169] Matthew 25:21 NIV.

Aviator Hero of the Vietnam War

A more recent example of fidelity can be found in the biography of John McCain, now a United States Senator and a past candidate for President of the United States. Regardless of political affiliation, many Americans consider him a war hero for his fidelity.

In October 1967 McCain was a naval aviator serving in the Vietnam War when he was shot down over North Viet Nam. Although he was badly injured, he received almost no medical care from his North Vietnamese captors. He was brutally tortured and held prisoner for more than five years.

In 1968, the North Vietnamese offered him early release, primarily because his father was a U.S. Navy admiral and it would be a major propaganda victory for them to release the admiral's son. In spite of his injuries, which even today make it impossible for him to raise his arms above his head, McCain refused the offer of release because other prisoners of war had been imprisoned for a longer time. He said they deserved to go home first. He knew that release meant escaping many more years of horrendous torture and starvation but he was faithful to his military oath and to his fellow prisoners of war who rallied behind him and were greatly encouraged by his fidelity.

Because of McCain's decision he is now known as a genuine American hero. He took the right action and is a living example of how to conduct ourselves during times of peace and tranquility and also times of war, regardless of the personal consequences.

FAITHFUL TO GOD'S EXAMPLE OF FIDELITY

Fidelity is a moral quality of being truthful, righteous, and trustworthy that stems from our understanding of God and our belief that He is faithful and true. For teachers and for our students it is important that we grasp with ever-increasing depth the fidelity of God toward us and respond to His character by becoming like Him.

Modeling Fidelity as a Teacher

In order to teach fidelity, teachers must first be people of fidelity. There is no greater teaching technique than modeling. If we cannot model the qualities of fidelity in our own lives, we cannot expect students to adopt fidelity in theirs. We need to develop a framework of thought that leads ultimately to the kind of person who has clearly grown up into the image of Jesus Christ. As we grow in our understanding of God and the grace and knowledge of Jesus Christ, we can fully incorporate essential fidelity into our lives.

As a teacher we must:

1. Be a person whom students will look up to and respect.

2. Demonstrate adherence to the principles of right and wrong in the loving manner of Jesus Christ.

3. Become an example of love, mercy, and conviction in all aspects of our lives.

4. Remain truthful, just, and faithful.

These traits might be easy to list, but they are not always easy to carry out. That is why it is so essential that as teachers we maintain an ongoing life of prayer and Scripture, seeking God in all that we do. These days it is sometimes easier to demonstrate our sinful nature than it is to take time to seek the Lord and maintain a level of maturity that makes it possible to think and act as Christ would do.

The privilege of teaching is a calling from God. As we interact with students and others, we are in the process of being sanctified. As we work out our sanctification in the process of teaching students, we are able to demonstrate the power of forgiveness and restoration, which are key components in the process of teaching fidelity.

God doesn't require us to be perfect but He does require us to be faithful. There is no greater demonstration of God's faithfulness than His fidelity and patience with the children of Israel as they wandered in Sinai for those many years before He allowed them to enter the Promised Land. As teachers we must hold on to His example so that we can be faithful in guiding our students through their personal deserts into their future land of promises.

DEVELOPING CHARACTER MEANS DEVELOPING FIDELITY

A holistic view of the Law of Fidelity encompasses the essence of moral behavior and includes every aspect of a person's character. Teachers have an obligation and a charge from the Lord Himself to help students to learn and internalize the character quality of fidelity. If fidelity is not learned at an early age and reinforced throughout the developmental years, it is unlikely that it will emerge in the later years, particularly in situations where it is tempting to take the easy way out and not be proactively trustworthy and faithful.

As teachers, we develop fidelity in the lives of our students on a day-to-day basis, helping them to internalize not only the knowledge of fidelity but the heart of fidelity, as well. We teach and encourage them to adopt those moral behaviors and beliefs that become the watchword of their very being.

Four Key Aspects of Fidelity

There are four key aspects to fidelity—workmanship, self-control, relationships, and empathy.

> **Workmanship**—becoming productive individuals who accept our responsibilities and are faithful to what we have been called to do

Self Control—giving up our rights in deference to the rights of others, not thinking more highly of ourselves than we ought to think and striving to mature in our faith and actions by controlling our natural desires

Relationships—getting along with others and working cooperatively, demonstrating loyalty and trustworthiness in all of our actions and encouraging others to fulfill their destiny

Empathy—putting ourselves in the place of others to understand their plight and reach out to them in a loving, faithful, and sensitive manner

Teachers can develop curriculum and activities that encourage and build fidelity in each of the four essential areas. The following guidelines are a primer for beginning to work toward the goal of developing fidelity in each of your students.

Workmanship—The Teacher's Role

1. Communicate clear standards and expectations, identifying the elements of good workmanship critical for success. Expectations should be high but obtainable.

2. Build on skills that students already possess.

3. Help them to set goals and focus on achieving those goals.

4. Encourage them to begin their work quickly and with purpose.

5. Teach students organizational skills that will facilitate the handling of difficult tasks.

6. Challenge students to finish on time, to be faithful to their tasks, and to stick with a task no matter how difficult it may be.

7. Help students define how they want others to see them.

8. Encourage cooperation among students as they undertake their assignments.

9. Celebrate success with your students.

Recognizing Students with Workmanship Traits

These characteristics will assist in identifying students with good workmanship traits:

1. Self-starter
2. Organized
3. Dependable
4. Perseverant
5. Decisive
6. Responsible
7. Motivated

Self-Control—The Teacher's Role

1. Show appreciation for respectful behavior.

2. Set expectations for practicing self-control.

3. Practice handling difficult situations such as those that produce anger.

4. Create a sense of pride and recognition when self-control is demonstrated.

5. Use role models to encourage self-control.

6. Help students to understand challenges, opportunities, and obstacles in their lives and the lives of others and teach them how to maximize their gifts and opportunities.

7. Help students develop self-evaluation skills and apply them realistically while encouraging their emotional growth.

Recognizing Students with Self-Control Traits

These characteristics will assist in identifying students with self-control traits:

1. Restrained
2. Principled
3. Committed
4. Accountable
5. Truthful
6. Open
7. Flexible

Relationships—The Teacher's Role

1. Create an atmosphere of respect, trust, and harmony in the classroom.

2. Make the classroom a safe and secure place to develop relationship traits and to learn to express ones feelings and values.

3. Build a sense of unity through cooperative activities.

4. Find ways to help students to get along with others and to be sensitive to one another's needs.

5. Help students to build trusting relationships and to develop the skills necessary to maintain them.

6. Teach students how to listen appropriately, negotiate, and express feelings in a way that enhances communication and builds up others.

7. Celebrate the building of relationship traits and commitment to each other.

Recognizing Students with Relationship Traits

These characteristics will assist in identifying students with relationship traits:

1. Forthright
2. Sensitive
3. Considerate
4. Loyal
5. Honest
6. Discreet
7. Humble

Empathy—The Teacher's Role

1. Teach students about the universal themes of life, love, justice, freedom, honor, integrity, and faithfulness in a practical manner.

2. Expose students through stories, videos, etc., to emotionally arousing situations that help them think about their feelings and examine their responses.

3. Use guided situations to lead them into a godly understanding of empathy and appropriate responses.

4. Model empathetic behavior and encourage students to remark on that behavior, identifying it as the right and sensitive thing to do.

5. Help students learn to reach out beyond themselves to help others and to understand their needs.

6. Help students to understand how to forgive and to extend forgiveness to others.

7. Create a classroom where empathy is the norm and not the exception.

8. Insure that students practice respect, courtesy, and appreciation by involving them in classroom activities that help put these traits into practice.

Recognizing Students with Empathy Traits

These characteristics will assist in identifying students with empathy traits:

1. Forgiving
2. Respectful
3. Non-judgmental
4. Trusting
5. Available
6. Kind
7. Sincere
8. Compassionate
9. Sympathetic
10. Understanding

CONCLUSION—BUILDING A NEW GENERATION OF HEROES

People who practice fidelity demonstrate a combination of all of these traits and are truly Christ-like in their behavior. We encourage you to use the guidelines provided to develop traits of fidelity in your students. Begin to integrate activities in your classroom that make fidelity-in-action such a normal, internalized response that when they are faced with overwhelming challenges they respond as heroes and true servants of Jesus Christ.

RESOURCES

Robertson, Pat. *The Secret Kingdom: Your Path to Peace, Love, and Financial Security.* Dallas: Word Publishing, 1992.

CHAPTER 8

THE LAW OF UNITY

By Joan J. Hoskins, Ph.D.
Faculty and Department Chair
Regent University School of Education

*"[Jesus] knew that the fulfillment of the purposes of God
would require unity. Without it, there would be no
flow of power to save the world and to perfect the people of God."*[170]

PAT ROBERTSON, *THE SECRET KINGDOM*

*One of the greatest challenges for educators today is to orchestrate
student diversity into a harmonious learning community.
Within the Secret Kingdom are strategies and principles that
resolve issues of culture and linguistic diversity and provide a
road map for educators to build unity and
access the benefits of God's invisible kingdom on earth.*

As I watch the children in a buzzing elementary school playground, I am quickly reminded of the diversity within school communities of the 21st century. The colors of their faces are as diverse as the colors of their bright summer clothes. The shades reflect a majority of brown and olive tones representing all regions of the globe including Asia, Latin America, Africa, the Middle East, and Europe.

According to the 2008 United States Census Bureau, the U.S. has more than 305 million people today.[171] In 2008, non-Hispanic whites made up about 74 percent of the population[172] and the Census Bureau projected that by 2042 non-Hispanic whites would no longer make up the majority of the population[173]. The percentage is expected to fall to 46 percent in 2050[174]. The report foresees the Hispanic population rising from 15 percent today to 30 percent by 2050.[175]

---

[170] SK, 202.
[171] U. S. Census Bureau, "United States ACS Demographic and Housing Estimates: 2006-2008, Data Set: 2006-2008 American Community Survey 3-Year Estimates, Survey: American Community Survey, accessed December 28, 2010, http://factfinder.census.gov/servlet/ADPTable?_bm=y&-qr_name=ACS_2008_3YR_G00_DP3YR5&-ds_name=ACS_2008_3YR_G00_&-gc_url=null&-redoLog=false&-_caller=geoselect&-geo_id=01000US&-format=&-_lang=en
[172] U.S. Census, American Community Survey.
[173] U.S. Census, American Community Survey.
[174] U.S. Census, American Community Survey.
[175] U.S. Census, American Community Survey.

Today African Americans make up 12 percent of the population; in 2050 they are projected to comprise 15 percent of the population. Asian Americans make up 5 percent of the population today and they are expected to make up 9 percent in 2050.[176]

Other statistics that demonstrate the growing diversity of culture and language in our school communities were captured by the 2009 *Digest of Education Statistics*.[177] Specifically, it reported that in 2008 some 21 percent of children ages 5-17 (approximately 10.9 million children) spoke a language other than English at home, and 5 percent (or 2.7 million) spoke English with difficulty.[178] Seventy-five percent of those who spoke English with difficulty spoke Spanish.[179]

> *The phrase "great American melting pot" once used to describe the incorporation of diverse religions and cultures into one American culture has become inadequate to represent the individuality of our diverse American nation.*

Today individual cultures are respected and individuals are encouraged to maintain their cultural identity, which has resulted in a new national cultural identity representing a mosaic from millions of unique pieces. Classrooms containing linguistically and culturally diverse students have the great promise of increasing our understanding of ourselves and other people and nations. However, this diversity inevitably presents educators with new challenges.[180]

> *These challenges and opportunities will drive the educational system to reform its methods of training teachers, educating children, and developing educational policies at all levels[181]. Now is the time for Christians to come forward with solutions based on the Law of Unity.*

BIBLICAL PRINCIPLES OF UNITY

Best-selling author and Christian Broadcasting Network (CBN) founder Pat Robertson describes universal Kingdom principles of Unity in his classic book *The Secret*

---

[176] U.S. Census, American Community Survey.

[177] T. D. Snyder, S.A. Dillow, and C. M. Hoffman, *Digest of Education Statistics 2009* (NCES 2010-012), National Center for Education Statistics, Institute of Education Sciences, U.S. Department of Education, Washington, DC (2009).

[178] Snyder, Dillow, and Hoffman, *Education Statistics*.

[179] Snyder, Dillow, and Hoffman, *Education Statistics*.

[180] Kathleen Trail, "A changing nation: The impact of linguistic and cultural diversity on education" (published in SEDL Letter Volume XII, Number 2, December 2000, Diversity in Our Schools: New Opportunities for Teaching and Learning), accessed September 12, 2010, http://www.sedl.org/pubs/sedletter/v12n02/2.html.

[181] Kathleen Trail, A changing nation.

Kingdom.[182] The Law of Unity declares that when individuals lay aside personal preconceptions and motives and focus on their agreement with others in Christ, consequently harmony and unity will prevail in any situation or relationship, irrespective of person or position. Unity will be an external manifestation of an internal agreement.

Unity in the Invisible Governs Unity to the Visible

This chapter will address the diverse linguistic and cultural mosaic of the classroom community from the perspective of the Law of Unity. This law, as described by Dr. Robertson, "is simple to understand, and for some, difficult to obey."[183] Like his other laws, it begins with God and His Word. Dr. Robertson says:

> "Perhaps the most powerful illustration of the creative power of perfect unity is found in God Himself. At the very moment of creation there was unity. 'Then God said, "Let *Us* make man in *Our* image, according to *Our* likeness." ' "[184]

Unity in the invisible Secret Kingdom governs unity in the visible world (in earth as it is in heaven).[185] Dr. Robertson points out that when God spoke at the point of man's creation He referenced the word "Us" in His dialogue as He shaped and formed man in "Our" image.[186] God's great creativity and power were released from a place of unity. Conversely, in the absence of unity, as seen in Genesis 3: 22-23, judgment followed man's disunity and Adam was sent out from the garden for his disobedience.

CULTURAL DIVERSITY AND UNITY IN THE EARLY CHURCH

From the beginning of time, God has provided principles of unity and harmony. His model is appropriately demonstrated among the unique members of the body of Christ. A study of the early church's experiences with conflict resolution provides an illustration of the power of unity.

Paul writes of the Christians at Corinth, "The body is a unit, though it is made up of many parts with different functions . . . so it is with Christ."[187] Paul himself experienced the benefits of unity produced in the diverse church at Antioch, where both Jewish and Gentile Christians worshiped God together:

---

[182] SK, 191.
[183] SK, 191.
[184] SK, 191. Emphasis as quoted.
[185] SK.
[186] SK, 191.
[187] 1 Corinthians 12:12 NIV.

"Now those who had been scattered by the persecution in connection with Stephen traveled as far as Phoenicia, Cyprus and Antioch, telling the message only to Jews. Some of them, however, men from Cyprus and Cyrene, went to Antioch and began to speak to Greeks also, telling them the good news about the Lord Jesus. The Lord's hand was with them, and a great number of people believed and turned to the Lord."[188]

Unity in the Church at Antioch

The multicultural diversity of the leadership and membership of the early church at Antioch are highlighted in Acts. 13:

"In the church at Antioch there were prophets and teachers: Barnabas, Simeon called Niger, Lucius of Cyrene, Manaen (who had been brought up with Herod the tetrarch) and Saul." [189]

DeYoung, Emerson, and Kim[190] emphasize the following cultural diversity of the Antioch congregation's prophets and teachers:

- Barnabas—a Jewish Levite
- Simeon, called Niger—a black African
- Lucius of Cyrene—a citizen of Cyrene in North Africa
- Manaen—a Jewish aristocrat brought up with Herod Antipas
- Saul (otherwise known as Paul)—a Jew raised in the Greek culture

CULTURAL UNITY AND DIVERSITY IN HIGHER EDUCATION

Based on my involvement in higher education over the past 12 years, I believe that schools and institutions of higher education have an opportunity to model and demonstrate these same characteristics of diversity in faculty/staff, curriculum, and student body. Within these diverse institutions of learning, we can teach and model biblical unity. We can learn lessons of conflict resolution and creative problem solving when we use the God-given human resources shared daily in our educational environment.

---

[188] Acts 11:19-21 NIV.
[189] Acts 13:102
[190] Curtiss Paul DeYoung, Michael O. Emerson, George Yancey, and Karen Chai Kim, "All churches should be multiracial—the biblical case," excerpt from *United by Faith* (*Christianity Today,* April 2005), accessed 2010, http://www.christianitytoday.com/ct/2005/april/22.33.html.

Biola University's Biblical Worldview on Diversity

Many institutions, including Christian colleges, have attempted to address diversity with a written statement included in the mission. However, many have not addressed the unity component or defined expectations for faculty and students from a biblical worldview. In contrast, Biola University has made great strides in the articulation of their biblical worldview on multiculturalism and diversity, as well as demonstrating the transforming power of unity as an outcome of internationally renowned student and faculty programs.

One exemplary program at Biola is the annual SCORR Conference—Student Congress on Racial Reconciliation—hosted by the Student Life Department. Glen Kinoshita, director of SCORR, describes the objectives and benefits to the participants of this conference, which is now in its 14th year:[191]

> "At this conference you will have the opportunity to meet one another, fellowship, dialogue and pray together for a weekend. Our diverse cultures, customs, styles of worship, and the different perspectives that we bring all add to the richness that makes up the vitality in the Body of Christ. It is essential for us to interact with one another. As we grow in Christ, we also grow to know and better serve one another.

> "This year's theme, 'One New Humanity' declares that as in the New Testament church, Jews and Gentiles were reconciled in Christ and that the wall of hostility had been torn down, so we are to be a testimony to the world. As people groups around the world have their differences and even hostilities, the Church is to display a reconciled people made up of peoples from every tribe, tongue, people and nation.

> "Through our sessions and interactions with one another we seek to grow in our vision for social justice and compassion for all peoples. We all play a crucial role in the building of the Kingdom of God on earth.

> "Because inner transformation leads to faithful action, it is vital that we learn, dialogue, pray, and grow...together. It is our hope and prayer that through this conference, we may stimulate and encourage one another to embrace the challenges of interacting in a more meaningful way."[192]

Power of Biblical Reconciliation

As previously discussed, the church was multicultural and multilingual from its early existence. We have learned from life experiences, Scripture, and church history that as people from various races, cultures, classes and conditions come to faith in Jesus Christ, He reconciles them to God and then we are reconciled to one another.

---

[191] Glen Kinoshita, "From the Director," Biola University Student Congress on Racial Reconciliation 2010, accessed 2010, http://studentlife.biola.edu/diversity/scorr-2010/about-scorr-2010.
[192] Kinoshita, Biola University.

> *The process of reconciliation and unity begins at the individual level and builds with each circle of relationship. At each stage, as people reach unity and harmony, we see God's power released and multiplied.*

Not only does this principle of unity highlight the diversity in the kingdom, but also it is a model for understanding the diversity of gifts in the body and how these all serve a unique purpose and function. Matthew 18:19-20 reflects a perfect example of God's power released and multiplied. The principle is revealed in the passage that states, "I tell you that if two of you on earth agree about something and pray for it, it will be done for you by the Father in heaven. This is true because if two or three people come together in my name, I am there with them."[193] Specifically, this scripture captures a perfect example of kingdom power being released to the world as a result of unity. Dr. Robertson states that the "full implication of the point is that when there is no unity of purpose, no crossover of barriers, then the power is not activated."[194]

The power of biblical reconciliation cannot be overlooked. It is a distinctive characteristic of unity found in the Kingdom as opposed to secular models of multiculturalism and diversity within organizations and institutions.

A great amount of research has been done within the Christian school movement using a character development approach as well as Restorative Disciple models,[195] both at the primary and higher education levels. As a Kingdom teacher, I have imparted my greatest lessons and wisdom through my actions to reconcile with a student following correction or rebuke. My intent in making the correction in student behavior is to reach out and provide a godly standard and to hold students accountable for their behavior in love. The visible results of the application of the Secret Kingdom principles have been enhanced classroom community, reconciliation between teacher and student, and an opportunity to demonstrate mercy within a public school environment.

CREATIVE PROBLEM SOLVING—BENEFIT OF DIVERSITY

Scripture affirms the diverse cultures and gifts found in the universality of church doctrine. God sent His message through the prophet Joel, "Even on my servants, both men and women, I will pour out my Spirit in those days."[196] At Pentecost, Peter's sermon referenced Joel's words in the environment of racial diversity.[197]

Geneva College offers this observation about the Bible's multicultural message in an article called "A Christian View of Diversity":

---

[193] Matthew 18: 19-20 NIV.
[194] SK, 83.
[195] Ron Claassen and Roxanne Claassen, *Discipline That Restores: Strategies to create respect, cooperation, and responsibility in the classroom* (Charleston, SC: BookSurge Publishing, 2008).
[196] Joel 2: 28-29 NIV.
[197] See Acts 2:17.

"It is fitting that this text, so rich in its multicultural implications, became the key text for the Apostle Peter's sermon at Pentecost, when people of some fifteen language groups first heard the gospel preached in their own native tongues (Acts 2:8 12, 16 21). Significantly, the Pentecost event did not involve a miracle of hearing, whereby each person was made to understand one language, but a miracle of speaking, whereby the apostles preached in many languages to the gathered crowds."[198]

At Pentecost, the apostles preached in many languages to the diverse crowd. The principle learned from these examples is that unity of heart released the creative ability and methods to communicate with the diverse cultures represented in this text.

Creative Resolution of Communication Conflicts in the Classroom

Elements of diversity in language and gifts are experienced daily in the multicultural classrooms of the 21st century. The Law of Unity provides an excellent strategy for addressing communication conflicts and misunderstandings rooted in linguistic and cultural diversity. When you are empowered to accomplish the goal of effective communication by the Kingdom principle of unity, you can resolve conflicts that arise between educators and parents that are compounded by challenges in language barriers by changing the focus to a unified objective for student success. This releases divine creative problem solving strategies.

It is critical, however, to understand and acknowledge that unity does not require uniformity or loss of self.

Maintaining Distinctiveness

The Bible clearly provides examples of unity without uniformity in two relevant domains—culture (Acts 11:19-26) and spiritual gifts (1 Corinthians 12: 12-13). In the early church, Jews and Gentiles continued to embrace their *natural birth* culture but rejected certain cultural practices that inhibited their ability to live as one in Christ (*spiritual birth*). For example, both ethnic groups ate and socialized together. For Jewish Christians this required them to give up an understanding that their ethnic identity necessitated separation from Gentiles. They had to risk being seen by their own culture as developing close relations with pagans when they were in fellowship with Gentiles who maintained their distinctiveness.

---

[198] Geneva University, "A Christian View of Diversity," accessed 2010, http://www.geneva.edu/page/diversity.

Significance of the Name "Christian" in the Context of Unity

The church members at Antioch could not be categorized or classified as one group or culture; therefore, a new culture of believers was born. The new term "Christian" is a perfect example of creative problem solving. A need to describe the culture following their spiritual reconciliation in Christ birthed the term "Christian" as a by-product:

> "The Book of Acts emphasizes the cultural diversity of the Antioch church, because it was here that the disciples were first called Christians (11:26). The newly coined term, meaning "Those of Christ," was invented to describe these believers in their unprecedented mix."[199]

Individuals within the school community can be encouraged to maintain their cultural identity while they nevertheless begin to find value in learning from other cultures and develop relationships around unified goals and purpose. Encouraging cultural identity in the school context and community opens doors and builds bridges.[200].

In the educational setting, this principle requires that you support your students in maintaining their family heritage while they simultaneously strive to integrate fully into mainstream society. Consequently, students will contribute in building a society that fosters unity through their unique diversity.

Paul teaches a simple lesson in 1 Corinthians 12 regarding diversity and the function of the gifts within the Kingdom. The passage assures us that our unique gifts can serve God's purpose, if collectively used. This message must be shared in the classroom among our students and parents.

Law of Unity and Learning Styles

In direct alignment with the Law of Unity is the awareness and appreciation of learning styles in the classroom for instructional and assessment success. Students preferentially take in and process information for understanding in many different ways—by seeing and hearing, reflecting and acting, reasoning logically and intuitively, analyzing and visualizing.[201] Not only are students taking in information differently, but instructors have preferences in teaching styles that are often related to a dominant learning style.

According to Richard Felder, ". . . some instructors lecture, others demonstrate or lead students to self-discovery; some focus on principles and others on applications; some emphasize memory and others understanding."[202]

---

[199] Geneva University, "A Christian View of Diversity," accessed 2010, http://www.geneva.edu/page/diversity.

[200] Colin Baker, *A parent's and teacher's guide to bilingualism,* 2nd ed. (Clevedon, England: Multilingual Matters, 2000).

[201] Richard Felder, "Reaching the Second Tier—Learning And Teaching Styles In College Science Education," 1993, J. College Science Teaching, 23(5), 286-290 (1993).
accessed 2010, http://www4.ncsu.edu/unity/lockers/users/f/felder/public/Papers/Secondtier.html .

[202] Felder, Second Tier, 289.

Understanding and appreciating an individual's intellectual style—how one best learns and how one best communicates from this vantage point—improves relationships within the class, thereby unifying the class and school environment.

STRATEGIES FOR THE EDUCATIONAL ARENA

The promises found within the fulfillment of unity principles can clearly be seen and applied to the classroom, parental relationships, and educational policy development. No greater release of God's power and purpose can be found from the collaboration of student, parent, and teacher in the learning environment. As these three participants agree on their purpose and ultimate goals for educational achievement, no barrier or obstacle is too great to overcome. Dr. Robertson observes:

> "Paul the apostle wrote of the fruit of the spirit that would grow in a climate of unity—love, joy, peace, patience, kindness, goodness, faithfulness, gentleness, self-control."[203]

Insignificant Differences and Inclusive Collaboration

How insignificant differences in culture and language become when we agree to walk the journey together—teaching one another, as Christ loves us, how to appreciate the special gifts and unique functions of those created in His image. This principle can be exemplified in an effective inclusion classroom scenario.

In many elementary school settings, the classroom is organized around an inclusion model for instruction of regular education and highly functioning exceptional students. In the ideal arrangement, the regular education class is taught by a general education teacher, a special education teacher, and a teacher's assistant. Often the exceptional student will participate in an out-of-room resource experience.

The most instructionally effective case scenarios are those where the parents, educators, and administrators share a common goal of achievement and use their special gifts and talents to support the instructional process in the regular classroom. This collaboration can appear almost seamless to the outsider but requires constant communication and collaboration to bring the diverse gifts into unity for a single purpose. While rich in the area of investment and time, the benefits to the student, whole class, educators, and parents can be immeasurable.

Each individual and gift brought together by unity releases an abundance of creativity and achievement beyond the individual's limited capacity.

---

[203] SK, 83.

116

Same Goal of Education in Every Culture

During my first year of serving as a school guidance counselor, several experiences with my students' parents allowed me to better appreciate this principle. Many of the parents at the school did not speak English or had limited proficiency in conversational English only. The parent-teacher conferences were spoken in Spanish with the students often serving as translators. However, from the very beginning, I realized one common thread with all of the students and parents within those meetings. Every parent expected their child to succeed. Many parents showed up at conferences, not knowing if they would even be able to understand the teachers, yet having a sincere desire to be a part of their child's education. After the realization that all parties were focused on the success of the student, we began to overcome our language challenges and found new creative ways of communicating. This experience taught me that regardless of the individual differences, the goal of educational success is the same in every culture. The single minded focus of these individuals or quest in purpose translated into peace and a high level of motivation.

Weakness and Disruption Result from Disunity

Unfortunately, this success story is not found in all educational settings where often parents find the diversity overwhelming and choose not to unite with the school system's efforts due to fear or frustration. As a consequence of this disunity among the student, parent, and school system, the opposite of the fruit of the spirit is released in the form of fear, lack of achievement, and frustration among all participants in the educational process. Unfortunately, the greatest loss is experienced by the student with a resulting negative impact on the community and society.

Christ said that any kingdom divided against itself is laid waste; and any city or house divided against itself cannot stand (Mark 3:25). Specifically stated, another universal principle highlights that unity produces strength and disunity produces weakness. Furthermore, the hatred and disunity often expressed between various races, ethnic groups, or social classes has ripped our society apart and continues to destroy communities, nations, and people.

COOPERATIVE LEARNING PRACTICES

The Bible carefully demonstrates that what is true for the individual is true for the organization, group, or nation. Therefore, the benefits and consequences of unity released for an individual hold true for a groups of students, schools, or communities. The instructional strategy of collaboration or cooperative learning is a practical application of these principles that can be used in the classroom or in staff-development activities.

Challenges of diversity and disunity can be addressed by implementing cooperative learning into any educational setting or environment.

Overview of Cooperative Learning

The practice of cooperative learning has undergone many years of validation in order to document its effectiveness and impact on achievement and learning experiences at all levels.[204] Hendry explains:

> "Cooperative learning is optimal when the class is divided into small groups of between three and five learners of varying ability, temperament, culture and gender to enable learners to interact with different people. A specific goal is set out for the group to achieve and they are told that each person's contribution is considered in the achievement of the goal. This is to ensure that no individual is carried by the others in the group."[205]

All group members must help the others to overcome problems and work collectively to finish the assignment.

Individual accountability must be designed as a
critical component of any task or assignment.

"For example, each person in the group is assigned a specific task to complete in order to attain the goal, as a result, if any one person in the group does not contribute, the assignment cannot be completed. By using this strategy, learners are taught the skill of decision making, leadership, good communication and conflict management." Just as with the diverse early church leaders, "conflict within this model can be *constructive* if it encourages the learners to regroup or unite around a solution; it can be destructive if learners are unwilling to change their opinion on a matter (disunity)[206]. It is the teacher's role to guide and facilitate the learning process. The teacher uses praise and encouragement to motivate participation and learning.

Multicultural Applications of Cooperative Learning

Cooperative learning is a valuable method to implement within a multicultural teaching situation.[207] As a result of this method, the learner receives the benefit of a more diverse view on the subject matter, improved self-concept, and a greater motivation to learn.[208]

---

[204] Roger T. Johnson and David W. Johnson, "Cooperative learning: two heads learn better than one," *Transforming Education* (IC#18) Winter 1988, 34, accessed September 12, 2010, http://www.context.org/ICLIB/IC18/Johnson.htm.

[205] Joan Hendry, "Addressing cultural diversity in the classroom" *Helium Magazine* (2002), accessed September 10, 2010, http://www.helium.com/items/964617-addressing-cultural-diversity-in-the-classroom?page=4.

[206] Hendry, cultural diversity, 4.

[207] Geneva Gay and Kipchoge Kirkland, "Developing cultural critical consciousness and self-reflection in pre-service teacher education," *Theory and Practice*, 42 (2003, Summer) (3) (Published by Taylor & Francis, Ltd.), 181-187, accessed September 10, 2010, http://www.jstor.org/stable/1477418.

[208] Felder, Second Tier.

Autonomous learning is encouraged by the fact that the teacher is there to guide and facilitate rather than to lead and control the learning process.[209] This practice reflects principles of unity and harmony that release the creative power of God into the educational experience of all learners in multicultural schools.

For example, "When students work together in small groups it also brings peer tutoring into play so students within an ethnic group who have a higher level of language skills can assist their peers in content comprehension."[210] I would say that God's creative power is released to achieve the goal.

Unfortunately, efforts at multicultural education often depend upon bringing peoples' diversity into a somewhat artificial harmony that seeks to minimize the uniqueness and distinctiveness of people. As Kingdom residents, our main approach focuses upon what we all share in common, which is our faith and our oneness in Christ.

LIFE STYLE INVITATION AND CONCLUSION

The invitation is given daily for educators to seek unity of purpose and demonstrate Kingdom principles to our local school and global community. Simple actions such as team membership, belonging to community groups, cooperative learning strategies, and even singing the national anthem are everyday practices that demonstrate our unity while maintaining our God-given gifts of diversity. Speak loudly with actions and begin to answer the prayer of Jesus in John 17:21, "Father, just as you are in me and I am in you. May they also be in us so that the world may believe that you have sent me."[211]

---

[209] Hendry, cultural diversity.
[210] Merlino, cultural diversity, 2.
[211] John 17:21 NIV.

RESOURCES

Baker, Colin. *A parent's and teacher's guide to bilingualism* (2nd ed.). Clevedon, England: Multilingual Matters, 2000.

Claassen, Ron & Claassen, Roxanne. *Discipline that restores: Strategies to create respect, cooperation, and responsibility in the classroom.* Charleston, SC: BookSurge Publishing, 2008.

DeYoung , Curtiss Paul, Emerson, Michael O., Yancey, George, and Kim, Karen Chai, "All churches should be multiracial—The biblical case," excerpt from *United by Faith* (*Christianity Today,* April 2005), accessed 2010, http://www.christianitytoday.com/ct/2005/april/22.33.html.

Felder, Richard (1993). Reaching the second tier: Learning and teaching styles in college science education. *College Science Teaching, 23*(5), 286-290.

Gay, Geneva, & Kirkland, Kipchoge (2003, Summer). Developing cultural critical consciousness and self-reflection in pre-service teacher education. *Theory and Practice*, 42 (3), 181-187. Published by: Taylor & Francis, Ltd. Retrieved on September 10, 2010 from http://www.jstor.org/stable/1477418

Geneva University, "A Christian View of Diversity," accessed 2010, http://www.geneva.edu/page/diversity.

Hendry, Jane. "Addressing cultural diversity in the classroom." *Helium Magazine* (2002). Retrieved on September 10, 2010 from http://www.helium.com/items/964617-addressing-cultural-diversity-in-the-classroom?page=4

Johnson, Roger and Johnson, David. "Cooperative learning: two heads learn better than one." *Transforming Education* (Winter 1988). Accessed September 12, 2010, http://www.context.org/ICLIB/IC18/Johnson.htm

Kauchak, Donald, P. and Eggen, Paul, D. *Introduction to teaching: Becoming a professional* (2nd ed). Upper Saddle River, NJ: Pearson Prentice Hall, 2005

Merlino, Rob, "Addressing cultural diversity in the classroom." *Helium Magazine* (2002), accessed September 25, 2010, http://www.helium.com/items/169369-addressing-cultural-diversity-in-the-classroom.

Robertson, Pat. *The Secret Kingdom: Your Path to Peace, Love, and Financial Security.* Dallas: Word Publishing, 1992.

Snyder, T.D., Dillow, S.A., & Hoffman, CM. *Digest of Education Statistics 2009 (NCES 2010-012).* National Center for Education Statistics, Institute of Education Sciences, U.S. Department of Education. Washington, DC (2009)

Stahl, Robert (1994). *The essential elements of cooperative learning in the classroom.* Retrieved from ERIC database (ED370881).

Trail, Kathleen (2000, December). "A changing nation: The impact of linguistic and cultural diversity on education." *SEDL News Letter, Diversity in Our Schools: New Opportunities for Teaching and Learning* 12(2), accessed September 12, 2010, http://www.sedl.org/pubs/sedletter/v12n02/2.html.

U. S. Census Bureau. *American Community Survey* (2008), accessed July 27, 2010, http://factfinder.census.gov/servlet/ADPTable?_bm=y&-qr_name=ACS_2008_3YR_G00_DP3YR5&-ds_name=ACS_2008_3YR_G00_&-gc_url=null&-redoLog=false&-_caller=geoselect&-geo_id=01000US&-format=&-_lang=en

CHAPTER 9

THE LAW OF CHANGE

By Hope Jordan, Ph.D.
Professor of Education and Department Chair
Regent University School of Education

"When the structures men build in the material visible world—whether in politics, law, business, science, health, social relations, education, and religion—begin to depart from the principles that characterize God's Spirit, the eternal, invisible kingdom begins to work quietly and secretly in the hearts of men to bring them new structures."[212]

PAT ROBERTSON, *THE SECRET KINGDOM*

"Do not be shaped by this world; instead be changed within by a new way of thinking. Then you will be able to decide what God wants for you; you will know what is good and pleasing to him and what is perfect."[213]

Last summer as I went to the beach with my Sony e-Reader—one compact piece of technology loaded with nearly 100 books—I was reminded of how the world is changing. Later, my son in Afghanistan joined me for lunch at Panera Bread via the Internet and we could see and hear one another as if we were actually in the same restaurant, instead of half a world apart. Technology plays such a large role in bringing modern society closer together that we can Skype or Twitter at any moment with virtually anyone almost anywhere in the world.

We live in a global society where social, political, economic, medical, financial, and educational events in other nations have an impact on our everyday lives. If we as educators expect to solidly ground our students and prepare them to succeed in this changing society, we must change, too. However, as Pat Robertson cautions in *The Secret Kingdom*, we must use wisdom and discernment as we initiate and implement change. He reminds us that God's laws never change and they will continue to govern this changing world.

He quotes from Ecclesiastes:

---

[212] SK, 215.
[213] Romans 12:2 NCV.

> "What has been will be again,
> what has been done will be done again;
> there is nothing new under the sun."[214]

Then Dr. Robertson follows with this statement from Malachi:

> "God has said, 'For I am the LORD, I change not.' "[215]

Dr. Robertson provides a framework and a challenge to each of us to see ourselves as potential agents of change when he says, "No one of us knows which people of the invisible kingdom are being prepared to change the visible kingdom."[216] Christian educators have an opportunity to be among those who bring stability to the changing world of education, but we must be transformed by God's Spirit.

First, seek Him with your whole heart and when you have allowed God to change you then you will have better discernment to know how He wants you to change education. You will be able to stand on a kingdom approach that goes deeper than the latest theory and is stabilized by principles that have stood the test of time.

HOW YOU CAN CHANGE EDUCATION FROM WITHIN

Secret Kingdom principles that operate in the invisible spiritual world are in place when the Law of Change is at work, whether those implementing the change are aware of them or not. Here are five principles that will help you to become one of God's agents of change in the realm of education:

1. Recognize that change begins with your own change of heart.

2. Remain open so that God can prepare you to be His agent of change.

3. As you encounter a problem in education, pray for discernment and ask God, "Should I become Your agent of change in this situation?"

4. Ask God to give you His mandate for action.

5. Keep God's principles in focus and stand firm in prayer as you move forward.

---

[214] Ecclesiastes 1:9 NIV.
[215] Malachi 3:6 NKJV.
[216] SK, 216.

- **Recognize that change begins with your own change of heart.**[217]

From the onset, you need to be sure that your motives are pure, your heart and mind are in the right place, and you are not bringing your own personal motives into the process of changing education. Therefore, your first step is to examine your own heart.

Jesus said, "No man puts new wine into old skins, lest the skins break and all be lost."[218] Dr. Robertson calls this principle "the governing Law of Change." He explains, "As we grow as individuals, each one of us develops habits, thought patterns, and conscious and unconscious attitudes that become more and more shaped by the secular world."[219] He adds, "It is impossible to reform a tired, cracked, wineskin to receive new wine. And it is impossible to reform our cracked, broken, sinful lives by religious exercises. That is why it is absolutely imperative that worldly persons who want God must first have a change of mind, turn from the old life, and then allow Jesus Christ to remake them into vessels suitable for the new wine of God's Spirit."[220]

- **Stay open so that God can prepare you to be His agent of change.**[221]

Change makes people uncomfortable, but people of faith realize that God's world (that includes our personal lives, our organizations, and our schools) is ever-changing. An awareness of this reality helps us to maintain that "new wineskin" approach that Jesus was talking about.

God will prepare you to introduce the right change at the right time and in the right place. As you develop, you may feel uncomfortable. Your human nature may cause you to question and worry, but take all of your worries and questions back to the Lord and stay open to receive His preparation. You can't force change until it is meant to take place but you also can't stop it if you have opened the door to God.

- **As you encounter a problem in education, pray for discernment and ask God, "Should I become Your agent of change in this situation?"**[222]

Is the Lord making you aware of corruption, apathy, incompetence, or another specific area in need of improvement? Perhaps you are God's agent to lead or facilitate change! In order to know the right direction, Christian educators need to pray for discernment with regard to both the problems and the solutions in modern education.

---

[217] SK, 220
[218] See Matthew 9:17.
[219] SK, 219.
[220] SK, 220.
[221] SK, 210, 212.
[222] SK, 211, 216.

You must know when to move forward or when to change routes. Sometimes as you proceed you may even determine that this is the wrong path for change or the wrong time or place and you must be able to determine when to quit.

- **Ask God to give you His mandate for action.**[223]

When it is time for change, action is needed. If God wants change to take place, He will provide the mandate for action. Often God prepares you for much more than you can imagine. Seek the Lord's wisdom and talk to trusted confidants. Ask questions, gather data, and ask yourself, "Is everything in place for me to go in the direction that God is leading?"

Remember, you can expect to encounter resistance that will require your persistence. There will be roadblocks as you proceed, so pray for discernment!

You cannot sit back and hope someone else will take the action that God has mandated for you to take. Too often people are frozen in a safe place as they wait for someone else to do the job that God has already given them. In his book *Fearless,* Max Lucado states, "When fear shapes our lives, safety becomes our god."[224]

Bruce Wilkinson says in *The Dream Giver* that we are each given a big dream but many never come close to achieving what God has intended as we let obstacles and fear get in the way.[225]

Take action based on the Lord's guidance and fear not.

- **Keep God's principles in focus and stand firm in prayer as you move forward.**[226]

Beyond initial action, further action is needed to continue to move forward.[227] All action, however, must be taken in the manner God wants you to proceed. You may think you should change an entire school system but the Lord may only want you to start with your school, grade level, or just your classroom. Be discerning and faithful as you maneuver on the path where the Lord would have you go, whether that path includes large or small changes.

For those working in the public schools, it is especially important to remain strong, stand firm, and be guided by the Lord rather than becoming changed by negative influences. Like Elijah who ended the three-year drought with earnest prayer, reach into the invisible world with repeated and earnest prayer![228] Look for God's principles and maintain them.

---

[223] SK, 210.
[224] Max Lucado. *Fearless: Imagine Your Life without Fear* (Nashville: Thomas Nelson, 2009), 23.
[225] Bruce Wilkinson, *The Dream Giver* (Colorado Springs, CO: Multnomah Books, a Division of Random House, 2003).
[226] SK, 217-218.
[227] SK, 213.
[228] SK, 218.

Dr. Robertson points out that in God's Spirit there is truth, justice, compassion, wisdom, liberty, free enterprise, moral self-restraint, and humble simplicity.[229] When these principles are obvious, there is a better chance that God's Spirit is present and you will be successful.

If you are God's agent and have used discernment as you proceed yet you are unable to make progress, you may be struggling against corruption or an ineffective organization. Even the smallest change can cause dissonance and be difficult. Don't be discouraged. God will send you what you need to make the change happen if it is His will. Don't give up.

There is constant pressure in educational settings to conform to the status quo. Sometimes you are expected to say, believe, or do only things that are acceptable to the general population or the mandate of the organization.

For example, the only acceptable discussion in some teachers' lounges and gathering spots may be negativity toward administrators, students, or teaching duties. Anything that is positive or enthusiastic may be greeted with cynicism and ridicule. Those who take initiative, uphold the cause of children with disabilities, or hold a political view counter to the culture of other teachers may be chastised or ostracized.

Everyone likes progress, but only a few feel comfortable with real change. The pressure is on within worldly systems to conform. Christians must continuously seek God's kingdom principles to bring true and lasting change.

Below are two examples of positive change in schools.

EPIPHANY SCHOOL—
MOBILIZING A COMMUNITY TO CHANGE EDUCATION

In 2005, award-winning author and philanthropist Nicholas Sparks along with his wife and associate Thomas McLaughlin saw the need for educational change in their community of New Bern, North Carolina.[230] They started by taking their vision to the community and asking some questions. It is not obvious whether these three people intended to use the principles from the Law of Change when they seeded what became the Epiphany School, but as you analyze the process they took, you can see that many of the supporting principles were in place.

First Nicholas Sparks asked the community what they thought about a faith-based school that inspired scholarship. By asking the community good questions, he utilized invisible spiritual principles to see if the community was open to change. In essence, as Dr. Robertson might say, he was looking for new wineskins to receive the new wine of change. Taking these steps he was already at Principle #2 by remaining open to what was new.

As a Board of Trustees formed and developed the school's mission, the members had to utilize discernment and stand firm in order to walk through all the difficulties that

---

[229] SK, 215.
[230] Nicholas Sparks' bio is online at www.nicholassparks.com/aboutnicholas.asp?PageID=4.

are inherent in starting a new school. The Epiphany School Mission reflects their focus on listening for God's voice as it opens with these words: "We are a community of faith and scholarship that challenges students to uncover and expand their unique God-given gifts." The first Core Value for the school also cites God as the Source and Summit of their existence.[231]

The founders of the Epiphany School saw a need to provide more options than those available to middle and high school students at that time in the New Bern, North Carolina, area. Using principles from the Law of Change they opened the new school in 2006 with 97 students in grades 6-10. The school has expanded to include grades 5-12 (as of Fall 2010) and 280 students. During a visit to the school, I was given a tour and spoke to David Wang (assistant head of school/Upper School director) about the school's success and growth that has necessitated expansion of the facility to include a vision for a new high school building in the near future.

In order to establish this new school with forward-thinking approaches, the founders had to start by recognizing a need for change (Principle #1) and were open ("new wineskins") for that change (Principle #2). As they developed their mission and vision they kept their focus on God as their source and utilized Principles 2-5 as they took action and stood firm to ultimately launch this innovative school.

Although the Epiphany School has only been in existence for a few years and data is therefore limited, they are already seeing academic success as measured through outcomes-based curriculum, the California Achievement Test scores, the PSAT scores, math test scores from a test that is normally given to incoming freshmen at East Carolina University, and the National Latin Exam scores. The students are doing well academically and most of the graduates go on to attend college.

The Epiphany School provides an example of a faith-based school that focuses on diversity and global awareness through academic studies, service, and international travel. It enhances scholarship through an emphasis on college preparation. This unique school shows promise for an exciting future as it utilizes principles of the Law of Change while it continues to grow.[232]

RADICAL INNER-CITY CHANGE— AMERICAN INDIAN PUBLIC CHARTER SCHOOL

Dr. Ben Chavis is an example of a public charter school principal who took such strong, successful actions to change an inner-city school in Oakland, California, that he now leads a national initiative using the principles he developed. Although we might not agree with all of his methods and personal opinions, we endorse his success as a positive example of change.

Ben Chavis grew up in the southern United States in an American Indian family

---

[231] Epiphany School Mission Statement at http://www.epiphany-nb.org/MissionandValues.html.
[232] For more information about the Epiphany School, please go to www.epiphany-nb.org. There is also a video clip of an interview with Nicholas Sparks on *The 700 Club* at http://www.cbn.com/cbnnews/us/2010/May/Nicholas-Sparks-Epiphany-on-Education/.

of sharecroppers. In his autobiography, *Crazy Like a Fox,*[233] he says that one of his grandfathers was a preacher and the other was a bootlegger. He says he learned something from both of them. When he was principal of the American Indian Public Charter School of Oakland, California (which had many nationalities, not just American Indians), he went to the neighborhood churches to get the pastors involved.

With his controversial style, he also communicated with local drug dealers. He then used those conversations to keep the kids in line by telling them that those tough guys on the streets would be watching them.

He motivated parents to take an unprecedented part in the success of the schools, including one visit to the neighborhood bar where he publicly chastised one of the mothers who missed his meeting. His technique worked as she never missed another meeting.

When he made his first, unannounced visit to the American Indian Public Charter School, where he had been asked to serve as principal, he saw a trash-infested mess with middle-school and high-school children wandering around and doing what they wanted, including having sex in a next-door building. He decided to take on the challenge. In a series of strong moves he transferred all of the older children to high schools so that he could focus on the middle school, ended socially sensitive classes, and launched tough academic courses. He placed each age group of students in one school room with the same teacher all day (like an elementary school model) and looped them—kept them with the same teacher as long as they were in the school.

Chavis says he understood from his background that minority children achieve the greatest results in a structured environment with discipline and accountability. He gives examples of church, sports, and the military to prove his point. He says that they are also strongly motivated by personal relationships and a family environment, which many of them lack at home. He created something similar to a family by placing them in one classroom for three years to develop the family-type constraints of a familiar environment among friends who hold one another accountable under firm but fair adults who are their teachers and role models.

Within one year Chavis had achieved outstanding success with his primarily Asian, Black, Latino, and American Indian students and soon won national awards. The first American Indian Public Charter School (AIPCS) won the U.S. Department of Education Blue Ribbon School award in 2006 under No Child Left Behind. The school found success through a back-to-basics approach of discipline, structure, hard work, and high expectations. This school achieved a 99.5 percent attendance rate and collaboration between school, community, and family.

Replication of a Successful School

Journalist Mitchell Landsberg of the *LA Times* reported on the academic excellence that became a consistent benchmark of schools replicating Chavis's system:

---

[233] Dr. Ben Chavis with Carey Blakely, *Crazy Like a Fox: One Principal's Triumph in the Inner City* (New York: New American Library, 2009).

"The Academic Performance Index (API), the central measuring tool for California schools, rates schools on a scale from zero to 1,000, based on standardized test scores. The state target is an API of 800. The statewide average for middle and high schools is below 750. For schools with mostly low-income students, it is around 650.

The oldest of the American Indian schools, the middle school known simply as American Indian Public Charter School, has an API of 967. Its two siblings—American Indian Public Charter School II (also a middle school) and American Indian Public High School— are not far behind. Among the thousands of public schools in California, only four middle schools and three high schools score higher. None of them serves mostly underprivileged children."[234]

In July 2007 Chavis retired after seven years as principal of the American Indian Public Charter School and now trains others to use the principles through the American Indian Model of Education (AIM-Ed). He is helping others in North America take failing schools to top performing schools through replication of the first model.[235] AIM Schools promote family culture, accountability, structure, high expectations, and free-market capitalism with a primary goal to enhance academic skills.[236] These schools also utilize student contracts, dress codes, and summer programs and all this results in some very impressive test scores—some of the highest in the state of California for schools with 97% free/reduced lunch and 98% minority populations.[237]

CHANGE EVIDENT IN 21ST CENTURY THEORY

Let's take a look at modern educational change as we apply biblical principles to contemporary education. Clayton Christensen, Michael B. Horn, Curtis Johnson, Tony Wagner, and James Comer are educational theorists who are leading the way in the recent discussion of change in schools.

Christensen, Horn, and Johnson suggest that disruptive innovation (a concept first introduced in business) is needed in order to change the way the world learns. In *Disrupting Class: How Disruptive Innovation Will Change the Way the World Learns*, the authors use change research and theory to reveal how customizing student-centric approaches by intrinsically motivating our students can maximize their potential.[238]

In *The Global Achievement Gap,* Tony Wagner elaborates on the need to overhaul our educational system with dramatically different schools. He proposes a need for more

---

[234] Mitchell Landsberg, "Spitting in the eye of mainstream education," *LA Times* (May 31, 2009), accessed 2010, http://www.latimes.com/news/local/la-me-charter31-2009may31,0,7064053.story.
[235] "American Indian Public Charter School," accessed 2010, http://www.aimschools.org/.
[236] "The AIM Model," http://www.americanindianmodel.org/AIM/AIM_Model.html.
[237] The AIM Model.
[238] Clayton M. Christensen, Michael B. Horn, and Curtis Johnson, *Disrupting Class: How Disruptive Innovation Will Change the Way the World Learns (*McGraw Hill, 2008).

and better lessons to enhance collaboration, critical thinking, adaptability, oral and written communication, entrepreneurialism, analysis, and creativity.[239]

Creating a new kind of school environment that considers societal impact and child development is James Comer's focus in *Leave No Child Behind: Preparing Today's Youth for Tomorrow's World.* Comer also emphasizes the importance of relationships in bringing change to schools.[240]

These theorists have opened new levels of discussion on change in schools. Their books are examples that underscore a few of the current hot topics surrounding the issues of educational change. There is a need to disrupt our contemporary educational practices and make changes in order to enhance academic achievement for all students. Identifying a need for change in any school setting is only the first step. It needs to be followed with action in order to put those changes in place and actually effect change. No one model for change will fit every school. Each educational community needs to decide what change is needed and exactly how to make those changes based on sound principles.

No matter what the specific needs of the community or whether the educational setting is public or private, *Secret Kingdom* principles of change are still in effect. Christian educators can utilize the principles of the Law of Change and intentionally reach into the invisible kingdom to impact change.

PERSONAL APPLICATIONS

Your first step in utilizing the Law of Change is to realize that change will take place and prepare yourself by making sure that your heart is in the right place—God's place. Prayer and reflection will help you to stay open to see how the Lord wants to use you in the change process. Use wisdom and discernment to determine what changes need to be made and how to implement those changes.

Ask yourself the following questions:

- Is my heart ready?
- Do I understand that God's world is ever-changing?
- Am I open and ready to change as a new wineskin?
- Am I working with others who are open and ready for change?
- Am I God's chosen agent for this change (am I the best person to do this job)?
- Do I have God's mandate for action?
- Am I pursuing God's preparation process?
- Am I using wisdom and discernment as I move forward?
- Is this the right time and place for action?
- Am I keeping truth, justice, compassion, wisdom, liberty, self-restraint and humility in mind as I proceed? Do I recognize these traits in others?

---

[239] Tony Wagner, *The Global Achievement Gap: Why Even Our Best Schools Don't Teach the New Survival Skills Our Children Need—and What We Can Do about It* (Basic Books, 2008).

[240] James P. Comer, *Leave No Child Behind: Preparing Today's Youth for Tomorrow's* World (Integrated Publishing Solutions, 2004).

- As I pray, reflect and ask for wisdom, do I have the strength to stand firm when needed so that I will not give up until this change takes place?

As you pray and meditate on these questions, you will begin to tap into the invisible spiritual kingdom and understand how you can become God's agent of change.

CONCLUSION

Most experts in the field of education agree that change is needed in our schools. Pat Robertson's Law of Change provides a framework for implementing positive change through the power of the invisible spiritual kingdom.

In this chapter we have looked at some suggestions and models from Clayton Christensen, Michael B. Horn, Curtis Johnson, Tony Wagner, James Comer, Epiphany School, Ben Chavis, and the U.S. Department of Education regarding what is needed to implement successful change. They all provide specific examples of educational change that work in conjunction with Pat Robertson's Secret Kingdom principles.

As a Christian educator, you may be working in a public school, a Christian school, or a home school. In every setting there is always room for improvement through positive change. Whether the changes you are making are at the classroom, school, district/division, state or federal level, Secret Kingdom principles still apply.

Perhaps God has destined you to design a model charter school or to implement instructional changes as a public school principal, as Ben Chavis did. Maybe you are on a path to do research, write, speak, and consult like James Comer. Maybe you are becoming aware of corruption, apathy, incompetence, or a need for major improvements in your setting and you will be God's agent for change. Be sure to keep taking your concerns to the Lord in prayer and He will lead you down the right path to the changes that you are to facilitate.

Our children and young people are unique and special creations and deserve the best possible education. Those who are called to teach and lead have a very important task. Combining the principles of the Secret Kingdom Law of Change with research-based best practices will result in change that leads our students on a positive path toward achieving 21st century skills.

Resources to Support Change in Schools

There are numerous resources available that encourage innovation – below are a few you might find helpful.

- U. S. Department of Education Web Site – this site discusses innovation and change in education and successful charter schools. They provide elements of successful charter schools and highlight K-8 schools that provide models for innovation in the 21st century. http://www2.ed.gov/admins/comm/choice/charter/index.html (highlights successful charter schools)

- KIPP (Knowledge is Power Program) Academy of Houston – This site highlights one of 82 KIPP Academies across the United States and has been recognized as one of U.S. News and World Reports Top High Schools http://www2.ed.gov/admins/comm/choice/charter/report_pg16.html#fourth (one of the 8 schools The KIPP ACADEMY in Houston)

- Online Charter Schools -- Technology is providing more opportunity for change in schools through online schools. CBN News did a report, *Online Charter Schools Proving Popular* which highlighted virtual academies. The on-line charter schools in this report are becoming very popular, particularly in Idaho and many support those who opt for home schooling. However, more and more public schools are also providing online options as tens of thousands of children take online classes. Online classes bring the best curriculum and subject experts to any location via the computer and often meet state requirements while providing content to pass state exams. Many of the best options also provide online interaction with instructors. These online schools provide alternatives to those who for health, academic, faith, or flexibility reasons prefer not to attend a traditional public school. http://www.cbn.com/cbnnews/us/2009/November/Online-Charter-Schools-Proving-Popular-/ (full report of online charter schools)

- Edison Learning – An organization that partners with schools to achieve school improvement. http://edisonlearning.net/

- Lexington Institute -- This organization has a mission to inform, educate & shape public debate. www.lexingtoninstitute.org

Video to Promote Discussion

Waiting for Superman -- http://www.waitingforsuperman.com/
The Lottery -- http://thelotteryfilm.com/
The Race to Nowhere -- http://www.racetonowhere.com/

RESOURCES

700 Club, "A School Principal's Triumph in the Inner City," accessed July 2, 2010,
http://www.cbn.com/cbnnews/us/2009/October/A-School-Principals-Triumph-in-
the-Inner-City/

700 Club, "Online Charter Schools Proving Popular," accessed 2010,
http://www.cbn.com/cbnnews/us/2009/November/Online-Charter-Schools-
Proving-Popular-/ (detailed report on online charter schools)

Technology is providing more opportunity for change in schools through online
schools. *Online Charter Schools Proving Popular* highlights virtual academies
such as one in Idaho. Many of these also support those who opt for home
schooling.

More and more public schools are providing online options as tens of thousands
of children take online classes. Online classes bring the best curriculum and
subject experts to any location via the computer and often meet state requirements
while providing content to pass state exams. Many of the best options also
provide online interaction with instructors. These online schools provide
alternatives to those who for health, academic, faith, or flexibility reasons prefer
not to attend a traditional public school and are an example of educational change
that require a new mindset (new wineskins).

700 Club, "Public Charter Schools," accessed 2010,
http://www.cbn.com/media/player/index.aspx?s=/vod/DBR141v1_WS.

American Indian Public Charter School

Mitchell Landsberg, "Spitting in the eye of mainstream education," *LA Times*,
May 31, 2009, accessed 2010, http://www.latimes.com/news/local/la-me-
charter31-2009may31,0,7064053.story.
"American Indian Public Charter School," accessed 2010,
http://www.aimschools.org/.
"The AIM Model," accessed 2010,
http://www.americanindianmodel.org/AIM/AIM_Model.html.

Chavis, Ben, with Blakely, Carey. *Crazy Like a Fox: One Principal's Triumph in the
Inner City.* New York: New American Library, 2009.

Christensen, Clayton M., Horn, Michael B., and Johnson, Curtis, W. *Disrupting Class:
How Disruptive Innovation Will Change the Way the World Learns.* McGraw
Hill, 2008.

Comer, James P. *Leave No Child Behind: Preparing Today's Youth for Tomorrow's World.* Yale University Press, 2004.

Epiphany School

> Main website: www.epiphany-nb.org
> Mission Statement: http://www.epiphany-nb.org/MissionandValues.html
> Video clip of an interview with Nicholas Sparks on "The 700 Club":
> http://www.cbn.com/cbnnews/us/2010/May/Nicholas-Sparks-Epiphany-on-Education/.

KIPP [Knowledge Is Power Program] Academy of Houston. Their website highlights one of 82 KIPP Academies across the United States and has been recognized in *U.S. News and World Report* Top High Schools. "America's Best High Schools Gold Medal Report," U.S. News and World Report (June 22, 2010). accessed June 22, 2010, http://www.usnews.com/sections/education/high-schools/index.html.

> See http://www2.ed.gov/admins/comm/choice/charter/report_pg16.html#fourth about one of the eight schools of the KIPP Academy in Houston.

Lucado, Max. *Fearless: Imagine Your Life without Fear.* Nashville: Thomas Nelson, 2009.

Robertson, Pat. *The Secret Kingdom: Your Path to Peace, Love, and Financial Security.* Dallas: Word Publishing, 1992.

Sparks, Nicholas. Nicholas Sparks' website: www.nicholassparks.com

U.S. Department of Education. "Innovation in Education: Successful Charter Schools," accessed May 1, 2010, http://www2.ed.gov/admins/comm/choice/charter/index.html. This U. S. Department of Education website discusses innovation and change in education and successful charter schools. It highlights K-8 schools that provide models for innovation in the 21st century.

Wagner, Tony. *The Global Achievement Gap: Why Even Our Best Schools Don't Teach the New Survival Skills Our Children Need—and What We Can Do about It.* Basic Books, 2008.

Wang, David. Personal Interview, June 15, 2010.

Wilkinson, Bruce. *The Dream Giver.* Colorado Springs, CO: Multnomah Books, a division of Random House, 2003.

CHAPTER 10

THE LAW OF GREATNESS

By Hope Jordan, Ph.D.
Professor of Education and Department Chair
Regent University School of Education

*"All people desire to be great. Because of human frailty, however,
this can turn out badly, especially if we think in terms of
comparison with others, for that usually spells pride."*[241]

PAT ROBERTSON, *THE SECRET KINGDOM*

*"The greatest among you will be your servant. For whoever exalts himself will be
humbled and whoever humbles himself will be exalted."*[242]

JESUS

When you enter the brightly lit corridors of Ocean Lakes High School (OLHS) in Virginia Beach, Virginia, you immediately sense a positive atmosphere and are surrounded by a feeling of respect. You are greeted with a smile and "How can we help you?" or "How are you today?" As you sign in, you are given directions to the location you seek or someone may actually walk with you to help you find your way through this large, modern building. Students, faculty, and staff you meet along the way greet you with "Good morning!" or "Good afternoon!" The school is clean and decorated with student work and awards.

OLHS is a public school model that follows key concepts highlighted by Pat Robertson in his chapter on the Law of Greatness in *The Secret Kingdom* and emphasized by many other authors.

I completed my public school career on a very positive note when I was blessed to have the opportunity to work at OLHS. It was relatively new when I began (only its third year of existence) so we did not have much history with regard to test scores. At that time there were fewer required tests but we had an excellent student leadership program, a successful magnet school, strong attendance and graduation rates, and teachers who were active and extended their support to students beyond the school day. Teachers at OLHS wanted to come early or stay late to work with the kids.

Having been in public schools for more than 15 years when I started teaching at OLHS, I had never experienced such a positive culture, such involved and supportive

---

[241] SK, 179.
[242] Matthew 23:11-12 NIV.

leadership, and such a group of devoted teachers. I was completing my own academic training in leadership at that time and was intrigued by this school and its leadership.

Student achievement and positive parent, student, and teacher ratings are key components of a school that aspires to greatness. A rewarding work environment and school culture are also important if a school is to remain successful. Recently I confirmed that Ocean Lakes High continues to be a school that portrays a welcoming atmosphere and encourages positive attitudes, leadership, and academic success. I investigated OLHS's current test scores (one important measure of high school success these days) and found that not only did this school make its AYP (Annual Yearly Progress) requirements, it also met or exceeded standards in all major academic areas including algebra, chemistry, biology, earth science, English/reading, geography, Virginia and United States history, geometry, world history, and writing.[243]

Ocean Lakes High is diverse with 33 percent "minority population" of the students having Asian, Black, Hispanic, or American Indian ethnicity. Their graduation rate for African Americans (85 percent), Caucasians (88 percent), and Hispanics (85 percent) is above both the state and district averages. They have a 96 percent attendance rate and when surveyed, students, parents, and teachers rated the school with a high quality of learning (more than 90 percent approval).[244]

Leadership of Greatness -- Humility and Service

The principal of OLHS while I was there was Jerry Deviney. His humility and service were traits that helped guide this large public high school to greatness and left a mark that remains at OLHS today. He encouraged these attitudes in his faculty who encouraged it in the students. He was one of the most humble principals I had ever met. While I taught in that school, I never heard him take credit for any of the school's successes. He was always quick to point out faculty, staff, or students who really deserved the praise.

Carolyn Thompson, a retired speech-language pathologist who culminated her career at OLHS, commented on the environment of greatness that existed under his leadership. She said, "Notwithstanding a remarkable facility with state-of-the-art educational technology and structural beauty, the pulse of that school is an exceptionally nurturing environment that supports, encourages, and expects excellence. This excellence extends not only to the parameters of the academic classroom but student deportment, emotional stability of the staff, and the genuine willingness to extend a safe learning environment to the students. Under Mr. D's [Jerry Deviney's] guiding hand, the Dolphin Code developed and flourished. He often stated, 'I selected the best of the best from numerous applicants and now I have to harness their energy.' He instinctively knew how to tap each of our strengths and watched the blanket of caring cover the student body. A

---

[243] Ocean Lakes High Test Results, accessed September 11, 2010,
http://www.education.com/schoolfinder/us/virginia/virginia-beach/ocean-lakes-high/test-results/.
[244] Ocean Lakes High Annual Report Card, accessed September 11, 2010,
http://www.vbschools.com/school_data/report_cards/0910/high/AnnualSchoolReportCard-OceanLakesHS.pdf.

testimony to that guiding principle is evident in the number of graduates who are current on staff."[245]

Cheryl Askew, who followed Jerry Deviney as principal of Ocean Lakes High School (she is principal there as of 2010), wrote the following about her predecessor:

"Jerry Deviney laid a foundation of greatness at Ocean Lakes High School and this foundation has continued to serve the school well some 17 years later. It has been a blessing to have been a member of the staff since we first opened the doors on September 7, 1994. My experience has been unique in that I came to Ocean Lakes as a teacher, moved to a computer resource position, then to an assistant principal position, and finally to become the school's second principal. Mr. Deviney has been my mentor throughout the process and it was through watching his leadership in action that I came to understand what it means to be a great principal. Every decision he made, every action he took started with the question, 'What is best for my students, my staff, and my school?' He never took credit for any good idea or successful program. He always sought to give others the spotlight—especially the students.

"Mr. Deviney often said that it is not the bricks and mortar that make a great school; it is instead the people inside the building working and learning together. That is the philosophy we have endeavored to continue since Mr. Deviney left six years ago. I remember very vividly my first staff meeting as principal. I told the staff that I knew I would never be Jerry Deviney, but that I understood and believed in the same ideals. His example was to put others before yourself, always be willing to work hard, and never compromise your values."

Ms. Askew provides a picture of the values of humility and service that Mr. Deviney exuded as he led OLHS through its early years but also speaks to her ongoing attitude of humility and service as she continues to lead. When I called her, I asked Cheryl to share what she is currently doing to keep the school on the right track and as you can see she, like Mr. Deviney, continues to give credit to others.

Hiring People with Qualities of Greatness

When I asked Jerry Deviney about his humble spirit and dedication to service, Mr. Deviney said, "I wasn't trying to be humble. I really believe that the staff deserve the credit. Be a cheerleader, hire the right people, create a climate, provide support, and get out of the way."[246] He said that excellent schools are built around successful faculty and he had taken great pains in choosing that initial faculty (many of whom still teach at the school). He said he was greatly influenced by William Purkey's "Invitational Education" model and the need for leaders to see their staff as able, valuable, and responsible. He found that if you see them as valuable and trust them, they flourish and will, for the most part, live up to your expectations.

---

[245] Personal Interview with Carolyn Thompson (September 12, 2010).
[246] Personal Interview with Jerry Deviney (September 21, 2010).

Like Jim Collins in *Good to Great,* he felt that getting the right people on the bus was most important. He chose people who were skilled, dedicated nurturers and smiled a great deal. They had a passion for education and a willingness to participate in extra-curricular activities—not because he required it, but because it was important.

Mr. Deviney said it is always easier to work with someone who by nature has a pleasant personality. Once you have talented, dedicated people, he noted that the only problem was keeping a handle on all their energy and helping them guide their great ideas to fruition. He likened it to holding the string on a bunch of helium balloons. He said he never had a lack of good ideas to work with in a school that had creative teachers. He finished our conversation in humility, as he had modeled all those years ago, by commenting on how lucky he was to have worked with such a great group of people in such a good school.

THE IMPORTANCE OF HUMILITY AND SERVICE

Mike Singletary, Football Hall of Famer and former coach of the San Francisco 49ers, models characteristics of greatness. The lessons of humility and sacrifice/service that he has learned can benefit teachers and educational leaders on a path to greatness.

As a born-again Christian, he tries to lead by example and both he and his wife believe in trying to make a positive impact on the community by giving back.[247] During an interview for "The 700 Club," Mike noted that he puts Christ first in his life and sets clear goals. He cries out to the Lord and listens for answers. He has learned that all the football glory he received early in his career only left him unfulfilled and that he needed to clean up a few things in his life (his language, some of the music he listened to, and how he treated others) in order to be all that God wanted him to be.[248] He said that first you need to humble yourself and be ready to sacrifice yourself to others in order to be a good father or a good coach.[249]

Longing to Be Great

Humility begins with removing competition between self and others. In his book *The Dream Giver,* Bruce Wilkinson posits that we are born with a God-given "Big Dream."[250] He describes this dream as a powerful, universal longing. He encourages individuals to identify their God-given dream and then focus on achieving that dream rather than focusing on what everyone else is doing. [251]

---

[247] "Mike Singletary," accessed September 23, 2010, http://www.answers.com/topic/mike-singletary.
[248] "Mike Singletary: Christ Means Everything," video from "The 700 Club," accessed September 21, 2010, http://www.cbn.com/media/player/index.aspx?s=/vod/SB85v2_Web_WS.
[249] Singletary, Christ Means Everything
[250] Bruce Wilkinson, *The Dream Giver* (New York: Multnomah Publishers, 2003), 6.
[251] Wilkinson, *Dream Giver.*

Similarly, Pat Robertson in *The Secret Kingdom* discusses the longing to be great.[252] Both authors emphasize the importance of following God's path as you fulfill your dream and achieve greatness.

Love of Learning

The truly humble are as open to new ideas and as pliable and teachable as a small child. Jesus said, "I tell you the truth, you must change and become like little children. Otherwise, you will never enter the kingdom of heaven. The greatest person in the kingdom of heaven is the one who makes himself humble like this child."[253]

Humility requires an ability to listen and a love of learning that come from the realization that we do not know it all and we continue to have so much more to learn. The truly humble are open to new ideas, are pliable, and have a teachable spirit. Even as accomplished adults, we are not all-knowing and what we know is miniscule compared with God's knowledge. That is humbling.

Dr. Robertson reminds us that children trust their parents and we need to trust God as our Father. He states, "Such total trust in the provision and protection of God is the first giant step toward greatness."[254] Adults who exhibit curiosity, are inquisitive, and trust the Lord are more likely to develop a stronger sense of humility.

Teachers and educational leaders with a love of learning and curiosity who trust the Lord and remain in awe of Him possess the biblical trait of humility and make huge strides in moving toward the biblical definition of greatness.

Professional Will, Mental Toughness, and Meekness

In *Good to Great*, Jim Collins presents traits of a Level 5 Leader that include self-effacement and a mix of personal humility and professional will.[255]

Similarly, the late Vince Lombardi, renowned Green Bay Packers football coach and devout Catholic, spoke of humility when he stated:

> "Mental toughness is many things. It is humility because it behooves all of us to remember that simplicity is the sign of greatness and meekness is the sign of true strength. Mental toughness is spartanism with qualities of sacrifice, self-denial, dedication. It is fearlessness, and it is love."[256]

---

[252] SK, 179.

[253] Matthew 18:2-4 NCV.

[254] SK, 181.

[255] Jim Collins, *Good to Great* (New York: Harper, 2001).

[256] Vince Lombardi quote accessed 2010, http://www.quoteland.com/author.asp?AUTHOR_ID=1182.

Service and Sacrifice for Others

Service is another key component of the Law of Greatness. Pat Robertson discusses the pros and cons of service in the world's eyes. From a biblical perspective he notes that "the secret of greatness is service."[257] When you focus on others regardless of your field or position—business, medicine, law, education, the ministry, etc.—you move in the direction of God's model for greatness. Dr. Robertson points out that those who sacrifice in the service of others are elevated to greatness while those who are vain and focus on self will be taken down by the Law of Reciprocity, because what they give will come back to them in kind, whether good or bad.[258]

SERVANT LEADERSHIP

Since *The Secret Kingdom* was first published, the concept of servant leadership has become popular both among those of faith and those in the secular world. Robert Greenleaf says that the servant leader should be a servant first, leader second—one who puts others first in an effort to help them grow.[259]

Christians expand on many of these concepts through biblical principles. For example, Churchleadership.org (a Francis A. Schaeffer Institute) provides a profile using the term "incarnational leadership,"[260] challenging Christians to go beyond service and lead the way as Christ led. Incarnational leaders empower servant leaders and work to increase the impact of the church as visionaries, entrepreneurs, architects, and builders.

Servant Leaders Today says that servant leaders intentionally do the right thing.[261] Some of the readings at this site present Jesus as the ideal model. If you study the life of Jesus—how He grew and what He did—you will find a model of a servant leader.

Jesus, Ideal Servant Leader

Here are 12 principles that shaped Jesus' life of service as described by Lloyd Elder in "Jesus, The Ideal Servant Leader":[262]

1. Development: The Nazareth Principle
2. Relationship: The Jordan Principle (see Luke 3:21-22)
3. Preparedness: The Desert Principle (see Matt. 4:1-11)
4. Purpose: The Homecoming Principle (see Luke 4: 17-21)

---

[257] SK, 184.

[258] SK, 189.

[259] Greenleaf Center for Servant Leadership, accessed 2010, http://www.greenleaf.org/whatissl/.

[260] "Incarnational Leadership, accessed December 29, 2010, http://www.churchleadership.org/pages.asp?pageid=66920.

[261] Servant Leaders Today, http://www.servantleaderstoday.com/index.htm.

[262] Lloyd Elder, "Jesus, The Ideal Servant Leader" (SL#53), adapted from SkillTrack® 1:2, accessed December 29, 2010, http://www.servantleaderstoday.com/_53.htm.

5. Discipleship: The Personnel Principle (see Matt. 4:19-20; 10:37-39)
6. Kingdom: The Mountain Principle (see Matt. 6:19-24, 33)
7. Service: The Towel Principle (see John 13:1, 4-5)
8. Mutual Love: The Radical Principle (see John 13:34-35)
9. Confrontation: The Temple Principle (see Matt. 21:12-13)
10. Redemption: The Cross Principle (John 19:16-18)
11. Power: The Resurrection Principle (Matt. 28:6-7; Acts 1:8)
12. Commission: The World Principle (Matt. 28:16-20)

These concepts can be found in greater detail at Servant Leaders Today[263] and are worth taking the time to develop and study further as you shape your own life of service.

UNDERLYING PRINCIPLES FOR THE LAW OF GREATNESS

The Law of Greatness starts with each individual possessing both a sense of humility and an obligation to service. Here are some of the key principles:

- *Filled with a sense of humility.* People of faith can hardly stand on God's earth and not be humbled by His power, wisdom and the beauty of His creation. Part of developing a sense of humility is maintaining that sense of awe and spending time listening to others. The ability to listen goes hand in hand with respecting others and maintaining an open spirit.

- *Maintaining childlike character.* Children are trusting and teachable. If our trust remains in the Lord and we remain teachable, we are more likely to maintain that childlike spirit. It is also important to maintain a sense of childlike curiosity and be open enough to ask questions.

- *Continuing a love of life and learning.* Innocence, transparency, enthusiasm, and authenticity all go hand-in-hand with that free and open spirit that supports a love of life and learning.

- *Remaining meek and poor in spirit.* Those who are poor in spirit realize that they do not know it all. This openness leads to a servant attitude and meekness—a sense of controlled strength. Equating meekness with weakness is a misconception. Meekness has a component of gentleness but is built on strength.

---

[263] Jesus, Ideal Servant Leader.

- *Serving others with a servant attitude.* Jesus' life and teachings show us that the secret of greatness is service. This requires the ability to put others first and be unselfish. On the night before His crucifixion, Jesus demonstrated a servant's attitude by washing His disciples' feet even though He knew one disciple would deny Him (Peter) and one had betrayed Him (Judas). Jesus exercised leadership when He challenged the disciples to imitate His example with others (John 13:1-17).

ACHIEVING GREATNESS IN YOUR EDUCATIONAL ENVIRONMENT

Greatness in education begins with greatness in individual educators like Jerry Deviney, Carolyn Thompson, and Cheryl Askew of Ocean Lakes High School in Virginia Beach. In order to achieve greatness in your educational setting, you first have to achieve God's greatness in your own life. The example of OLHS shows how schools exhibit sustainable greatness in good part because they lead with humility and service.

As you strive to achieve greatness in your educational environment, ask yourself these questions.

1. Do I have a big dream on my God-given path?
2. Am I competing with myself instead of others as I strive to improve and reach God's goals?
3. Am I as teachable as a small child as I realize how much I have to learn?
4. Do I have a passion for life and a love of learning?
5. Do I trust the Lord?
6. Do I put others first and really care about them?
7. Do I understand the components of servant or incarnational leadership?
8. Am I remaining in prayer and reflection while I focus on God's goals?

Through prayer and reflection, as you answer these questions, God's goals for you will become more obvious and your path will be revealed.

CONCLUSION

Today, more than ever, students need leaders in administration and in the classroom who are able to take them to greatness. The biblical perspective of greatness starts with personal humility and putting service first. Educational leaders who trust in the Lord and remain humble and teachable provide examples of greatness and are able to guide students, faculty, and staff to their full potential.

Cheryl Askew pointed out that most visitors to OLHS mention how students carry themselves, the respect they have for each other and the staff, the spirit of collaboration among the teachers and the genuine sense of caring. These are traits developed under a leadership of humility and service that can take all schools to greatness.

Dr. Robertson concluded his *Secret Kingdom* chapter on the Law of Greatness by saying, "The nation that does the most for others will be the one growing in greatness."[264]

I present a similar challenge to our educational leaders. Which school has teachers and leaders who can do the most for others on their destined path toward greatness?

---

[264] SK, 190.

RESOURCES

700 Club. "Mike Singletary: Christ Means Everything." Accessed September 21, 2010.
http://www.cbn.com/media/player/index.aspx?s=/vod/SB85v2_Web_WS.

Collins, Jim. *Good to Great.* New York: Harper Collins, 2001.

Elder, Lloyd. "Jesus, The Ideal Servant Leader" (SL#53), adapted from SkillTrack® 1:2.
Accessed December 29, 2010. http://www.servantleaderstoday.com/_53.htm.

International Alliance for Invitational Education, http://www.invitationaleducation.net.

Robertson, Pat. *The Secret Kingdom: Your Path to Peace, Love, and Financial Security*
(Dallas: Word Publishing, 1992).

Wilkinson, Bruce. *The Dream Giver.* New York: Multnomah Books, a division of
Random House, 2003.

CHAPTER 11

THE LAW OF RESPONSIBILITY

By Don Finn, Ph.D.
Associate Professor
Regent University School of Education

*"I am always stopped momentarily when I read the words of James
regarding teachers: 'Let not many of you become teachers, my brethren,
knowing that as such we shall incur a stricter judgment.'*[265]
*"Those who have been shown enough to teach can
be expected to practice what they teach, at the very least.
The office carries a great responsibility."*[266]

PAT ROBERTSON, *THE SECRET KINGDOM*

"Much will be required of everyone who has been given much."[267]

During the first year of our marriage (which was the last year of my undergraduate program), my wife Laurie Ann and I worked at a child care center. She was hired as the director and I worked with the school-aged kids in the after-school program. Although my studies were preparing me to teach middle- and high-school students, I welcomed the opportunity to work with younger children on the way to my long-term vocation.

The children under my care came from various income brackets and family situations. Some had a mom and dad at home. Others came from blended families with stepparents and others from single-parent households. Regardless, most of the kids—both boys and girls—wanted the attention of the "guy teacher."

Because of my upbringing in a single-parent household, I could understand their desire for a positive male role model. My parents separated when I was five and my older sister, younger brother, and I were raised by our mother. My friends had both a mom and a dad and I remember thinking that I was the only child experiencing the pain of not having a dad in the home.

At the time of my after school program employment, I had already reconciled and reestablished my relationship with my dad—mainly driven by the faith I found in Christ at 19 years of age. Through prayer and study, the Lord had helped me to work through the hurt feelings and low self-image of my childhood, so I looked for opportunities to be used of God to sow blessings into the lives of the students.

---

[265] James 3:1 NASB.
[266] SK, 177.
[267] LUKE 12:48 HCSB.

The Lord impressed on me the importance of being patient and understanding, particularly in instances where kids who were "disadvantaged" became the targets of ridicule or were shunned by the others. God put a special love in my heart for them and He rewarded me with the skills and talents to work with all types of kids. I did my best to be "prayed up" and ready to bless the children as the Lord prompted me by being a role model of fairness and charity.

Much Will Be Required of Everyone Who Has Been Given Much

Jesus makes it clear that those whom God has favored with His blessings have a responsibility to share blessings with others because this furthers the Kingdom of God. Those who follow the laws of the Kingdom will experience prosperity and strength, but God did not intend for us to keep these benefits for our own gain and benefit.[268]

This is especially pertinent for those who teach. When teachers give of themselves in Jesus' name, they set in motion a "cycle of blessing" (financial, material, spiritual, etc.) from investing in the lives of others! This mindset is ingrained. We teach to add value to the lives of others and to our society.

We take Jesus' words as our responsibility:

"For unto whomsoever much is given, of him shall be much required: and to whom men have committed much, of him they will ask the more."[269]

WATCHING FOR OPPORTUNITIES TO BLESS OTHERS

In Luke 12:35-40, Jesus shares a story with His disciples on the value of being prepared. He uses the example of servants who keep their lamps burning in order to welcome their master home at any time. Jesus said:

"Be dressed for service and keep your lamps burning, as though you were waiting for your master to return from the wedding feast. Then you will be ready to open the door and let him in the moment he arrives and knocks."[270]

Like these servants, we stay watchful for opportunities to bless others. We already belong to the household of the Lord, but in order to please our Master, we stay ready to move whenever He prompts us to share something.

God's obedient servants receive great rewards for being ready to answer this call:

---

[268] SK, 165.
[269] Luke 12:48 KJV.
[270] Luke 12:35-36 NLT.

"The servants who are ready and waiting for his return will be rewarded. I tell you the truth, he himself will seat them, put on an apron, and serve them as they sit and eat! He may come in the middle of the night or just before dawn. But whenever he comes, he will reward the servants who are ready."[271]

LEADERSHIP RESPONSIBILITIES OF A TEACHER

The first chapter of James describes the heavy responsibility that God has placed on leaders, including those who teach. Teachers must practice what they teach in order to demonstrate godly obedience and to avoid being "judged more strictly":

"Not many of you should presume to be teachers, my brothers, because you know that we who teach will be judged more strictly."[272]

Responsibility to Parents

According to the doctrine of *in loco parentis* established since the early days of American education, teachers and administrators teach, discipline, and care for students as if they were their own children. Webb, Metha, and Jordan note that:

"Traditionally it was accepted that school officials had considerable authority in controlling student conduct. Operating under the doctrine of *in loco parentis* (in place of a parent), school authorities exercised almost unlimited, and usually unchallenged, discretion in restricting the rights of students in disciplining students."[273]

WEBB, METHA, AND JORDAN, *FOUNDATIONS OF AMERICAN EDUCATION*

The school and its employees are charged with caring for the minors in their charge while on school grounds and involved in school activities. Sometimes, news reporters highlight disciplinary aspects of this doctrine in a negative way, but although it has been weakened in some court challenges, *in loco parentis* is the law and is a responsibility that God takes seriously.

Responsibility to Be a Godly Example

Teachers and administrators serve as examples to the students, their parents, and the community. The Apostle Paul challenges those who desire to lead as elders in the church

---

[271] Luke 12:37-38 NLT.
[272] James 3:1 NIV.
[273] L. Dean Webb, Arlene Metha, and K. Forbis Jordan, *Foundations of American Education*, 6th ed. (Upper Saddle River, New Jersey: Merrill, 2010), 307.

(or overseers or bishops) to live a life that is above reproach, be faithful to their wives, exercise self-control, live wisely, have a good reputation, be able to teach, be gentle and not be quarrelsome, not love money, manage their own families well, and have children who respect and obey them. Paul adds that people outside of the church should be able to speak well of them so that they will not be disgraced and fall into the devil's trap.[274]

Responsibility as a Steward of God's Blessings—*Noblesse Oblige*

As the Lord increases His favor, He also increases responsibility. To illustrate this point in *The Secret Kingdom*, Pat Robertson briefly discusses the writings of Gaston Pierre Marc, a French duke who in the early 19th century wrote a two-word statement in a collection of maxims and reflections: *"Noblesse oblige."* Translated, that means "nobility obliges" or "nobility obligates." This idea did not originate with Marc. In fact, it can be traced back to the ancient Greeks. However, this concept states that it is the obligation of people in high rank, position, or favor to behave nobly, kindly, and responsibly toward others.[275] Anyone who lives in America is blessed with a standard of living, opportunities for educational attainment, and access to resources that are among the highest in the world. Do you consider yourself noble? A person of privilege? What will you do with your blessings as a responsible person? *Nobility obliges.*

Responsibility to Serve

Pat Williams, senior vice president of the Orlando Magic basketball team, motivational speaker, and author, notes that in addition to being placed on earth to serve God, we have another mission, a higher calling. He says, "He also placed you here with a mission to love and serve the people around you."[276] That means serving your family and your supervisors but also those under your supervision, other teachers, administrators, and students. How do you do this? Williams says:

> "Your mission in life—your unique calling from God—involves the way you live out your love for God and your love for other people.
> As someone once put it, your mission in life is the place where your deep gladness in God meets the deep hunger and need of the world.
> Your purpose in life is to glorify God by obeying his calling and his will for your life."[277]

PAT WILLIAMS, *SENIOR VICE PRESIDENT, ORLANDO MAGIC*

As God's people, we are servants in the household of the Lord. The Master has called us to obedience to carry out His mission. This mission is fueled by the hunger He has placed in us by His Holy Spirit. We carry out our mission with gladness deep within,

---

[274] See 1 Timothy 3:1-7.
[275] SK, 169.
[276] Pat Williams, *How to Be Like Jesus* (Deerfield Beach, FL: Faith Communications, 2003), 335
[277] Williams, *How to Be Like Jesus*, 335.

knowing we are serving our heavenly Father as Jesus did while on earth. This service requires an intense focus. Williams continues:

> "Do you have the same intense focus on your calling, on God's plan for your life that Jesus had? Are you pursuing God's strategy for your life with laserlike focus and intensity? Has God called you to teach needy children in the inner city? Then focus on God's plan for your life. . . . Jesus was able to focus with intensity because he knew the irreplaceable value of a moment. He never 'killed time,' because he knew that time was precious. A single moment, once passed, would never come again."[278]
>
> PAT WILLIAMS, *SENIOR VICE PRESIDENT, ORLANDO MAGIC*

Nobility obliges and the Lord gives great rewards.

Responsibility to Be True to Your Faith

As a first year teacher, I remember the excitement and energy that greeted me each morning as I woke up and got ready for work. (I know you may not believe it, but I did!) I knew that God had placed me, a young guy from Connecticut, into a middle/high school (grades 6-12) in a farming community in southwest Virginia.

After I graduated with a bachelor's degree from a Virginia university, my new wife and I were open to moving back to Connecticut. After all, our family and friends were there. However, we wanted to be in God's will so we had looked to Him for opportunities and He had sent us here.

My first teaching assignment was to begin the school year as a long-term substitute social studies teacher. The regular teacher had become very ill at the end of the previous academic year. My responsibility was to teach one seventh grade U.S. history class and four sections of ninth grade world geography.

One of my anxieties on entering that job was concern over how my students and co-workers would accept this young man from Connecticut. I quickly found that my concerns were unfounded because I "clicked" immediately. It became evident to me that I was in my element being a teacher. I worked hard at that job. I kept late hours. On a few occasions, I had to be asked to leave by the custodians who needed to close the building and set the alarm. I truly loved my job!

My principal had to pass my classroom on his way to the parking lot in the afternoon and would sometimes reach into the room and shut off the lights and tell me to go home. I knew that I was working a temporary job and that the teacher would eventually return, but I wanted to give it my all.

I met a few times with the teacher who was still slowly recovering. He was the yearbook co-sponsor and on occasion he would come by the school to

---

[278] Williams, *How to Be Like Jesus,* 335-336.

assist with some tasks. Truthfully, it was challenging to see him because I was becoming so attached to the job and to the kids, but I knew that the job was his and I was his fill-in. I would sit with him and talk about the kids and how I hoped he would get well enough to come back and work with them, but all the while I was experiencing internal conflict.

In the spring of the academic year, the teacher felt well enough to return. This proved to be difficult for me and the students. We had less than a week to transition. The kids were sad to see me go and I was sad to leave, but I had to do it.

Since I knew the teacher had experienced hardship and his journey had been a difficult one, I felt the Lord prompting me to share the Gospel with this man who had been through so much. After all, Paul calls us "Christ's ambassadors":

> "We are therefore Christ's ambassadors, as though God were making his appeal through us. We implore you on Christ's behalf: Be reconciled to God. God made him who had no sin to be sin for us, so that in him we might become the righteousness of God."[279]

I had come from a background that was largely non-religious. During my childhood, my family would attend church from time to time, mainly on Easter and Christmas, but none of us truly knew God. Now that I had a true faith in Christ and was attending a church that taught biblical truth, I was determined to represent Jesus in all I did.

On my last day, I left the teacher a tract that I had picked up from my church about trusting in the Lord during difficult times. Based on some of our discussions in the past, I had a strong sense that he did not have a personal relationship with God. I attached a brief note to the pamphlet and told him that, despite his health issues and trials, I knew that God cared for him and wanted to help him through his difficulties.

After I left the students behind, I was deeply saddened. I was able to pick up work as a substitute teacher in the county to keep me busy, but it wasn't the same! Then, less than three weeks after I left the job, I received a call from my principal. In short, he told me that the teacher's health had not improved as much as he had hoped. If I wanted the job, I could finish the academic year teaching in his place. I gladly accepted. I wondered what progress they had made in the curriculum and what graded assignments they had completed. I was elated to return the following day and the kids were happy to see me. There was so much to do!

However, my joy was short lived. On my desk, along with various notes about the progress of each class and lesson plans and other miscellaneous items, I found the tract that I had left for the teacher just a few weeks earlier. It had a sticky note with a brief message and an arrow pointing to the name of my church that was printed on the back. The note said, "Don, I almost got involved with the people at this church when I was in college. . . . thankfully I got out in time to be 'saved.' "

---

[279] 2 Corinthians 5:20-21 NIV.

I was saddened by this note because this man was not only rejecting the church, he was also rejecting God and the gifts of comfort and peace that faith in Him can bring. This moment was poignant because just over a year later, the teacher lost his battle with the disease and I fear he died without ever knowing Christ as his Savior. Although that was nearly 20 years ago, I still think about it from time to time and it always saddens me.

Like the Thessalonians in Paul's day, I had been persecuted for my faith (see 1 Thessalonians chapter 1), something I had not experienced before. It hurt deeply because although I was a young believer, I knew of the liberating power found in trusting Christ. I had experienced the freedom and relief of being forgiven for past mistakes and sins because of God's goodness. This was the first time that someone had outright rejected God's truth in a personal way, but it made me more determined than ever to press on and share my faith because of the eternal impact of everything I did as Christ's ambassador.

ETERNAL IMPACT OF ONE TEACHER'S OBEDIENCE

In April 1855, a teacher named Edward Kimball entered Holton's Shoe Store in Boston, looking for one of the students from his senior high Sunday school class. He found him working in the stock room wrapping shoes.

After a brief discussion about the Lord, Kimball prayed with this young man to receive Christ as his personal Savior. This student, Dwight L. Moody, would go on to become one of the greatest evangelists of all time.

Moody worked with an evangelist named J. Wilbur Chapman. Chapman later hired Billy Sunday, the baseball player turned evangelist, to hold a revival in Charlotte, North Carolina, in 1924. At the end of that meeting, he helped organize a group called the Christian Men's Club, which in 1934 called in the evangelist Mordecai Ham to hold a revival in Charlotte.[280]

Rev. Ham's revival lasted for several weeks. In the audience for several of the meetings was 16-year-old Billy Graham. Graham described in his autobiography the conviction he felt listening to Ham's words and how he and his schoolmate Grady Wilson had dealt with the discomfort:

> "Grady and I had both decided on a strategy to avoid the frontal attack by Dr. Ham. We had signed up for the choir, which sat on the platform behind the preacher. Neither of us could sing, but we could move our mouths or hold a hymnbook in front of our faces for camouflage. As choir members, we were safe from Dr. Ham's accusatory stare. . . . As a teenager, what I needed to know for certain was that I was right with God. I could not help but admit to myself that I was purposeless and empty-hearted. . . . And then it happened. . . . Dr. Ham finished preaching and

---

[280] Stan Toler and James Baldwin, *Devotions for Sunday School Teachers* (Kansas City, MO: Beacon Hill Press, 2002), 15.

gave the Invitation to accept Christ . . . his song leader, Mr. Ramsey led us all in 'Just As I Am'—four verses. Then we started another song: 'Almost Persuaded, Now to Believe.' On the last verse of that second song, I responded. I walked down to the front, feeling as if I had lead weights attached to my feet, and stood in the space before the platform."[281]

BILLY GRAHAM, DESCRIBING THE STORY OF HIS CONVERSION

Graham told how a local tailor, J.D. Prevatt, put his arm around him and led him in the sinner's prayer. He wrote, "I believe that was the moment I made my real commitment to Jesus Christ."[282]

Billy Graham is one of the greatest evangelists of all time. Through his ministry, countless millions of people have come to know Christ as their Lord and Savior. Graham has counseled presidents from Harry S. Truman through George W. Bush. But what if Edward Kimball had not obeyed the prompting of the Holy Spirit to seek out his Sunday school student, Dwight L. Moody, in Boston in 1855? The chain leading to Billy Graham's salvation and later answering God's call to preach the Gospel would have been broken and possibly never would have happened!

Think of the lives you touch as a teacher every day in your classroom. Who knows how many more lives your students will touch because of your investment in them? As they watch your life, you have a responsibility to represent fairness, charity, and Christian love. You may never know until eternity the impact of your words and deeds.

WWJD—WHAT WOULD JESUS DO?

Throughout the New Testament, God deplores those who hear His word and do not do it—and then wonder why they don't see power in their lives. In the 1990s, the book *In His Steps* by Charles M. Sheldon, written in 1896, was reintroduced and gained wide popularity in Christian circles. It is the story of the Rev. Henry Maxwell, pastor of First Church in the fictional town of Raymond, and his chance encounters with an out of work "tramp." These encounters lead the pastor and his congregation to make a pledge not to act or make any decisions without first asking themselves, "What would Jesus do?"

In the Preface, Sheldon wrote, "It is the earnest prayer of the author that the book may go its way with a great blessing to the churches for the quickening of Christian discipleship, and the hastening of the Master's Kingdom on earth."[283]

---

[281] Billy Graham, *Just as I Am: the Autobiography of Billy Graham* (San Francisco: HarperCollins Worldwide, 1997), 28-29.

[282] Graham, *Just As I Am*, 29.

[283] Charles M. Sheldon, *In His Steps* (Chicago: Advance Publishing Company, 1897; also available through Google Books), 4.

With the return of the book to a new generation 100 years later, that prayer seemed to be answered. It was common to see bumper stickers, t-shirts, and bracelets with the letters WWJD (What Would Jesus Do?) as a reminder to followers of Christ to consider what Jesus would do or how He would act in any situation. I was no exception to this trend. I was challenged to live my life as a true disciple of Christ. I purchased and wore a WWJD bracelet every day for some time and it served as a daily reminder to me that I am Christ's representative and that I should act accordingly. This became particularly useful at times in my job as a teacher.

After my year ended as a long-term substitute teacher, I put in my application to take on the job full-time. I went through an interview process with school district officials and the building principal and assistant principal. There was plenty of competition but eventually I was hired for the position. My principal later told me that he was impressed with the rapport I had developed with my students and colleagues and with the time that I spent after hours during that first year working on lesson plans and assignments.

I went on to work in that school for another seven years, teaching students in the seventh, eighth, ninth, eleventh, and twelfth grades. I was able to see them grow and mature and they saw the same in me! During that time, I completed my master's degree and was offered a position at a university across the state. Things moved quickly, but God had opened the doors and by faith my wife and I and our young family stepped out and made the move.

Upon my departure, the outpouring of appreciation from my students was wonderful. One student in particular gave me a touching send-off. I had taught Amanda in middle school and in the ninth and eleventh grades. She was a beautiful, kind young lady who had grown up in a Christian home. Her father had passed away the year before, but she was adjusting well, thanks to her faith in Christ and the support of her church. She gave me a card in which she wrote something to the effect of "Mr. Finn, I hope you and your family do well in your new job. Thank you for being a godly example to your students, even without saying a word. Amanda."

We often hear how teachers are barred from sharing their faith in public schools, but it is possible to live out your faith by being consistent and righteous in your conduct and dealings with students. In order to do your job effectively and to represent Christ in spirit and in truth, you should always consider the question "What would Jesus do?" Because we are His disciples, we are responsible to represent Him well in all we do:

> "We must not just please ourselves. We should help others do what is right and build them up in the Lord. For even Christ didn't live to please himself. As the Scriptures say, 'The insults of those who insult you, O God, have fallen on me.' Such things were written in the Scriptures long ago to teach us. And the Scriptures give us hope and encouragement as we wait patiently for God's promises to be fulfilled. May God, who gives this

patience and encouragement, help you live in complete harmony with each other, as is fitting for followers of Christ Jesus."[284]

RESPONSIBILITIES BEYOND THE CLASSROOM

As Christ's disciples, we are responsible to live a life that glorifies God. Teachers are public figures held to a high standard of conduct as mentioned earlier in James 3:1. As public figures and as Christ's representatives, it is our duty to try our best to be upstanding citizens who reach out and participate in daily life in a way that honors Him.

Successful and Still a Sunday School Teacher

In 1946, S. Truett Cathy and his brother Ben entered the restaurant business when they opened the Dwarf House in Hapeville, Georgia. In 1967, Truett opened his first Chick-fil-A restaurant in Atlanta's Greenbrier Mall that has since grown into a multi-billion dollar business with more than 1,400 locations that in 2009 generated $3.2 billion in sales.[285] What may not be as well known is that for more than 50 years, Truett Cathy has served as a Sunday school teacher for middle school boys.

In his book *Eat Mor Chikin: Inspire More People* he shares many stories about how his work with young people fueled his desire to reach out and help those in need by being a positive role model. In 1984, he and his wife Jeannette established the WinShape Centre Foundation that places a special emphasis on building up responsible young people. In cooperation with Berry College in Rome, Georgia, the foundation provides college scholarships for young people, particularly for high school employees of Chick-fil-A. WinShape also provides opportunities for foster children that include long term foster homes and summer camps for 1,900 foster children each year.[286] In his words:

> "Nearly every moment of every day we have the opportunity to give something to someone else—our time, our love, our resources. I have always found more joy in giving when I did not expect anything in return."[287]

TRUETT CATHY, FOUNDER OF CHICK-FIL-A

---

[284] Romans 15:1-5 NLT.

[285] Chick-fil-A, Inc. Fast Facts http://truettcathy.com/pdfs/CFAFastFacts.pdf (accessed December 9, 2010).

[286] S. Truett Cathy, *Eat Mor Chikin: Inspire More People,* (Decatur, GA: Looking Glass Books, 2002).

[287] Cathy, *Eat Mor Chikin*, 11.

CONCLUSION

God's blessings carry responsibilities, but being obedient to the Lord through the Law of Responsibility brings unspeakable joy that leads us to great places. Pat Robertson writes, "Give and it will be given to you. Fulfill your responsibility at your current level if you would rise to a higher one. Blessing carries responsibility."[288] Fellow educator, I challenge you to take that responsibility, run with it, and see where God will lead you!

---

[288] SK, 177.

RESOURCES

Robertson, Pat. *The Secret Kingdom: Your Path to Peace, Love, and Financial Security* (Dallas: Word Publishing, 1992).

CHAPTER 12

THE LAW OF MIRACLES

By Elizabeth Hunter, Ed.D.
Assistant Professor, K-12 Special Education and
Director of Research on Learning
Regent University School of Education

*The "Law of Miracles . . . governs the question of God's willingness to
disturb His natural order to accomplish His purpose. When He does
disturb that natural order, the result is a miracle, a contravention of the
natural laws through which He usually works moment by moment.
He overrides the way in which things normally operate."[289]*

PAT ROBERTSON, *THE SECRET KINGDOM*

Miracles happen every day in the Secret Kingdom, even when you are a teacher in the public schools. Some years ago Dr. Alan Arroyo asked his class of graduate students at Regent University if anyone had a testimony of God's love and miracle-working powers in a public-school setting. One woman stood up. She described a situation from the previous year when she had encountered a principal who was rude and arrogant and did not seem to care about the students or the teachers. After hearing a sermon on praying for her enemies, she and another Christian teacher began praying for the principal. She said, "I did not like him one bit but I prayed for him anyway."

Slowly but surely, this two-teacher prayer team began to see changes in the unfriendly principal. He became kinder and more considerate. Eventually, he began to listen to the teachers' concerns. The school environment began to change from negative to positive. An on-the-job miracle had occurred when God intervened and answered prayer.

Interestingly, that was not the end of her story. She said that as she continued to pray for her principal she became aware that he, like her, was not married. The more she prayed, the more her affection grew. She ended her story by saying, "And we are getting married at the end of the month!" God does bring us favor with God and man when we believe in miracles.

You can experience miracles in your life in any setting because of the Secret Kingdom Law of Miracles.

---

[289] SK, 221.

Reaching into the Invisible Kingdom

As you have been reading in previous chapters, Pat Robertson reveals universal Kingdom principles from the Bible in *The Secret Kingdom*. Meditate on the Scriptures and you will begin to believe that it is within your grasp as an educator to preserve and uphold Jesus' great message of a Kingdom with two facets—one visible and another invisible.[290]

Dr. Robertson writes:

"Jesus brought the kingdom with Him, and He left tangible and very real evidence of the kingdom in our hands when He was taken up into heaven. When Christ went ahead to prepare a place for us, He fully expected us to claim the rights and privileges of our citizenship from that moment on.

"Jesus taught that the kingdom has two dimensions: the immediate and visible, which we see, and the invisible kingdom, which we do not see now but which will be fully revealed at the close of this age. From beginning to end, the Bible teaches that these two dimensions are real and very powerful."[291]

As an educator, you have the opportunity to use the power and authority of Jesus that flows from the invisible Secret Kingdom to create miracles in your own life[292] and the lives of your students. If you expect favor and success for your students,[293] you will get exactly what you expect. You can bless your students in visible ways with God's love here on earth. You can teach children how to experience miracles in their lives every day.

FIVE ATTRIBUTES OF SUCCESS THROUGH MIRACLES

Pat Robertson names several attributes that contribute to your success in creating miracles in your life: **Forgiveness, Faith, Love, and Hope**. These theological virtues are the foundation of Christian moral activity and are character qualities associated with a mature Christian life.

The Attribute of Forgiveness

Forgiveness is the most important key to releasing miracles in your life and it is the most important of the Christian attributes. Remember the Golden Rule[294] and Jesus' words about forgiving others seventy times seven.[295] Pardon, excuse, absolve, and exonerate

---

[290] SK, 37.
[291] SK, 37.
[292] SK, 222, 224.
[293] Luke 2:40
[294] Mathew 7:12. Mathew 22:39, Luke 6:31 KJV.
[295] Matthew 18:21-22 KJV.

yourself and others. Forgiveness is just not a religious term. Psychologists often list forgiveness as a component of a mentally and emotionally satisfying life. Therefore, you can teach children about forgiveness in any setting.

The Attribute of Faith

Faith is the place to begin if you want to understand how the Kingdom works. Pat Robertson calls it the "umbrella of faith." Faith is your covering as you seek what is necessary to find miracles and success in your life. Keep your eyes on the Lord and believe, never doubting. Speak what you believe.

The Salwen family of Atlanta, Georgia, is busy living out their faith in the way Jesus did—serving others in deed, and not just words. They took a great leap of faith and sold their two million dollar house and other amenities and donated half of the proceeds to charity. Because of their generosity, the "Epicenter" in Ghana is a community that has a health clinic, food storage facility, meeting place, and a bank. They are now sponsoring an elementary school in Ghana. Each student is given a scholarship to attend and complete their education. Together the family traded material things for a deeper level of connectedness and trust. The Salwen children understand that they are part of a bigger world and already understand their responsibility to give back to the world community. Their lives are a demonstration of faith leading to a modern-day miracle and the miraculous intervention of God in their lives.

Faith is a Christian moral virtue given by God's grace. It flows from obedience to the First Commandment[296] to love God with your heart, soul, strength, and mind. It is a gift of God and a human act. God invites your response and freely assents to share the truth that He has revealed. When you as a believer give personal adherence to the truth of God, you find out that with God all things are possible. You remember to live in faith because without faith you cannot please God.[297]

The Attribute of Love

Love is the greatest virtue.[298] It is depicted in the Old and New Testaments by people who love God above all others for His own sake. God commands those of us who love Him to love our neighbors as ourselves out of our love for Him. He gives us the love between a man and a woman that results in the holy union of marriage—an expression of God's love for the men and women that He created.

Pat Robertson writes about the power of love to solve world crises:

"Our principal weapon in the crises we face in the world is love and love operates only in a state of forgiveness and reconciliation. Pettiness must go, and jealousy and pride and lack of concern for others, and neglect of the poor and needy."[299]

---

[296] Romans 13:22-23.
[297] Hebrews 11:16.
[298] 1 Corinthians 13.
[299] SK, 229.

The Attribute of Hope

Hope is the Christian virtue of unlimited expectations. You desire and expect from God both eternal life and the grace you need to attain it[300]. By God's grace you reach the goals you hope for. God's unmerited favor is available to you. Nothing is impossible to you when God is with you.[301]

THE MAJOR HINDRANCE TO MIRACLES

In *The Secret Kingdom*, Pat Robertson explains that the major hindrance to miracles and supernatural success in your life is unforgiveness.

"Men and women, Christian and non-Christian, carry grudges. Any power of God within them is eaten up by resentment.
"Is it any wonder that we see so little of the miraculous intervention of God in the affairs of the world?"[302]

Unforgiveness creates a cloud of sin between you and God that obstructs your view and prevents miracles from occurring in your life and your work as an educator. Miracles are available, but unforgiveness causes bitterness and resentment that are roadblocks to miracles. However, if you let go of your unforgiveness and let God do His miracles you will be blessed and pass on the blessing. Have faith. Believe in God's Word. Trust Him and never doubt.

"[Abraham] staggered not at the promise of God through unbelief; but was strong in faith, giving glory to God; And being fully persuaded that, what he had promised, he was able also to perform."[303]

ENCOURAGING MIRACLES IN SCHOOLS THROUGH THE ATTRIBUTES

The attributes of forgiveness, faith, love, and hope that lead to miracles can directly be taught in both Christian and secular settings. Even in settings where you are unable to pray openly, quote Scripture, or talk directly about God there are ways to model and encourage students to practice virtues that set the stage for miracles to happen in their

---

[300] 1 Cor. 13
[301] Luke 1:37
[302] SK, 227.
[303] Romans 4:20-21 KJV.

lives. Below are some general suggestions that, with the help of divine wisdom, you can adjust to your particular settings.

Teaching Forgiveness

Teach forgiveness by example until your students see the connection between forgiveness and treating others the way they would want to be treated. Teach them vocabulary about compassion, sympathy, empathy, feelings and sensitivity, kindness and tenderness, affection and concern for others. Design lesson plans that teach the development of a moral compass. Teach your students to do the right thing, because it is the right thing to do. Instruct your students in proper etiquette, social relationships, and conflict resolution skills.

Teaching Faith

As an educator, you can model faith for a miracle to your students by speaking positive and optimistic words of expectation. When you have faith the size of a mustard seed[304] and believe, see, and refuse to doubt, you will see that your students catch your attitude of excitement, even in settings that prohibit the direct teaching of Scripture. Remember to live in faith. Without faith you cannot please God.[305]

Modern-day miracles happen every day and are available to every person in every walk of faith. Some examples are chronicled in books and videos like Miracles in Our Midst.[306]

Teach your students to have faith that if they work hard toward a goal, they will reach it. Have high and reasonable expectations for every student and tell them what you expect because you know they are capable. Once they understand the concept of faith in themselves and others introduce faith in larger terms. Design lesson plans where students will respond to literature, art, and movies where faith was a factor in people's successes. Pascal, Handel, Bach, Newton, Columbus, Joan of Arc, Mother Teresa, and Martin Luther King, Jr., all had faith in someone greater than themselves. Put on a play using an appropriate script that addresses faith. Encourage your students to trust and never doubt, to act as they believe even if they cannot see the desired outcome yet.

Teaching Love

The Bible says that the greatest virtue is love.[307] Give your students examples of the testimony of God's love and miracle powers demonstrated in public school settings. Teach your students to move in God's love and favor and to expect His miracles to work

---

[304] See Luke 17:6.
[305] See Hebrews 11:6.
[306] Grizzly Adams Productions, http://www.grizzlyadams.com/public/home/index.cfm, accessed 2010.
[307] See 1 Corinthians 13.

through them. You can teach your students to express love for others through good works that result from their love of God.[308]

Pat Robertson says:

"Our principal weapon in the crises we face in the world is love, and love operates only in a state of forgiveness and reconciliation. Pettiness must go, and jealousy and pride and lack of concern for others, and neglect of the poor and needy."[309]

God wants to bless you and your students and He often does that when you give and receive love. You will block your faith if you speak of doubts, fears, and failures. *Speak* the positive words of God's love and honor for his children as you teach your students. Talk about how love means to care for someone or something even if it means personal sacrifice. Have your students' journal what love means to them. Guide them through the biblical meanings as directly as you can for your given setting.

Teaching Hope

Teach your students to remember their successes and accomplishments as they work toward their goals so that they will have hope. Teach them to expect, trust, anticipate, look forward to, and expect great things that they desire, aspire to, dream, and plan. Speak words of encouragement. Have students write a plan describing their goals and dreams for their future. Help them to set life goals. Teach them how to hope for and work toward successful careers and lifestyles. Help them to find their purpose.

Teaching All of the Attributes

Talk about how love means caring for someone or something and that caring can be demonstrated in tangible, active ways. Teach them how to help others thus creating hope. Forgiveness and faith are needed to overlook various differences and trust that our charitable efforts will produce results. Miracles can start as a heart's desire that is acted on in faith and the outcome can be the transformation of a person or a whole community on the other side of the world or right next door. Miracles can emerge from social consciousness ideas like Pay it Forward[310] and non-profit organizations like Habitat for Humanity[311] and TOMS Shoes.[312]

Introduce the concept of philanthropy, aid organizations, charitable trusts, aid gifts, and donations. Teach the vocabulary of help, assistance, offerings, kindness, humanity, compassion, and generosity. Plan community projects that will result in benefits to others. Have student's research local organizations that offer services to fill a specific need in the community. Invite guest speakers from these organizations, including

---

[308] Judges 5:31.

[309] SK, 229.

[310] Catherine Ryan Hyde, *Pay It Forward* (Riverside, NJ: Simon and Schuster, 2000).

[311] Habitat for Humanity, http://www.habitat.org, accessed 2010.

[312] Blake Mycoskie, TOMS Shoes, http://www.toms.com, accessed 2010.

faith-based groups. Have students listen for the miracles that happen in peoples' lives when they are shown love through charity.

MIRACLES IN OUR PERSONAL LIVES

Jack—A Lesson in Faith

When our newborn son Jack was sent home from the hospital nursery with the diagnosis of failure to thrive, my husband Michael and I were devastated. The hospital had given up and Jack was being sent home to die. We believed them and were heartbroken. It seemed that we had forgotten our faith. We began to doubt ourselves and that God would pull us through this.

Our son's pediatrician, Dr. Shoaibi, an expert in children's internal health from India, took me by the shoulders and said, "Mrs. Hunter, where is your faith?" I was overcome with emotion as I looked into his dark almond eyes. It was a pivotal moment for me. It was like being sucked rapidly through a narrow dark vacuum and suddenly being thrust into the brightest light of realization! I was grieving before the fact! I had believed the circumstances. I had let doubt and the visible realm beat me down.

It flooded back to me that when God brings you to these trials He does see you through to the end. I had forgotten. God is faithful. He wants us to be faithful, too. We just have to ask our Father for grace and mercy. My husband and I immediately began to pray together and to affirm God's glory. We asked for forgiveness. We thanked God for the wonderful four months we had been blessed to have our son in our lives. Our three daughters joined us in prayer. We needed a miracle.

As soon as we arrived home, Michael stripped everything off of Jack and we examined his emaciated, frail, 3.7-pound body, looking for anything we could find that would allow Jack to be readmitted to the hospital. There! His feet were like tight, fat little footballs; swollen and painful looking. Yes! Edema! It was a new symptom. Jack was immediately admitted back into the hospital. Dr. Shoaibi's original diagnosis of pyloric stenosis was confirmed this time. Jack was immediately rushed into the operating room. Forty-five minutes later he was in recovery. Jack has been thriving ever since.[313]

Expect miracles, believe in miracles. Have faith and always praise God!

Jack—A Lesson in Hope

Confusion, incorrect information, negative assumptions and fear on the part of experts and much of society were motivating factors that influenced how we dealt with our son's life. The Down Syndrome population or any other individual to be targeted as a result of their health issues is a judgment made too quickly and often without the perspective of hope, and should be more closely examined.

---

[313] Elizabeth Hunter, "Waking Up With Jack" collective material (2009).

When Jack was three years old, we were facing the inevitable open heart surgery to close the hole in his heart that we had been monitoring since his birth. We put off this terrifying operation as long as we could until Jack was strong enough to undergo this serious procedure. We remained hopeful and were faithful in prayer and claimed Jack's total and complete healing. Our pediatric cardiologist, Dr. Schneider, would pray with us as he treated Jack for this heart defect. Every few months as we viewed the echocardiogram images, we would bless Jack's heart and pray for a successful surgery.

The day arrived and we were to look at one last echocardiogram picture before the operation. I tried to be hopeful, but I was terrified of losing my baby. We needed a miracle in our lives. Our son needed to be healed through this surgery. We got down on our knees and prayed for that miracle. We asked the Lord to guide the surgeon's hands and to bless everyone who would be part of this dangerous surgery.

We watched as the technician placed the sensor patches on Jack's little body. Dr. Schneider exclaimed, "I cannot explain it, but the hole in Jack's heart is closed." We were astonished to see that the echocardiogram image revealed the hole in Jack's heart was closed. He looked at us and continued with a smile, "But we all know why." God went a step better and cured Jack without the surgery. Praise God! Our hope was restored. God wants to work miracles through all of us.[314]

Jack—Believe in Miracles

As the family of a child diagnosed with Down Syndrome and other health issues, we were terrified by the implications that Jack may never eat, talk, walk, or function on his own. Some experts said that it would be futile to try to raise Jack at home. We were told that Jack would not go to school. We had experienced many healing miracles in Jack's life. We needed another kind of miracle in this new situation.

We did not accept the real world perception of what Jack was going to be able to do. We turned our hearts to the Lord. We thanked God every day for such a gift, a boy like Jack. He was a pleasure in our lives. Our priest and fellow parishioners prayed with us to find the solutions for Jack's schooling. Not only did we believe that Jack would go to school, he would go to regular school with his same age peers.

Education experts were totally against any of our ideas about inclusion into regular classrooms as an option for Jack. In Kindergarten, Jack was placed in a self-contained classroom with one teacher and seven other children who could not speak either. It made no sense to us! We knew Jack had more going on inside than he could communicate. We knew that Jack needed to interact with people who could communicate normally. We had been strong-armed into leaving Jack to sit silently with other silent children. A special educator stepped up and told us that we were right. It had just been easier for everyone to put Jack in the self-contained class.

As we watched Jack's persistence in his early struggles through life, we observed that the more he participated in everyday activities the more he began to function like everyone else. We prayed for a miracle. We prayed as a family that Jack would be able to attend regular school in an inclusive setting.

---

[314] Hunter, "Waking Up With Jack."

A public school principal and a fellow parishioner who had known Jack since his birth approached us and asked if we would consider placing Jack in her public school where she was beginning a new inclusive special education program. We were amazed at God's intervention. Our prayers had been heard. All of a sudden it was easy. Jack was happy and learning in school. He was in a classroom with same aged peers. The whole school was learning sign language because of Jack. Because of this experience everyone knows him and refers to us as Jack's father or mother when we they greet us at the store.

Jack surprises us every day with his new talents and leaps in cognitive, emotional, and psychological development. Jack is just like any other child who expresses strength, power, and heart. Although developmentally delayed, Jack potty trained himself and makes the Honor Roll. Jack became a Cub Scout and crossed the bridge to become a Boy Scout. He received the sacrament of First Holy Communion. When Jack takes the Eucharist, he signs, "Thank you, Jesus." We brag that Jack has more chromosomes than his classmates![315] Jack experienced four successful years in this elementary school environment.

When the administration and teachers changed in Jack's school, a similar conflict began as we prepared Jack for middle school classes in the school. We were up against even stronger opponents this time. We continued to pray for miracles in this situation. God continued to intervene and placed the right people in the right place to help Jack be the best person he could be. We were always being reminded of God s grace in this situation as parents and teachers alike approached us and told us that they had been praying for Jack and our whole family. Our experiences have led to increased expertise in special education and further research into the issues of equality and fair treatment of all children. We have been affirmed that God wants to work miracles through us in our lives. He wants to use us for his glory. Yes, miracles do happen, even in the public school.[316]

CONCLUSION

Teachers, you have been charged to access the Secret Kingdom through forgiveness, faith, love, hope, and charity. Jesus Christ said to have faith in God. Believe that God exists and trust in Him. Pray to know His purpose and will in your life. Use the Law of Miracles to create miracles in others' lives.

You can be a witness to others of God's miracles in your life. We have heard of countless occasions where teachers prayed for students and parents during their prayer time with results that could not be explained through normal occurrences. There was the student who suddenly behaved after being taken off medication or the parent who actually was friendly and open at conference time after several rough meetings. Those are the types of miracles that have resulted from teachers' prayers over the years.

Teachers, remember that when others witness your faith they become more open to tell you that they believe as you do. You can show them by example that you are a believer and a witness to the truth. Pray and act as if what you pray is going to happen.

---

[315] E. O'Neill Hunter and Elizabeth M. Hunter, "Our kid has more chromosomes than your kid does," *VA CEC Research to Practice K-12 Scholarship e-journal* (2010).
[316] Hunter, "Waking Up With Jack."

What you say has the power to convince your students that God is real. Speak positive affirmation to the children that you teach. Scripture tells us that Jesus stilled a storm by what He said. By speaking, He raised three dead people, cast out demons, cleansed a leper, and healed a Roman officer's servant from a remote location[317].

You have been charged to access the miracles in the Secret Kingdom through your faith. Jesus Christ said we must have faith in God. Believe that God exists. Trust in Him. Pray to know His purpose and will in your life. Use the Law of Miracles. Model for students what it means to expect and experience miracles, even when you cannot directly testify about Who performed those miracles. Point out miracles when you see them happen in their lives and perhaps within the classroom itself. You and your students can view your school differently and live in a new and amazing way through miracles.

---

[317] SK, 225.

RESOURCES

Robertson, Pat. *The Secret Kingdom: Your Path to Peace, Love, and Financial Security* (Dallas: Word Publishing, 1992).

CHAPTER 13
THE LAW OF DOMINION

By William F. Cox, Jr., Ph.D.
Professor, Founder—Christian Education Programs
Regent University School of Education

"When man, through Jesus, reasserts God's dominion over himself,
then he is capable of reasserting his God-given dominion
over everything else"[318]

PAT ROBERTSON, *THE SECRET KINGDOM*

The dominion perspective on education and teacher behavior is often under-appreciated in academic endeavors, even though much of schooling and academic equipping in general is rooted in the dominion mandate. As Pat Robertson emphasizes in *The Secret Kingdom*, the principles of God's kingdom depend in many ways on their alignment with the Law of Dominion for proper fulfillment.

God's Dominion Mandate to Man

One of God's earliest recorded statements was giving humans dominion over all the earth:

> "And God said, Let us make man in our image, after our likeness: and let them have dominion over the fish of the sea, and over the fowl of the air, and over the cattle, and over all the earth, and over every creeping thing that creepeth upon the earth.

> "So God created man in his own image, in the image of God created he him; male and female created he them.

> "And God blessed them, and God said unto them, Be fruitful, and multiply, and replenish the earth, and subdue it: and have dominion over the fish of the sea, and over the fowl of the air, and over every living thing that moveth upon the earth."[319]

This charge from God was unique to man. Although God expected all living beings to reproduce and multiply, only man was charged with ruling over God's entire creation (except, of course, over other humans). This dominion charge was so important that it preceded His statement to humans to reproduce and multiply.

---

[318] SK, 242.
[319] Genesis 1:26-28 KJV.

Internal Dominion—Jesus Christ and the Holy Spirit

Dominion-taking does not actually begin with *external* dominion—taking over the environment of the earth. Instead, it begins with *internal* dominion—each person taking over their inner environment—namely, over self. The external, earthly, or natural dominion that God wants ultimately cannot properly occur until mankind first takes dominion over himself.

In large measure, much of what is taught in school is intended to equip people to take dominion over the natural environment, but because of the fallen nature of mankind, unless students are first equipped for dominion-taking by taking dominion over self, the results will not reflect God's intention for this earth. And, as the Bible reveals, particularly in the New Testament, this can occur only with the help of the Holy Spirit.

Individuals only receive the internal help of the Holy Spirit when they have a personal relationship with Jesus Christ. In fact, Jesus did not die primarily to restore the dominion-taking abilities of mankind. Instead Jesus died to restore the relationship between God and each and every person. God desires that humans would live and rule interdependently with Him. In order for that to happen, the individual must first take dominion over the contrary internal motivation that wants to live independently of God.

God's plan for man's dominion-taking role seems to be crucial to His desire for the well-being of earth and its inhabitants. It fulfills God's desire to bring His kingdom to earth. Since Satan does not want God's kingdom to come to earth, this plan creates a spiritual tension. As history reveals, Satan set out with the chief intent to subvert man's internal dominion-taking, since that would directly affect the intimate relationship that God desired to have with his image-bearers. Once Satan prevents intimacy with God, it secondarily affects earthly dominion-taking.

To say it differently, messing up dominion-taking over the non-human environment is nowhere near as catastrophic as messing up intimacy between God and humans, which results from failed dominion- taking over self.

THE DOMINION PERSPECTIVE ON EDUCATION

What implications does this have for education? In order for teachers to achieve the proper focus on teaching external dominion-taking in line with God's desire for earth, they first need to be guided internally by God Himself. Although they need to be competent in both the subject matter to be imparted to students and the pedagogical skills required for the act of teaching, it is even more important that they help their students to become self-controlled.

Implications of the Law of Dominion for Educators

Here are five implications of the Law of Dominion for educators.

1. Teachers need to possess dominion over self in order to model the qualities of Jesus to others and particularly to students.

2. Teachers need to possess dominion over the skills and procedures of teaching.

3. Teachers need to possess dominion over competence in the content they teach that is to be mastered by the students.

4. Teachers need to build into students qualities that reflect the character of Jesus so that the students' attributes parallel those of their teachers.

5. Teachers should enable their students to master content-related skills, attitudes, and understandings in order to take dominion over that range of activities for which God has made them responsible.

Requirements for Teachers

Here is another presentation of the requirements for teachers in these areas under the Law of Dominion. While the order of progression below may seem intuitively obvious, by chapter's end we will see the high value of a professionally counter-intuitive order.

1. Content competence

2. Suitable presentation of content

3. Spiritual competence

     3a. Modeling obedience to God's Word

     3b. Being a representative of God to the students.

1. Content competence. First, without doubt, content competence for teachers is a must. It is the reason why teachers are employed and why children attend formal schooling. Whether teachers are being interviewed for employment, tenure, or promotion, they must demonstrate competence in their subject matter or discipline. This goes without saying. It really is a no-brainer. In fact, there is no place in education for a teacher who lacks content expertise to impart to students.

2. Suitable presentation techniques. The next area of concern is the highly related matter of the teacher's ability to present the academic content in a way most suitable for students to learn. Most adults have experienced, at one time or another, the boring and often frustrating instance of being taught by someone fully competent content-wise but lacking in creative delivery of the content. While this type of environment sometimes stimulates a student to persevere and learn anyway, this is not what the education profession (and students) consider an optimum learning environment.

Clearly, teachers using fruitful teaching techniques improve the academic attainment of students,[320] but strangely, the teaching profession does not have a solid understanding of what techniques to use and when.[321] Generally speaking, the more learned the instructor becomes in educational methods, the greater benefit to students. However, beyond that, the causative nature of teacher behavior on student learning lacks professional certainty.

Obviously, some teachers are "better" than others simply because they are naturally gifted at teaching, but for the most part, training and practice are crucial to improve good teaching. A good teacher explains a complex topic to a novice (such as setting up a spreadsheet) different from the way an expert explains a complex topic to another expert.

What seems to be coming clearer in teacher impact research is that what constitutes teaching competence (i.e., dominion) is that artful mix of the mechanics of teaching plus the wisdom to know what method to use and when.[322] On reflection, it is no wonder that dominion in the area of teaching competence is difficult to acquire. After all, there are more than 16 types of teaching methods, 22 types of learner variables, and an equal amount of learning outcomes, not to mention the differential relationship these factors have with various types of content typically taught in school.[323]

All this is to say that for a teacher to have dominion over his/her profession, content competence and suitable presentation techniques are absolutely essential. However, there is a third vital area to consider.

3. Spiritual competence. The third area of dominion in teaching skills may be the least acknowledged yet perhaps most important in a quality-of-life sense. This has to do with biblical matters.

To do justice to this topic, we digress momentarily to examine student/learner dominion-taking. Just as there are skills associated with fruitful teaching, there are skills associated with fruitful learning. For instance, there are cognitive skills associated with perceiving, attending, storing, and recalling information.[324] There are skills particular to learning different kinds of subject matter, such as learning how to write poetry vs. learning inferential statistics. And there are skills associated with the various kinds of learning outcomes expected[325] as well as skills associated with mental operations such as comparing, contrasting, identifying issues, and examining assumptions.

Important as all these skills are, of far more eternal significance are the skills, attitudes, and understandings students need to acquire regarding spiritual matters. This is the area in which we would expect Christian teachers to excel.

---

[320] James H. Stronge, Pamela D. Tucker, and Jennifer L. Hindman, *Handbook for Qualities for Effective Teachers* (Alexandria, VA: Association for Supervision and Curriculum Design, 2003).

[321] Frank B. Murray, ed., *The Teacher Educator's Handbook* (San Francisco: Jossey-Bass, 1996).

[322] Linda Darling-Hammond, *The Flat World and Education* (White Plains, NY: Teachers College Press, 2010).

[323] Frank B. Murray, "Explanations in Education," in *Knowledge Base for the Beginning Teacher,* ed. M.C. Reynolds (New York: Pergamon Press, 1989), 1-12.

[324] Robert M. Gagne, *The Conditions of Learning,* 3rd. ed.. (New York: Holt, Rinehart & Winston, 1997).

[325] Benjamin S. Bloom (Ed.), *Taxonomy of Educational Objectives: Handbook I* (White Plains, NY: Longman, 1956).

This remaining topic takes us all the way back to the Garden of Eden. It relates to learning how to represent the King of the universe while being tempted to depart from that privilege. There are at least two dimensions to this matter.

3a. Modeling obedience to God's Word. One area relates to teaching students obedience to God's word. This includes mastering difficult issues like obedience to authority and demonstrating other character traits that are appropriate in both Christian and secular school environments.

3b. Being a representative of God to the students. The other dimension relates to personally representing God to students who are often not very mature in that matter themselves. It includes being conformed to the nature of Christ, not taking offense, forgiving even if forgiveness is not reciprocated, and many other areas that first require the teachers' spiritual competence before they can enable student competence.

Regarding the first issue, Christian teachers—as with all Christians—are in the ongoing process of sanctification and are hopefully at a much more advanced stage than their students in the process of dying to self.[326] Obviously, great self-dominion is needed before you can be a character mentor to others.[327]

Regarding the second matter, children, no matter what age, often act in ways that test the patience of adults. As representatives of God to their students, Christian teachers should be at such a level of maturity that they do not reciprocate when confronted with immaturity of character in troublesome students. Instead, Christian teachers are expected to display the very nature of Christ to them.

As seen in many award-winning movies about successful teachers in ghetto conditions, the teacher who loves, edifies, and holds the students to high but fair expectations invariably succeeds wonderfully beyond the students' past performances and future expectations.

CONCLUSION

Far more is involved than might be expected when applying the Law of Dominion to the field of education. It is not just about teaching students content such as mathematics, communication, and history so that they can rule over the natural environment. In fact, this is just the tip of the iceberg, so to speak, in terms of equipping them to govern as regents and ambassadors of the King to bring His kingdom to earth.

Teachers need competence or dominion-equipping ability far beyond their content specialty. They need to overcome their own disobedient nature that the sin of Adam passed on to all future generations. There are forces that try to prevent us from taking proper dominion over our weaker nature. Thus we see the high value of a professionally counter-intuitive order that begins with the spiritual condition of the teacher as the first priority.

Ultimately, dominion-taking in education involves far more than taking dominion over the natural world. It involves the extensive range of spiritual competence needed to

---

[326] Galatians 2:20; Philippians 3:10-11.
[327] James 3:1.

exercise dominion over the unseen but powerful spiritual realm. Most important, it relates to taking dominion over the hindrances to being effective teachers, to be able to exercise dominion in the way God expects. Educators, you have a wonderful opportunity through this Law to get closer to God yourself and thus be a model dominion taker to others.

In the final analysis, this means that self-discipline under Holy Spirit guidance is the ultimate dominion issue in education because it is the ultimate issue in all of life.

RESOURCES

Robertson, Pat. *The Secret Kingdom: Your Path to Peace, Love, and Financial Security* (Dallas: Word Publishing, 1992).

Part III
How Educators Should Live and Practice

Part III

How Educators Should
Live and Practice

CHAPTER 14

SPECIFIC APPLICATIONS FOR EDUCATORS

By Helen R. Stiff-Williams, Ed. D.

Professor and Director of Center for Character Education and Civic Development

Regent University School of Education

"I have become convinced that wisdom is the key to the secrets of the kingdom of God. It leads to favor. But the starting point is humility."[328]

PAT ROBERTSON, *THE SECRET KINGDOM*

"If you want to know what God wants you to do, ask him, and he will gladly tell you, for he is always ready to give a bountiful supply of wisdom to all who ask him; he will not resent it."[329]

By way of launching this chapter, I will orient you to my beliefs as a Christian and how my faith has informed this writing. As an active Christian, I believe in God, the Father; Jesus Christ, the Son of God; and the Holy Spirit. Further, it is my belief that the Holy Bible is an ageless, living document capable of helping you to see your purpose for living, which makes the Bible relevant for all generations. My understanding and application of the Holy Scriptures, along with Dr. Pat Robertson's book *The Secret Kingdom,* served to guide the preparation of this chapter. I aim to show practicing educators how contemporary, evidence-based, professional practices are most appropriately and effectively implemented through morally-guided principles, such as those identified by Dr. Robertson and found in the Holy Bible.

The primary purpose of this chapter is to link the principles of the Secret Kingdom to the lives and professional practice of educators and others who work with children and youth to improve the quality of service. This chapter will describe ten principles and present illustrations related to evidence-based educational strategies that foster change and improvements within various K-12 school settings. Teachers and other educators who apply these Kingdom principles can meet their purpose in life and improve the quality of their professional practice.

---

[328] SK, 103.
[329] James 1:5 TLB.

Professional Performance Standards

This chapter aims to support educators in the examination of their personal behavior and professional practice, with the goal of identifying changes that will raise the awareness of teachers regarding their moral responsibility for working with learners and increase the academic success of all students. To support the use of the Secret Kingdom principles in educational practice, each law has been converted to a professional performance standard that defines specifically what educators should know and be able to do as a practitioner.

As a self-help experience, this chapter engages the user in activities for personal and professional development that are selected on the basis of grounding in contemporary research findings and best practices in education. Specific self-help professional development activities located in the Appendices will be notated throughout this chapter.

After studying the content of this chapter and completing the accompanying professional development activities in the Appendices, you should be able to demonstrate the behavior of an inspired leader and change-agent, an ethical and morally-guided practitioner, a supportive and caring professional, and a highly motivated, skillful educator.

The Educator's Moral Obligation

Teaching is a deeply moral activity. Fenstermacher described the moral nature of teaching in this way:

> "What makes teaching a moral endeavor is that it is, quite centrally, human action undertaken to regard other human beings. Thus, matters of what is fair, right, just, and virtuous are always present. Whenever a teacher asks a student to share something with another student, decides between combatants in a schoolyard dispute, sets procedures for who will go first, second, third, and so on, or discusses the welfare of a student with another teacher, moral considerations are present. The teacher's conduct, at all times and in all ways, is a moral matter. For that reason alone, teacher is a profoundly moral activity."[330]

To professionals with a moral purpose, the Holy Scriptures advise: "It would be better to be thrown into the sea with a millstone hung around your neck than to cause one of these little ones to fall into sin."[331] I can think of no stronger warning about an educator's moral responsibility and obligation than the words written in the Book of Luke and corroborated in Matthew 18:6 and Mark 9:42. The Scriptures warn us who teach the young that there will be a heavy penalty for corrupting them. Failure to deliver appropriate instruction that supports the preparation of our youth is a professional obligation that comes with eternal consequences.

---

[330] Fenstermacher in Goodlad, Soder, and Sirotnik (1990), 133.
[331] Luke 17:2 KJV.

As a further statement of the moral responsibility of teachers, we should be strongly reminded of the precept of the physicians' Hippocratic Oath: "First, do no harm."[332] Consistent with scriptural expectations, the calling to serve as a teacher demands that the work be done to the highest standard. To teach at a high standard means that you must "do no harm" and serve as though your professional performance will have an impact on your eternal status.

APPLYING KINGDOM PRINCIPLES FOR PERSONAL AND PROFESSIONAL CHANGE

By applying Kingdom principles, an educator can expect to see change on multiple levels.

Becoming a better person. On one level, an individual educator following these Kingdom principles will experience personal growth and in this context become a better person. According to recent authors, becoming a better person means becoming a happier, more fulfilled individual who is attaining his perceived purpose in life.[333] Jesus implied that becoming a better person means following the commandments to wholeheartedly love God and others.[334]

Becoming a better educator. On another level, change will be evident in the professional practice of the persons involved in education. Practitioners who know and apply Kingdom principles will become more skilled in the implementation of the education process.

Improving outcomes of educational organizations. Educators in leadership roles will gain insight about how to change educational organizations to improve the outcomes of the education process. Leaders will see how to make changes in the people and the culture that result in increased student achievement and other outcomes.

Kingdom principles are capable of shaping and improving educators to become influential leaders, morally-guided, ethical and caring professionals, and expert educational practitioners.

APPLYING KINGDOM PRINCIPLES TO THE EDUCATION PROFESSION

The ten laws of the Secret Kingdom have critical importance in the field of education and can guide educators to new heights of professional effectiveness. Figure 1

---

[332] MedicineNet.com.
[333] Warren 2002; Covey, 2004.
[334] Mark 12:29-31.

identifies each law, provides a brief description of the law as it was explained in the original *Secret Kingdom*, and, in the third column, describes how each law can be directly applied to practices within the education profession.

Figure 1

HOW THE LAWS OF THE KINGDOM INFORM EDUCATIONAL PRACTICE		
Law →	Description of the Law	→ Importance for Educational Practice
Law of Use	*"If talents and abilities are not used, you will lose them."*[335]	Teachers should be able to identify their own talents and abilities and use these strengths to achieve success as they work with learners. Educators should also possess the skills and understandings to identify students' talents and abilities and to design instruction that addresses the diverse needs and interests of students.
Law of Reciprocity	*"Give and it will be given to you." "Expressions of kindness will yield kindness in return, while expressions of criticism will produce criticism in return."*[336]	Teaching and learning is a purely reciprocal process. It is important to understand that teaching is a "giving" profession. When effective teaching is done, effective learning will occur. Teaching has not happened until learning has occurred. When teachers contribute in positive ways to the success of the learners, students will contribute to the accomplishment of the goals of the teacher.
Law of Perseverance	*"Success in life comes through industry. . . . Industry refers to dedication, commitment, patience, self-discipline, and hard work that bring positive results."*[337]	Educators should demonstrate industriousness through dedication, commitment, patience, and self-discipline. These values should also be taught to students. Teachers should undertake to work hard to achieve positive results. Students should demonstrate these values throughout their educational experience.
Law of Unity	*Great creativity occurs where there is unity, agreement, and harmony.*[338]	Educators should establish a culture of unity, agreement, and harmony within classrooms and schools, recognizing that a positive, supportive culture influences learning outcomes and student achievement. Creativity and success occur under positive, supportive conditions.

---

[335] SK, 137.
[336] SK, 113, 114.
[337] SK, 153.
[338] SK, 192.

Law of Fidelity	*"Whoever can be trusted with very little can be trusted with much; and whoever is dishonest with very little will also be dishonest with much."*[339]	Trustworthiness and honesty should be demonstrated at all times. Recognize that the eyes of the youth are constantly upon educators. Dishonesty and infidelity will lead to growing problems for one's career and service in the profession.
Law of Change	*"No man puts new wine into old skins, lest the skins break and all be lost."*[340] *"God is always the same; His plan is always the same. But the vehicles, the organizations, and techniques of carrying out His program will always be changing."*[341]	Education in the 21st century is markedly different from any previous generations. Educators should keep abreast of professional developments and embrace change with the full understanding that new, evidence-based practices will result in advancements and the best outcomes. All classroom operations and instructional procedures should be grounded in current research and best practices.
Law of Greatness	*"The greatest person in the kingdom of heaven is the one who makes himself humble like this child."*[342]	Educators and leaders must be humble, open, and receptive to new ideas and innovations to be successful. These behaviors must be demonstrated toward the students being served as well as colleagues, supervisors, and others in authority to foster collaboration, cooperation, and inspiration that lead to the mutual accomplishment of goals.
Law of Responsibility	*"Jesus made it clear that with blessings also come responsibilities. He summed it up succinctly: 'unto whomsoever much is given, of him shall be much required.'"*[343]	Persons gifted as teachers and leaders are morally obligated to perform with the highest quality. Like the ministry, the teaching profession is considered to be a "calling," which means that eternal rewards and consequences will be based upon the quality of one's service. Educators have an awesome responsibility to teach (serve) all youngsters to the best of their ability.
Law of Miracles	*Override the way in which things are normally done to achieve a greater outcome.*[344] *Miracles point out the mysteries and unexplainable things of science such as bumble bees flying when their bodies far outweigh their wings and birds migrating 7,000 miles non-stop.*	Given the huge influence that they have upon the lives of others for the future of the nation, educators and leaders should be agents of change through innovation to achieve exceptional outcomes. They should seek to achieve the miraculous transformation of students. Incredible change and improvement in the lives of many can be achieved over the course of an extended career in education.

---

[339] SK, 203.
[340] SK, 210, ref. Luke 5: 36-38.
[341] SK, 210.
[342] SK, 180, ref. Matthew 18:2 NCV.
[343] SK, 165, ref. Luke 12:48 KJV.
[344] SK, 221.

Law of Dominion	*"God wants man to have authority over the earth. He wants him to rule the way he was created to rule."* [345]	Educators and leaders should use their authority in responsible ways and recognize their moral obligation to treat others with dignity and honor. By virtue of professional position, teachers have authority over the youngsters in their charge. This authority should not be used to abuse youngsters or corrupt the educational process.

Professional Standards Derived from Kingdom Laws

The ten laws of the Kingdom given above can be converted to professional standards that guide the practice of educators. Figure 2 identifies each of the ten laws and its corresponding professional performance standard. The description of how each law can be applied in the education field is presented as a "standard" or statement of expectation for professional practice. Biblically grounded and structured to be consistent with professional best practices in education, the new standards describe what educators should know and be able to do to achieve improved student academic outcomes and the spiritually-guided development of youths.

Figure 2

KINGDOM PRINCIPLES CONVERTED TO PROFESSIONAL PERFORMANCE STANDARDS	
10 Kingdom Principles	**10 Standards for Educators**
Law of Use	**Standard 1:** Maximize the use of talents and abilities.
Law of Reciprocity	**Standard 2:** Operate with the full awareness of the inherent effects of reciprocal relationships.
Law of Perseverance	**Standard 3:** Demonstrate industriousness through dedication, commitment, patience, and self-discipline.
Law of Unity	**Standard 4:** Maintain and work within a culture of unity, agreement, and harmony because these factors directly influence outcomes and the attainment of success.
Law of Fidelity	**Standard 5:** Demonstrate trustworthiness and honesty at all times.
Law of Change	**Standard 6:** Embrace change with the understanding that new, evidence-based practices result in advancements and the best outcomes.

---

[345] SK, 237.

Law of Greatness	**Standard 7:** Demonstrate being humble, open, and receptive to new ideas and innovations to achieve success.
Law of Responsibility	**Standard 8:** Demonstrate the moral obligation to perform to your best ability.
Law of Miracles	**Standard 9:** Be innovative to achieve exceptional outcomes.
Law of Dominion	**Standard 10:** Use authority in responsible ways and recognize the moral obligation to treat others with dignity and respect.

These professional performance standards refer to how teachers and leaders should operate in their day-to-day practice. It is important to note that meeting these standards in one's daily practice can yield results far beyond typical or average outcomes. By applying the Kingdom standards, educators will be able to see incredible improvements and remarkable outcomes.

As a first step in engaging the self-help experience through this chapter, you should complete the pre-assessment of your beliefs and professional practices in education *(Figure 3)*. Then complete the self-assessment instrument to determine your baseline on the professional standards *(Figure 4)*. After completion of the self-assessment, you should use the results to guide your use of the series of professional development activities in the Appendices.

You are encouraged to work systematically through all of the exercises to achieve the best outcomes for the book. However, on the basis of individual ratings for items on the pre-assessment, you can identify areas for increased emphasis and concentrated professional development to improve your performance in specific areas.

Figure 3

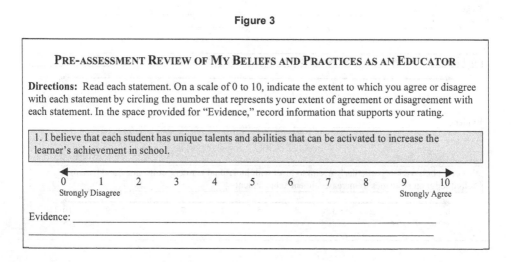

PRE-ASSESSMENT REVIEW OF MY BELIEFS AND PRACTICES AS AN EDUCATOR

Directions: Read each statement. On a scale of 0 to 10, indicate the extent to which you agree or disagree with each statement by circling the number that represents your extent of agreement or disagreement with each statement. In the space provided for "Evidence," record information that supports your rating.

1. I believe that each student has unique talents and abilities that can be activated to increase the learner's achievement in school.

0 1 2 3 4 5 6 7 8 9 10
Strongly Disagree   Strongly Agree

Evidence: _____
_____

2. I believe that the quality of my teaching directly impacts the level of each student's learning within my classes.

```
        0    1    2    3    4    5    6    7    8    9    10
        Strongly Disagree                         Strongly Agree
```

Evidence: _____

_____

3. I believe that I am industrious, such as being meticulous in lesson planning and instructional delivery, to maximize learning for each student in my classroom.

```
        0    1    2    3    4    5    6    7    8    9    10
        Strongly Disagree                         Strongly Agree
```

Evidence: _____

_____

4. I believe that I establish and maintain a positive, caring culture within my classroom/school that directly contributes to each student's success in learning.

```
        0    1    2    3    4    5    6    7    8    9    10
        Strongly Disagree                         Strongly Agree
```

Evidence: _____

_____

5. I consistently demonstrate trustworthiness and honesty in fulfilling my responsibilities as a teacher/school leader.

```
        0    1    2    3    4    5    6    7    8    9    10
        Strongly Disagree                         Strongly Agree
```

Evidence: _____

_____

6. I look for and apply new evidence-based practices known to increase student achievement.

```
        0    1    2    3    4    5    6    7    8    9    10
        Strongly Disagree                         Strongly Agree
```

Evidence: _____

_____

7. I don't believe it is particularly useful to meet with individual learners, colleagues, and parents to solicit input on strategies to increase student achievement.

```
        0    1    2    3    4    5    6    7    8    9    10
        Strongly Disagree                         Strongly Agree
```

Evidence: _____

_____

---

8. A moral commitment to perform my teaching and/or school leadership duties to the highest standard influences the quality of my professional performance.

| 0 | 1 | 2 | 3 | 4 | 5 | 6 | 7 | 8 | 9 | 10 |

Strongly Disagree   Strongly Agree

Evidence: _____

_____

---

9. I seek out innovative practices and strategically apply new research-based developments to increase the performance of my students.

| 0 | 1 | 2 | 3 | 4 | 5 | 6 | 7 | 8 | 9 | 10 |

Strongly Disagree   Strongly Agree

Evidence: _____

_____

---

10. I use my authority in responsible ways and I treat each student with dignity and respect.

| 0 | 1 | 2 | 3 | 4 | 5 | 6 | 7 | 8 | 9 | 10 |

Strongly Disagree   Strongly Agree

Evidence: _____

_____

To summarize this discussion, you are encouraged to complete the Summary of Performance Standards and Self-Assessment that follows *(Figure 4)*.

In the first column is one of the ten Standards for Educators.

In the second column, rate yourself according to each standard. Based upon these ratings, identify where you see a need for professional development to make improvements in your performance.

In the third column, write narrative comments about the areas needing improvement that you have identified. Likewise, identify those standards on which you rated yourself as performing strongly and requiring less attention for professional improvement.

Figure 4

SUMMARY OF PERFORMANCE STANDARDS AND SELF-ASSESSMENT

Directions: Use the results of your pre-assessment to identify which of the standards will require additional time and attention for your professional improvement. For each standard, record your corresponding numerical rating in Column 2. Next, record notations in Column 3 that indicate how you might engage professional development experiences to increase your performance on any low-rated standards.

Standards for Educators	Your Rating	Focus on Professional Development
Standard 1: Maximize the use of talents and abilities.		
Standard 2: Operate with the full awareness of the inherent effects of reciprocal relationships.		
Standard 3: Demonstrate industriousness through dedication, commitment, patience, and self-discipline.		
Standard 4: Maintain and work within a culture of unity, agreement, and harmony because these factors directly influence outcomes and the attainment of success.		
Standard 5: Demonstrate trustworthiness and honesty at all times.		
Standard 6: Embrace change with the understanding that new, evidence-based practices result in advancements and the best outcomes.		
Standard 7: Demonstrate being humble, open, and receptive to new ideas and innovations to achieve success.		
Standard 8: Demonstrate the moral obligation to perform to your best ability.		

Standard 9: Be innovative to achieve exceptional outcomes.		
Standard 10: Use authority in responsible ways and recognize the moral obligation to treat others with dignity and respect.		

As a result of the performance assessment, you now have a perspective of how to focus your attention for improvement in your professional practices. Strategic professional development activities in the targeted areas will yield measurable increases in student performance. As you continue with this chapter, you will see evidence of value-added strategic changes capable of boosting the achievement of all students.

Power of Secret Kingdom Laws as Professional Performance Standards

The next section describes how each of the ten professional performance standards derived from the ten Secret Kingdom principles can be applied in educational settings. Educators will see how to apply these standards to improve interpersonal relationships with colleagues, increase student achievement outcomes, and create and maintain a work culture that is positive and supportive for all members. Further, application of the ten professional standards is linked to current evidence-based practices in the field of education. Thus, by using these standards, educators will experience spiritual guidance and confirm that the recommended practices are grounded in educational research and best practices.

LAW OF USE—MAXIMIZING EVERYONE'S TALENTS AND ABILITIES

Pat Robertson indicates that if you do not use your talents and abilities, you will lose them. A corollary to this point is this: The use of your talents and abilities is a way to unbelievable advancement and incredible success.

The first professional standard emerges from the Law of Use with particular attention to maximizing the talents and abilities of everyone.

Appendix B, Exercise 1. On the personal level, begin a process of self-analysis to identify your talents and abilities and determine how to maximize the use of all of your gifts. Go to Appendix B and complete Exercise 1, "Learning Styles Inventory," to identify your strengths. How can you use what you are good at doing to make a difference for yourself and others? To what extent are you using your talents and abilities? Are you working in a profession that maximizes their use? If not, consideration

187

should be given to a career change. If the results of your self-analysis indicate that you *are* working in the profession that matches your talents and abilities, the expectation is that you will seek ways to maximize the use of your strengths.

Teachers who apply their talents and abilities in the classroom can plan and deliver the highest quality of instruction. For example, if you are talented as an artist, you should use your artistic talent in the classroom. Engaging your personal talents and abilities increases your sense of personal satisfaction and ability to respect the diverse strengths and interests of learners within the classroom. This will manifest itself in the differentiation of instruction that corresponds with the students' interests and abilities.[346]

In practice, the teacher will conduct an assessment of students to identify their interests and abilities. The findings from such assessments will be used to plan and deliver instruction in the classroom. When class work is centered upon the learners' interests and involves their strengths and abilities, student engagement increases and achievement rises.[347]

Figure 5 illustrates the increased effects of combining the talents and abilities of teachers and students.

Figure 5

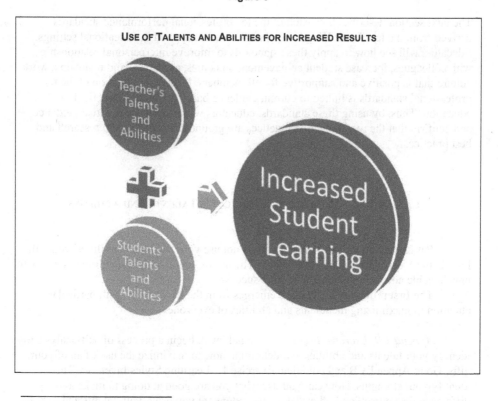

USE OF TALENTS AND ABILITIES FOR INCREASED RESULTS

---

[346] Tomlinson, 2008.
[347] Hattie, 2009.

188

During the delivery of instruction in the classroom, teachers should help students to recognize, appreciate, and use their God-given talents and abilities. Learning experiences that engage learners in routine use of worksheets thus become inherently unacceptable. Such experiences do not offer adequate opportunities for students to use their different talents and abilities.

Identifying Talents and Abilities

Teachers should provide learning experiences and professional support that help students to develop a positive attitude toward their strengths and abilities. By simply describing talents and abilities as what you are really good at doing, students can be engaged in identifying their strengths. It is also important to help students understand that they must respect and honor the differing talents and abilities of other learners. Talents and abilities can differ markedly among individuals and they develop by an incremental process that occurs over time.

According to authorities such as Howard Gardner (1983) and Thomas Armstrong (2009), human strengths and intelligences can be organized into eight categories:[348]

- Linguistic intelligence ("word smart")
- Logical-mathematical intelligence ("number/reasoning smart")
- Spatial intelligence ("picture smart")
- Bodily-Kinesthetic intelligence ("body smart")
- Musical intelligence ("music smart")
- Interpersonal intelligence ("people smart")
- Intrapersonal intelligence ("self smart")
- Naturalist intelligence ("nature smart")

Based upon the preceding eight intelligences, a simple assessment has been provided for use in determining the strengths of your students. Engage your students in completing the assessment to identify their strengths or intelligences and their corresponding subject preferences.

Appendix B, Exercise 2. Go to Appendix B to locate Exercise 2, "Match Learner Intelligences with Subject Preferences." To identify other aspects of your students' learning styles, you are encouraged to invite them to complete this tool. After analyzing the learning styles of students, as emphasized previously, teachers should design lesson activities, instructional strategies, and teaching materials that correspond with the diversity of learners within the classroom.

---

[348] Howard Gardner (1983) and Thomas Armstrong (2009).

Talents and Abilities Exercise

Analysis of a student's talents and abilities can begin with a simple exercise that engages the learner in selecting areas of strongest interest from a list. A student can read through the following list of activities and select his/her first choice by placing number one (1) on the line to indicate strongest preference, number two (2) on the line for a second preference, and number three (3) to indicate a third preference.

> **Instructions.** Record your preferences, using the numbers 1, 2, and 3 to indicate your first choice, second choice, and third choice.
>
> _____ I like solving mathematics problems.
> _____ I like writing poetry.
> _____ I like drawing pictures.
> _____ I like to take nature walks.
> _____ I like making mechanical models.
> _____ I like solving crossword puzzles.
> _____ I like to listen to music every day.
> _____ I like to exercise every day.

For a complete analysis of your talents and abilities, complete a reputable comprehensive analysis using one of the free multiple intelligence assessment tools available online through an Internet search. Through the completion of one of these free tools, I learned that my strongest areas of intelligence were "intrapersonal," "linguistic," and "interpersonal." These results were generally consistent with the findings from other multiple intelligence assessment instruments that I completed.

Identifying Learning Styles

When there is clear evidence of the alignment of the components of instruction that support the diversity of intelligences and learning styles, teachers can maximize the use of the talents and abilities of individual students. Such deliberate and strategic planning yields increased student learning even from the most challenging students.

Learning through kinesthetic experiences. For example, a teacher might know that several students in the class have bodily-kinesthetic intelligence and learn best through kinesthetic experiences. In this case, the teacher should plan instructional activities that involve physical movement to facilitate learning instead of teaching approaches that singularly involve listening.

Learning through differentiated instruction. Differentiated instruction is one common label used to describe the professional practice of designing teaching strategies and materials to support the diversity of learners. As presented in an interview with Rebore (2008), Tomlinson described differentiated instruction as what teachers do "to address students' particular readiness needs, their particular interests, and their preferred ways of learning. Of course, these efforts must be rooted in sound classroom practice—

it's not just a matter of trying anything. There are key principles of differentiated instruction that we know to be best practices and that support everything we do in the classroom. But at its core, differentiated instruction means addressing ways in which students vary as learners."

Hattie's (2009) comprehensive meta-analysis of the relationship between learning style strategies and student achievement established a slightly stronger than average effect size for this teaching approach. There is sufficient research evidence to demonstrate that teaching to address learning styles based upon students' gifts and talents will have a favorable impact on student achievement.

LAW OF RECIPROCITY

The Law of Reciprocity describes inter-related factors in everyone's lives. In *The Secret Kingdom*, Dr. Robertson uses the act of giving to explain the Law of Reciprocity. "Give, and it shall be given unto you."[350] As you give to others, you can expect proportionally that others will give to you. In considering the real-life application of this principle, it is important to understand that it is operating in the spiritual realm. Hence, we, as human beings, are not in charge of causing this giving and receiving to occur. We operate knowing that God has created this process with an inherent, proportional giving and receiving relationship.

The Law of Reciprocity operates in the same manner as Newton's third law involving the use of force: If a body exerts a force on a second body, then the second body exerts an equal and opposite force on the first. Stated in another way, Newton's Third Law indicates that for every action, there is an equal and opposite reaction.[351]

The Law of Reciprocity operates within the physical and non-physical realms. Consider the reciprocal relationship involving human interactions. The most important take-away from this principle is the understanding that how we treat others will be returned in how others treat us. Dr. Robertson explains, "Expressions of kindness will yield kindness in return; expressions of criticism will produce criticism in return."[352]

With consideration of Newton's third law of force and Robertson's Law of Reciprocity, the teaching and learning process is a reciprocal operation. The amount of "force" for instructional quality produces a reciprocal amount of thrust in student learning and achievement.

The forces of instructional quality are identifiable as the quality of relationships with students, careful lesson planning, use of research-based instructional strategies, and the application of effective assessment techniques. Teachers who manifest a positive, caring relationship with students can expect to receive in return positive, caring behaviors from students.

---

[349] Tomlinson, 26.

[350] SK, 116, ref. Luke 6:38 KJV.

[351] Newton's Laws: Third Law, n.p.

[352] SK, 114.

191

Reciprocal Relationships

See Figure 6 for an illustration of the reciprocal relationship between quality of teaching and quality of learning.

Figure 6

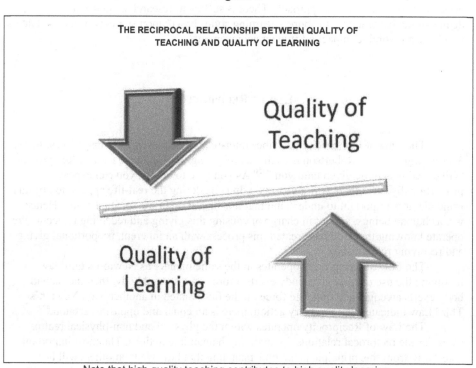

Note that high quality teaching contributes to high quality learning.

Planning Strategically for Positive Outcomes

Strategic planning typically begins with an essential phase of conceptualizing desired results and then determining the kind and amount of "force" you will need to apply to achieve the specific results. Each action you take will receive an equivalent reaction. When you choose to act positively, you can expect to receive an equivalent positive reaction. On the other hand, when you choose to act negatively, you can expect to receive an equivalent negative reaction.

For example, to achieve a particular outcome in working with colleagues, you strategically determine how you can interact with them in a positive way that will yield the results you seek. To increase student achievement, you strategically plan the amount and quality of instruction that will produce positive results. Through meta-analysis of research studies on teachers' relationships with students, Hattie provides compelling evidence for increasing student achievement by establishing and maintaining positive relationships.

Law of Reciprocity Applied to Course Content

The teacher can perform a great service to students by pointing out occurrences of the Law of Reciprocity because the law's influence cuts across disciplines and subject matter as well as being revealed in everyday life. History shows us what happens when communities and nations try to work together but also the reciprocal results when they are at war. Literature is rich with characters who reap what they sow, for better or for worse. Algebra teachers use the Law of Reciprocity when they instruct students to perform the same operation on one side of the equation as the other. Biological studies reveal symbiotic relationships between animals and plants, such as the pilot fish and sharks.

Appendix C, Exercise 3. Standard 2 requires educators to operate with full awareness of the powerful inherent effects of reciprocal relationships. Complete the listening assignment in Appendix C, Exercise 3, "Engaging in Communication as a Reciprocal Relationship." Note how this promotes understanding of the inherent effects of reciprocal relationships.

Appendix C, Exercise 4. Next, since it is equally important for learners to acquire this understanding, you will find an exercise for students in Appendix C, Exercise 4, "Student Understanding of Reciprocal Relationships."

LAW OF PERSEVERANCE

Perseverance is a character trait of educators who demonstrate dedication, commitment, patience, and self-discipline and as a result can expect incredible personal and professional achievements and success.

t is commonly said that character is defined by who you are and what you do when no one is looking. For professional educators, perseverance manifests itself in completing professional duties to the highest standards, even when no supervisor is monitoring your work performance. It is demonstrated by promptly grading students' work to provide essential feedback, even though this duty might not be a favored activity. In this instance, the educators' personal desire to excel at the job drives their desire to provide prompt feedback on student's performance with input that helps them advance to improved learning outcomes.

How do we know that improved learning outcomes will result? Prompt student feedback on performance, i.e., promptly graded and returned student work, is an evidence-based practice that contributes to improved student performance.[353]

Through a process of reflection and analysis, you can personally assess the extent of your perseverance as an educator. As a practical exercise, you can self-assess the extent to which your commitment to professional duties is demonstrated and the overall quality of your performance is completed.

Self-examination can begin with a few reflective questions such as these:

- To what extent have you established a culture of perseverance and faithful relationships with learners that assure them of your best interest in their achievement?
- To what extent do you modify instructional strategies to address the different learning needs and preparedness of students within your classroom?
- Do you expect all students to learn regardless of your selection of instructional strategies and tools used in the delivery of instruction?

As I wrote these questions, I found myself examining my own teaching practices and considering ways to refine my instructional practices. You are invited to do the same reflection and analysis.

Teaching Character Development

Dedicated teachers plan and intentionally address the character development of students within their charge[354] at all grade levels. I recommend teaching character development alongside instruction of state and/or national standards curriculum. This approach promotes the integration of student character development with standards of instruction delivered daily. In this way, teachers inculcate values and behaviors that will contribute to the students' lifelong success. Receptive learners can be expected to accept responsibility for their work and become committed to its completion, demonstrate high levels of engagement in learning, and engage in corrective actions to achieve short term and long term goals.

Four Steps of Reciprocal Instruction

The 21st century skills of problem-solving and critical thinking can be taught through routine reciprocal instruction in the classroom. This involves students in taking the lead in their own learning. An instructional strategy developed and popularized by Palinscar and Brown during the 1980s[355] described the technique of reciprocal instruction as engaging four steps:[356]

---

[353] Hattie, 2009; Marzano, 2005.
[354] Lickona, 2004.
[355] Marzano (2005).
[356] Marzano (2005), 42.

1. Summarizing
2. Questioning
3. Clarifying
4. Predicting

As students learn to problem-solve and think critically about completion of work, industriousness and perseverance are facilitated as they state the facts of a situation (summarizing), analyze possible paths forward (questioning), reconsider the facts of the situation (clarifying), and determine the way forward (predict). *All* students should be taught to think strategically as soon as the learners are developmentally ready to assimilate the process, probably not later than age eight.

Implementing the Law of Reciprocity, students take turns asking questions and then answering others' questions. A give and take, action and reaction pattern takes place. Students stimulate thinking by asking questions and they are also stimulated to think when it is time for them to answer the questions.

Relationship between Effort and Achievement

Another research-based strategy to help students to increase industriousness and perseverance is the relationship between effort and achievement.[357] This strategy engages students in measuring how much effort is put into a task in order to achieve results. Students are taught to measure elements such as the amount of time they engage in study and the number of relevant action steps they complete in relationship to the results of their efforts. In reflecting upon the outcomes of their efforts, they are able to see that the amount of engaged time and the number of relevant action steps is directly related to their results. By understanding the relationship between effort and achievement, students can see how industriousness and perseverance are necessary for the achievement of desired outcomes –not only in the classroom but also in life!

Appendix D, Exercise 5. Go to Appendix D to complete Exercise 5, "Assessment and Instruction of Student Industriousness." Use Exercise 5 to evaluate the extent to which you perceive that your students practice industriousness and to self-assess the extent to which you emphasize and teach students how to practice industriousness in school and their daily lives.

Appendix D, Exercise 6. With additional emphasis on Standard 3, a second tool is available in Appendix D to assess your personal practice of industriousness as a professional educator. See Exercise 6, "Educator's Self-Assessment of Industriousness," for the opportunity to examine the quality of your professional practices. Are there duties and practices that you could improve to raise your level of professional performance?

---

[357] Marzano, 2005.

LAW OF UNITY

School leaders, teachers, superintendents, and school boards are under attack for the poor showing in student achievement in America. A few decades ago, we were the leader in education among industrialized nations of the world. Today, America has fallen far down in the rankings.

To improve educational systems and America's ranking, educational visionaries like Hargreaves and Shirley (2009) advise that our approach to change requires working together to solve problems and make improvements instead of competing to determine winners and losers.

Dr. Robertson's Law of Unity proposes the same approach to success by stating that "great creativity occurs where there is unity, agreement and harmony."[358] Thus a professional standard emerges that requires educators to maintain and work within a culture of unity, agreement, and harmony because these factors directly influence outcomes and the attainment of success.

School leaders have a responsibility for creating and maintaining a culture of unity for all stakeholders of the organization where students, teachers, parents, and others are fully vested in the success of what transpires within the school setting. This begins with effective communications among the various groups, beginning with students and teachers and extending to parents, staff members, central office administrators, and others.

Within the learning setting, creating a sense of unity involves having each student feel wanted, supported, and valued for their importance. Any intentional or unintentional behaviors, actions, or communications that divide members of the classroom or learning group will undermine the sense of community and have a negative effect upon student learning.

As the authority within the classroom, teachers must maintain a culture that is unifying and not divisive. Likewise, school leaders are compelled to establish and maintain a positive and supportive school-wide culture as a first order of business. Deal and Petersen (2009) declared that the "school should be a place to create a sense of community; each student should be able to realize his or her potential; each student should feel fulfilled; each teacher should feel fulfilled; each parent should experience joy in watching their child learn and grow."[359]

Effective communication and conflict resolution are skills essential for success in the 21st century workplace.[360] Teachers can teach students how to be effective communicators, including the use of negotiation skills, and how to develop effective interpersonal relationships and social skills, such as conflict resolution, etc.

Schaps, Battistich, and Solomon[361] found, through their research with the Child Development Project, that a strengthened sense of community was a key to the growth of students. A positive, supportive school culture was associated with fostering "academic

---

[358] SK, 191.
[359] Deal and Petersen (2009), 70.
[360] Johnson and Johnson, in Bellanca and Brandt, 2010.
[361] In Zins, Weissberg, Wang & Walberg (2004).

motivation and aspirations, desirable character-related outcomes, social and emotional learning, and avoidance of problem behaviors."[362]

Within the classroom setting, teachers should establish and maintain conditions that are supportive of the development of each learner. For this to happen, the classroom culture must be positive and uplifting for each student. There should be opportunities for students to serve in leadership roles, offer input into the management of the classroom, make selections for learning approaches, and interact with other learners. Schaps, Battistich, and Solomon, (in Zins, Weissberg, Wang, &Walberg, 2004) explained that students need regular opportunities for self-direction, along with input into decision-making. Their rationale was grounded in this way.

> "People are invested in the choices they make for themselves; they feel little personal responsibility for the choices made for them. When students have a genuine say in the life of the classroom—class norms, study topics, conflict resolution, field trip logistics, and so on—then they are committed to the decisions they have been trusted to make and feel responsible for the community they have helped to shape."[363]

In planning for instructional delivery, teachers should make routine use of cooperative learning as a teaching strategy because of its usefulness in reducing the sense of competition among students and fostering a sense of unity to promote the success of all learners."[364] Through effective use of cooperative learning strategies, students are afforded the opportunity to use their talents and abilities, resulting in an increase in engagement in learning. Through different meta analytical research studies, Marzano (2005) and Hattie (2009) determined that cooperative learning is one of the most effective instructional strategies for increasing student achievement.

Appendix E, Exercise 7. Standard 4 requires that educators be proficient at maintaining and working within a culture of unity, agreement, and harmony because these factors directly influence outcomes and the attainment of success. In Appendix E, Exercise 7, "Assessment of Aspects of School/Classroom Culture" is a professional development exercise for assessment of an educator's proficiencies in maintaining and working within this type of culture.

LAW OF FIDELITY

Pat Robertson uses verses from the Book of Luke in the Holy Scriptures to identify the Law of Fidelity. Grounding the law in Luke 16: 10-12, Robertson quotes, "Whoever can be trusted with very little can also be trusted with much, and whoever is

---

[362] Schaps, Battistich, and Solomon in Zins, Weissberg, Wang & Walberg (2004), 202.

[363] Schaps, Battistich, & Solomon, In Zins, Weissberg, Wang & Walberg (2004), 191.

[364] Johnson & Johnson (1994).

dishonest with very little will also be dishonest with much."[365] Thus, the Law of Fidelity is about trust and honesty.

To explain the importance of the principles of trustworthiness and honesty as these qualities impact the educational process, this writer will illustrate how fidelity is so very important in carrying out an experimental research study. In brief, a researcher uses an experimental study to determine if a treatment, also referred to as an intervention, makes a difference when administered to a sample of subjects.

As a practical illustration, imagine that I am the researcher and I want to determine if a particular reading program will increase the reading performance of fourth grade students. To conduct such a research study, I, as the researcher, will need teachers to implement the reading program, study subjects who will be the fourth grade students, and the treatment that is the reading program.

One important factor that will impact the results or outcome of the research study will be the extent to which the teachers actually use the reading program as it was designed to be implemented. Honest and trusting implementation of the reading program is called "fidelity" in the implementation of the treatment. The reading teachers' implementation of the academic program with fidelity will greatly impact the results or the students' reading achievement to be measured at the conclusion of the instructional time period. If the teachers responsible for implementing the reading program fail to implement the program as it was designed and intended to be used, then it is reasonable to expect that student achievement in reading will not measure up to the results projected for the reading program. Thus, the fidelity of the teachers' implementation of the reading program will impact student learning in reading.

Now that "fidelity" has been explained in terms of a research study, it is possible to transfer the same understanding about this factor to application of the teaching process within classrooms and schools. Educators who implement the instructional process with fidelity are far more likely to see positive results represented as increased student learning in their classrooms.

On the other hand, educators who poorly implement the instructional process will not see the kinds of measured results in terms of student achievement. Hence, one can see how important it is to have fidelity, referring to consistent and high-levels of trustworthy and honest professional behaviors, in the implementation of the instructional process.

If educators want all students to learn and achieve to high levels of performance, then there must be evidence of consistent, high-quality instruction on the part of all involved in delivering instruction. Fidelity in the implementation of the instructional process must be evident throughout the system.

Appendix F, Exercise 8. Standard 5 requires that educators demonstrate fidelity (trustworthiness and honesty) in the instructional process at all times. Appendix F, Exercise 8, "Self-Assessment of Fidelity of Instruction," engages educators in evaluating their conformity to aspects of Standard 5. When staff members increase in trustworthiness and honesty within the educational setting, students will benefit from high quality instruction and see these virtues modeled, leading students to inculcate the values and demonstrate higher performance.

---

[365] SK, 203-204, ref. Luke 16:10 NIV.

LAW OF CHANGE

According to Dr. Robertson, the Law of Change in the Secret Kingdom is rooted to chapter 5 of the Book of Luke in the Holy Scriptures. Dr. Robertson's rule advises: "No man puts new wine into old skins, lest the skins break and all be lost."[366] Robertson further advises: "God is always the same; His plan is always the same. But the vehicles, the organizations, and the techniques of carrying out His program will always be changing."[367]

The Law of Change can be conceptualized into this professional standard for educators:

Embrace change with the understanding that new, evidence-based practices result in advancements and the best outcomes.

This standard will be further explained in this section and the discussion will also describe the role and responsibility of educators for implementing appropriate changes that fulfill their obligations.

Over the course of the history of education, "change" has been a common expression used to describe efforts to improve the processes aimed at increasing the literacy of the American citizenry. Thomas Jefferson posited that an educated citizenry is critical to the sustainability of the American form of democracy. Hence, the critical importance is established for the viability of the American educational process.

Over the centuries of American history, K-12 education has undergone dramatic change, including transformation from one-room rural school houses to modern complexes that serve thousands of students. Although facilities have evolved, recent change initiatives in American education have been focused upon curriculum—the "what" to be taught to K-12 students. The curriculum changes have emerged as academic standards that establish performance expectations for K-12 students in America. At the time of this writing, approximately ten years of individually state-mandated curriculum standards are evolving into a set of common core curriculum, to be agreed upon by individual states within the nation.

With further consideration of contemporary educational practices, the most radical K-12 change is described as "school turnaround" that involves a virtual 180 degree shift in the direction and outcomes of a school. School turnaround aims to change the lowest performing schools and increase student achievement in schools where learning is most dismal.

---

[366] SK, 210, ref. Luke 5: 36-38.
[367] SK, 210.

Increasing Student Achievement Compared to Other Nations

Contemporary school change efforts or transformation procedures are aimed at improving America's educational system to increase the achievement of students during the 21st century.

The Race to the Top Initiative of the Obama Administration was conceptualized to give incentives to states and school districts to undertake reforms such as closing achievement gaps, increasing teacher and school leader effectiveness, adopting the national common core standards, turning around the lowest performing schools, and engaging the use of data systems for educational programming.[368]

This federal reform initiative could increase the national achievement in K-12 education so as to re-position America from its current devastatingly low position near the bottom of the list of industrialized nations. It seeks to improve educational systems and thereby raise the achievement of students so that America can once again be competitive with the top industrialized nations

The low ranking of American students is evidenced by the 2009 report of PISA, Program for International Student Assessment, that assesses both in and out of school learning for tenth graders (15 year olds) in the 34 mostly industrialized nations that compose the Organization of Economic Cooperation and Development (OECD).

Reflecting on the achievement of students from Japan, Korea, the United Kingdom, Australia, China, and Germany, the PISA results indicated:

> "In mathematics literacy, the U.S. average score (487) was lower than the OECD average score (496). Among the 33 other OECD countries, 17 had higher average scores than the United States, 5 had lower average scores, and 11 had average scores not measurably different from the U.S. average. In reading literacy, the U.S. average score (500) was not measurably different from the OECD average (493) or scores from previous PISA assessments. Among the 33 other OECD countries, 6 had higher average scores than the United States, 13 had lower average scores, and 14 had average scores not measurably different from the U.S. average."[369]

Framework for 21st Century Learning

This nation continues to be confronted with the realization that its K-12 educational program must be substantially modified to address the readiness of students for employment in the 21st century workplace. Educators must continue to make changes to classroom curriculum, expand the use of technology in learning, and increase instructional emphases in areas that have previously been overlooked, relegated or even perhaps dismissed as unimportant.

---

[368] U. S. Department of Education (2009).

[369] IES, Newsflash (2010).

As an exercise to heighten your awareness of the school and classroom changes to be implemented for 21st century workplace readiness, consider the student outcomes included in the Framework for 21st Century Learning:

- **Core Subjects and 21st Century Themes** (Core subjects include English, reading or language arts, world languages, arts, mathematics, economics, science, geography, history, government and civics. The 21st Century Themes include Global Awareness; Financial, Economic, Business and Entrepreneurial Literacy; Civic Literary; Health Literacy; and, Environmental Literacy.)

- **Learning and Innovation Skills** (creativity and innovation; critical thinking and problem-solving, and communication and collaboration)

- **Information, Media and Technology Skills** (Information Literacy, Media Literacy, and ICT Literacy)

- **Life and Career Skills** (Flexibility and Adaptability, Initiative and Self-Direction, Social and Cross-Cultural Skills, Productivity and Accountability, Leadership and Responsibility.[370]

Appendix F, Exercise 9. Standard 6 requires educators to: "Embrace change with the understanding that new, evidence-based practices result in advancements and the best outcomes." To analyze your professional practices related to knowing and applying current research-based practices, you should complete Exercise 9 in Appendix F, "The Skillful Teacher—Use of Research-Based Instructional Strategies." This will help you to change your focus to future professional development experiences that will increase your readiness for delivery of instruction for student learning in the 21st century and support the preparation of students for 21st century workplace readiness.

LAW OF GREATNESS

The Secret Kingdom Law of Greatness is based on the Book of Matthew: "The greatest person in the kingdom of heaven is the one who makes himself humble like this child."[371] From the foundation of the Law of Greatness, professional performance Standard 7 emerged: Demonstrate humbleness, openness, and receptivity to ideas and innovations to achieve success. To be humble, open, and receptive, one has to eliminate arrogance and any sense of superiority.

It is the servant demeanor of Mother Teresa that one must personify—particularly to support needy students within our school settings. Positioning oneself as a servant

---

[370] Partnership for 21st Century Skills (2009).
[371] SK, 180, ref. Matthew 18:2-4 NCV.

establishes a relationship with the learner that eliminates threat, reduces anxiety, and encourages the learner to contribute to his/her own academic success. With barriers removed, the teacher is able to instruct and the student is able to learn.

Systemic Character Education

Humbleness, openness, and receptivity need to be evident throughout the organization. All members of the organization should manifest these behaviors towards internal and external stakeholders of the organization. To reap the maximum effect of such a change, a cultural transformation must occur. To achieve such a depth and breadth of transformation, consider Systemic Character Education for changing classrooms, schools, and even the entire school district.

Systemic Character Education[372] involves changing the culture of schools to emphasize a "customer" relationship with students, parents, and other stakeholders. Success in the business profession is largely based upon the quality of customer relationship. The "customer" relationship in education is one of humbleness, openness, and receptivity towards others.

To assure their success, businesses invest a major portion of their budget in training their personnel in customer relationships. Like businesses that operate with customer relationships among its highest priority, educational organizations need to be transformed by the adoption of a similar priority for the relationship with students and parents and other stakeholders.

Aimed at bringing into reality the written mission and vision statements of schools, Systemic Character Education was conceptualized as an approach that would address the most serious problems evident in our schools: student disengagement in the classroom, discipline problems, students dropping out of school, achievement gaps, attendance and truancy problems, and low student achievement. With systemic problems endemic to the nature of low-performing schools, the solution had to be capable of transforming all aspects of the organization.

Through years of study of the professional literature on school improvement, along with several years of examination of the Character Education Partnership's National Schools of Character and the federal grant-funded schools and districts of the Partnerships for Character Education Program, this solution emerged to the systemic problems in America's schools.

Character education programming incorporates these processes:

1. Changing students by addressing their character development delivered through integrated standards-based instruction

2. Creating and maintaining a "customer relationship" school culture

3. Development of teachers as caring professionals

4. Widespread use of research-based instructional strategies that increase student learning.

---

[372] Stiff-Williams (2007).

By using these four components of Systemic Character Education, educational organizations can be transformed to prepare increasing numbers of students for success in the 21st century.

Appendix H, Exercise 10. To assess your demonstration of caring teacher behaviors to meet Standard 7, you are encouraged to go to Appendix H and complete Exercise 10, "Self-Assessment of Caring Teacher Behaviors." As was the case for the preceding self-assessments, your results on the self-assessment of Caring Teacher Behaviors can be used to modify personal behaviors and guide procedural changes within your classroom or school.

LAW OF RESPONSIBILITY

The teaching profession is believed to be a calling upon the life of those who choose to serve. Accepting the calling to teach is accompanied by the moral obligation to perform to one's best ability. Thus, the Secret Kingdom Law of Responsibility is framed as a professional performance standard that requires one to comply with a moral commitment. Teachers and educational leaders are morally obligated to demonstrate the highest quality of performance.

How should educators focus upon this expectation? An examination of proficiency in instructional delivery is a useful starting point. Refer to Figure 7 for seven essential considerations for planning and implementation of the instructional process.

The seven considerations include:

1.) **Curriculum Standards.** Planning for the delivery of instruction should begin with consideration of curriculum standards that establish "what" to be taught and "how" the instruction should be delivered.

2.) **Learner Objectives.** Based upon the selected curriculum standards, measurable objectives are written to be able to judge the extent to which each learner achieves the targeted outcome.

3.) **Instructional Delivery.** With consideration of the curriculum standards and the learner objectives, appropriate evidence-based instructional strategies will be used to support student accomplishment of the targeted outcome.

4.) **Learner Activities.** With consideration of the needs and interests of the students, the teacher facilitates learning activities that engage the learners in the "work" of accomplishing the targeted outcomes.

5.) **Formative Assessments**. To identify students who need additional instruction or time to "work" to accomplish the targeted outcomes, the teacher collects feedback on the extent of learning of each student.

6.) **Follow-up Instruction and/or Summary.** Based upon the data from the formative assessments, the teacher provides supplemental instruction to identified students to assure their attainment of the targeted outcomes.

7.) **Summative Assessment.** Finally, students will demonstrate their accomplishment of the targeted outcomes through a high-value demonstration of new learning acquired during the teaching and learning experience.

Figure 7

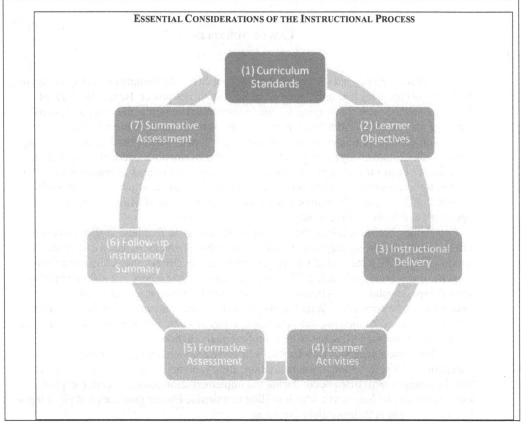

ESSENTIAL CONSIDERATIONS OF THE INSTRUCTIONAL PROCESS

(1) Curriculum Standards

(2) Learner Objectives

(3) Instructional Delivery

(4) Learner Activities

(5) Formative Assessment

(6) Follow-up Instruction/ Summary

(7) Summative Assessment

The Secret Kingdom Law of Responsibility and its related professional performance standards compel educators to accept responsibility for demonstrating the highest quality of instruction. Darling-Hammond[373] emphasized the importance of high quality classroom instruction as being directly related to student learning. Further, Viadero (2003) explained the importance of high quality classroom instruction as essential for closing achievement gaps among groups of students within America's schools. At the core of high quality instruction is planning and implementation of the seven essential components of the instructional process.

Appendix I, Exercise 11. To determine your proficiency with implementation of effective instructional procedures for 21st century teaching and learning, access Appendix I and complete Exercise 11, "Gauging Readiness for Teaching for 21st Century

---

[373] Darling-Hammond (2000; 2001; 2009; 2010).

Instruction." Continue to be mindful that your results can be used to plan professional development experiences for increasing your proficiencies.

LAW OF MIRACLES

Miracles go beyond the realm of the acts of man. My thoughts instantly go to God and those occurrences that only manifest as a result of His power. Hence, the Law of Miracles was the most challenging for me to conceptualize into a relevant professional standard for educators. After much prayer, I felt led to read and connect to the professional literature related to innovations—new concepts and practices on the cutting edge of educational change that yield important improvements in student achievement. As a result of this process, a professional standard emerged related to innovations. After all, Dr. Robertson makes it clear that "He overrides the way in which things normally operate."[374] As a result, the professional standard for the Law of Miracles expects that educators will be innovative to achieve exceptional results.

Hattie (2010) explained the "attributes of innovation that lead to above average effects" in the following way: Innovation occurs when a teacher makes a deliberate action to introduce a method of teaching, curriculum, or strategy that is different from what he or she is currently using. The aim is to encourage teachers to see their teaching as related experimental designs because then the benefits of the increased attention to outcomes can be accrued.[375] With the understanding that "innovation" does not need to refer to "miracles" of the God-delivered type, educators can now pursue innovations that can make a powerful difference in their professional practice.

Innovation occurs in various stages of professional activity, including conceptualization, initiation, implementation, and evaluation, with Hattie pointing out that the changes most often occur during the implementation phase.[376] Hattie explained that anyone can be innovative who is willing to examine his/her practices and elicit input to guide changes in their standard practices.

Hattie described the shift in mindset for innovation in these words:

> "The most critical attribute, however, is that when undertaking an innovation there is a heightened attention to its effects, to feedback to the teacher about the effects of the innovation, and to a focus on the learning intentions and success criteria from any innovation. Innovations carry the risk of failure; innovations help us free ourselves from the structured life and schemes that are created around us. It is this searching for that which is not working, and those students for whom you are not being successful; it is the heightened sense of seeking feedback, the increased attention to the principles of evaluation (discerning that of merit and worth), and the focus on how to seek the evidence of disconfirmation of the teaching so as to improve it that are important. . . .

---

[374] SK, 221.

[375] Hattie (2010), 251.

[376] Hattie, 251.

"When teachers seek evidence that their teaching may *not* have been successful, then the desirable lens of success is in place. The teaching may *not* be successful for all students, for all parts of the learning intentions, towards all aspects of the success criteria; and even our goals, level of challenge, and processes of both effortful and conduct engagement may need to be constantly questioned."[377]

Innovation that leads to markedly improved outcomes begins with the search for change in one's day to day practices. Dr. Robertson's Law of Miracles has been conceptualized into the professional standard that requires educators to be innovative to achieve exceptional results. Based upon the insight about innovation as provided by Hattie, educators should undertake the process through self-examination of their professional practices and the solicitation of input from stakeholders.

Appendix J, Exercise 12. Please go to Appendix J and undertake Exercise 12, "Conduct Action Research: Elicit Ideas to Design Innovations for Success." By completing Exercise 12 you will collect important information from key stakeholders that will be useful for initiating innovations in your professional practice. You will gain insight about steps to apply to make changes to increase student learning within your classroom or school setting—activities resulting in improvements in your professional practice.

LAW OF DOMINION

The Law of Dominion yielded professional Standard 10 that guides us to know that authority must be used in responsible ways, recognizing that people in charge have a moral obligation to treat others with dignity and respect. Dr. Robertson identified the Law of Dominion as emanating from Genesis 1: 26-27: "God wants man to have authority over the earth. He wants him to rule the way he was created to rule."[378]

From the Law of Dominion, practicing educators should recognize their authority over others and those with whom they work and should respond by respecting others as authority figures. However, it is clear from the New Testament Scriptures that authority is most appropriately demonstrated through a mutual exchange of dignity and respect for all parties involved. Further, through evidence-based practices in the field of education, it is known that absolute authority is destructive to organizational effectiveness. Hence, authority must be recognized within educational settings in a climate of mutual respect and shared decision-making.

In the classroom, the teacher is the authority figure. In this setting, it behooves the teacher to be in charge of the assigned youngsters. With the full recognition of the teacher as the authority figure in the classroom, Schaps, Battistich, and Solomon (in Zins, Weissberg, Wang, and Walberg, 2004) provide research evidence of the importance of

---

[377] Hattie, 251.
[378] SK, 237.

democratic principles on student growth and development in educational settings. Hence, the teacher who manages the classroom as a dictator will not achieve the student achievement results that are desired. It behooves the classroom teacher to establish and maintain a positive and caring classroom culture where students have choices for some learning tasks and input into the rule-making for operations.

The Law of Dominion does not imply mindless obedience on the part of anyone. In fact, this writer is adamantly opposed to any practice of mindless obedience to any human authority. Such a practice conflicts with the Judeo-Christian principles upon which America has been created.

I encourage educators to respect authority but shared leadership is the optimum approach to the management of educational institutions. Shared leadership means that formal avenues exist for teachers to have input into the decision-making processes[379] within the educational organization. Leaders and managers and other persons in authority positions should facilitate the decision-making process by inviting input from members of the organization and deriving consensus about the most appropriate way forward. Such a process can only be facilitated through attitudes of mutual respect and agreement about the value of others' opinions.

For school leaders, some of the well-known and field-tested avenues of input by members of the organization include data teams,[380] school improvement teams,[381] and PLCs or Professional Learning Communities.[382] All schools should be organized and operated to include formal groups that process member input into decision-making.

Just as schools are managed most effectively by including input from teachers and other members of the unit, classrooms should be managed with input from students.[383] Although teachers possess the authority to "rule" the classroom, the research indicates that a positive, supportive classroom culture where student input is welcomed forms the most effective learning environment. When teachers abuse their authority, are offensive to students, and disregard the needs and interests of learners, the resulting negative classroom culture undermines the teaching and learning process.

Fenstermacher (1990) explained how the moral behavior of teachers can have a direct impact upon all learners within the classroom:

> "... the morality of the teacher may have a considerable impact on the morality of the student. The teacher is a model for the students, such that the particular and concrete meaning of such traits as honesty, fair play, consideration of others, tolerance, and sharing are 'picked up,' as it were, by observing, imitating, and discussing what teachers do in classrooms."[384]

In proposing ways teachers serve as both moral agents and moral educators, Fenstermacher posited that teachers "act morally, holding oneself up as a possible model—at first a model to be imitated, later a model that will be influential in guiding the

---

[379] Fullan (2001).

[380] Reeves (2003).

[381] Reeves (2006.

[382] DuFour (2004).

[383] Zins, J., Bloodworth, M., Weissberg, R., & Walberg, H. (2004).

[384] Fenstermacher, In Goodlad, Soder, &Sirotnik (1990), 133.

conduct of one's students."[385] Given this understanding, educators must be constantly aware of their actions and speech when students are present.

Appendix K, Exercise 13. As a professional development activity that addresses Standard 10 about tempering the use of positional authority and acting in morally responsible ways, read the case study in Appendix K. It describes one adult's personal recollection of disrespect and offensiveness by teachers during the K-12 educational experience. It is important to note the writer's vivid recall of the offenses. It is a powerful story that continues to reflect the sting of pain inflicted upon a child. By completing Exercise 13, "Case Study Analysis: Moral Use of Authority and Respectful Treatment of Others," educators can heighten their awareness and sensitivity to unchecked authority and the enduring negative effects of unprofessional practices.

POST-ASSESSMENT OF THE PROFESSIONAL STANDARDS

At the beginning of this chapter, you were introduced to the professional performance standards based upon the Kingdom principles. In addition, you were invited to complete a pre-assessment of the ten professional standards to evaluate your initial status and identify areas for professional development to improve your performance.

The importance of each professional standard has been described within identifiable sections within the chapter. As part of the explanation of the importance of each standard, research-based support was provided to emphasize the relevance of each standard for improvement of the teaching and learning process within today's schools. Further, each explanation of a standard was prepared to establish its capability for improving educational services for the most challenging students in our schools. The rationales for the standards are designed to guide educators to change recognizable aspects of their professional practices to lead to increased student engagement and learning.

Appendix L, Exercise 14. After reading about the importance of the ten professional standards based on Kingdom principles and completing the related professional exercises, you will be able to reflect new knowledge and understanding through the post-assessment. Go to Appendix L to locate and complete Exercise 14, "Post-Assessment of Secret Kingdom Professional Standards for Educators." Hopefully, if you had the opportunity to complete the readings and development exercises over time, your newly adopted behaviors and practices will be reflected in your post assessment.

In summary, the importance of these standards in guiding professional practices of educators cannot be overstated. Arguably, it can be said that the future of our nation rests upon improving the education of the American populace.

---

[385] Fenstermacher, In Goodlad, Soder, &Sirotnik (1990), 134.

CONCLUSION

The American educational system must be changed to better serve K-12 students. The call for change through this book is different from the typical challenge to establish curriculum standards, integrate technology, establish charter schools, and modernize school buildings. Undoubtedly, these changes are important and can improve educational services for students in most communities. However, this approach to educational reform directs attention primarily to those on the frontlines—K-12 teachers and school leaders. The performance standards for educators provide directional changes to improve the dispositions, professional skills, and proficiencies of educators.

Statistical Evidence of the Need for Change

Here is some compelling evidence to support the need for change in the American educational system.

- An estimated two-thirds of all U.S. high school students admit to "serious" academic cheating while 90 percent admit to **cheating** on homework, according to a survey by the Rutgers Management Education Center and researcher Donald McCabe. Cheating scandals have recently stunned three high-performing high schools across the nation where the pressure for students to achieve may be at its greatest.[386]

- In 2003, 12 percent of students ages 12-18 reported that someone at school had used **hate-related words** against them (i.e. derogatory words related to race, religion, ethnicity, disability, gender, or sexual orientation). During the same period, about 36 percent of students ages 12 to 18 saw hate-related graffiti at school.[387]

- Twenty-one percent of students ages 12 to 18 reported that **street gangs** were present at their schools in 2003. Students in urban schools were the most likely to report the presence of street gangs at their school (31 percent), followed by suburban students and rural students (18 and 12 percent, respectively).[388]

---

[386] Susan Donaldson James, "Cheating Scandals Rock Three Top-Tier High Schools. National Survey Finds Two-Thirds of Students Admit Cheating." Retrieved from http://abcnews.go.com/US/story?id=4362510&page=1. (Accessed 12/20/10).
[387] "Indicators of School Crime and Safety 2004, Executive Summary," Indicator 14. Online at http://nces.ed.gov/pubs2005/crime_safe04/.
[388] School Crime and Safety, Indicator 15.

- In 2003, students in grades 9-12 were asked about using **drugs on school property**. In the 30 days prior to the survey, 5 percent of students reported having at least one drink of alcohol on school property[389] and 6 percent reported using marijuana.[390]

Josephson Institute in Los Angeles—statistics from FOX interview in 2008: 30 percent of surveyed students reported **stealing** from a store, 23 percent stole from a friend or close relative, 60 percent cheated on a test, and 33 percent used the Internet to **plagiarize** (regarding teenagers/adolescents).[391]

- Every year from 1998 to 2002, **teachers were the victims** of approximately 234,000 total nonfatal crimes at school, including 144,000 thefts and 90,000 violent crimes. On average, these figures translate into a rate of 32 thefts, 20 violent crimes, and 2 serious violent crimes per 1,000 teachers annually.[392]

- "Issues such as **discipline, disaffection, lack of commitment, alienation, and dropping out** frequently limit success in school or even lead to failure. . . . The teaching force need training in how to address social-emotional learning to manage their classrooms more effectively, to teach their students better, and to cope successfully with students who are challenging."[393]

- Many students indicate their reasons for being **absent from school or skipping classes**, and/or **dropping out of school**, are associated with feelings of alienation. Put simply, many students say that no one at the school cared about who they were as individuals.[394]

- 160,000 children stay home every day because of bullying.[395] Another study found that as many as 160,000 students go home early on any given day because they are afraid of being bullied.[396]

---

[389] School Crime and Safety, Indicator 17.

[390] School Crime and Safety, Indicator 18.

[391] 2006 Josephson Institute Report Card on the Ethics of American Youth: Part One – Integrity Summary of Data. josephsoninstitute.org/pdf/ReportCard_press-release_2006-1013.pdf Accessed 12/20/10)

[392] Source: U.S. Department of Education's National Center for Education Statistics and the Indicators of School Crime and Safety: 2004 http://nces.ed.gov/pubs2005/crime_safe04/ "Annually, over the 5-year period from 1998 to 2002, teachers were the victims of approximately 234,000 total nonfatal crimes at school, including 144,000 thefts and 90,000 violent crimes (rape, sexual assault, robbery, aggravated assault, and simple assault) (Indicator 9). Accessed 12/20/10)

[393] Zins, Bloodworth, Weissberg, & Walberg in Zins, Weissberg, Wang, & Walberg, 4.

[394] Thompson (2006).

[395] American Medical Association (AMA) Source: Journal of the AMA 286 (April 25, 2001).

[396] #9 Pollack W. Real boys: rescuing our sons from the myths of boyhood. New York (NY): Henry Holt and Company, LLC; 1998." Understanding School Violence, Fact Sheet, 2010 www.cdc.gov/violenceprevention/pdf/SchoolViolence_FactSheet-a.pdf

- In October 2001, some 3.8 million 16- through 24-year-olds were **not enrolled** in a high school program and had **not completed high school (status dropouts)**. These individuals accounted for 10.7 percent of the 35.2 million 16- through 24-year-olds in the United States in 2001.[397]

- Five out of every 100 students enrolled in high school in October 2000 **left school** before October 2001 without successfully completing a high school program.[398]

- *21st Century Workplace Skills.* A national survey of employers determined that students graduating from America's high schools, two- year colleges, and four-year colleges do not possess the job readiness skills that businesses want in entrants to the workplace. Of particular note was the lack of readiness in the areas of the soft skills – referring to areas such as interpersonal communications, collaboration, ability to work on teams, responsibility, taking initiative, etc.[399]

Using the content of this chapter, you can see how many of these systemic problems can be addressed by engaging change based upon the Kingdom principles and the performance standards for educators. This change process transforms teachers, school leaders, counselors, parents, and policy makers who serve and are responsible for the students within the school system. Through application of the Kingdom principles and the professional performance standards, educators can develop the know-how to transform learning environments and increase the success of K-12 learners. Through use of the performance standards, educators can be transformed through understanding of the importance of a positive, supportive learning culture necessary for all students to learn and succeed in school.

Further, through emphasis on the performance standards and the accompanying professional development exercises, educators will be prepared to ratchet up their delivery of instruction in K-12 classrooms. Most importantly, the Kingdom principles and corresponding performance standards will transform teachers by causing them to raise their expectations for all learners and, simultaneously, boost their commitment to delivering high quality instruction that improves learning.

Use of the professional performance standards through a school-wide improvement initiative or for individual professional growth will result in changes that can contribute to measurable changes in student learning. Through the transformation of educators within schools, systemic improvements will occur in the American educational process. The transformation of educators will begin to reduce the alarming statistics that illustrate the dysfunctional nature of the American educational system.

In closing, my challenge to each person who reads this book is to sow consistently into the life of at least one youngster with whom you work during each year of your service as a teacher, parent, counselor, school leader, or other advocate. If there are 1,000 readers of this book who apply the professional performance standards as they work with

---

[397] Source: NCES Report (2002).
[398] Source: NCES Report (2002).
[399] Partnership for 21st Century Skills (2008).

children and youth, then thousands of lives will be substantively impacted in positive ways each year. If there are 100,000 readers who apply the performance standards as they work with youngsters, then 100,000 children's lives will be positively changed each year. If 100,000 adults apply the Kingdom principles and/or the educator's professional performance standards to the lives of 100,000 children and youth each year and serve a different child over the course of ten years, just imagine the impact! The Kingdom principles will have an impact of "miracle" proportions!

RESOURCES

ABC News, 2/29/08 Cheating Scandals Rock Three Top-Tier High Schools, National Survey

Armstrong, T. (2009). *Multiple intelligences in the classroom* (3rd ed.). Alexandria, VA: ASCD.

Barton, P.E. (2006). The dropout problem: Losing ground. *Educational Leadership*, 63(5), 14-18.

Battistich, V., Solomon, D., Watson, & M., Schaps, E. (1994). *Students and teachers in caring classrooms and school communities.* Retrieved from http://www.devstu.org/about/articles.html

Bellanca J. & Brandt, R. (eds.). (2010). *21st century skills: Re-thinking How Students Learn*. Bloomington, Ill: Solution Tree Press.

Benninga, J.S., Berkowitz, M.W., Kuehn, P., & Smith, K. (2006). Character and academics: what good schools do. *Phi Delta Kappan*, 87(6), 448-452. Retrieved from ProQuest Education Journals database.

Berkowitz, M.W., & Bier, M.C. (2006). What works in character education. *Journal of Research in Character Education*, 5(1), 29-48. Retrieved from ProQuest Education Journals database.

Brimi, H. (2009). Academic instructor or moral guides? Moral education in America and the teacher's dilemma. *The Clearing House*, 82(3), 125. Retrieved from ProQuest Education Journals database.

Character Education and Civic Engagement Technical Assistance Center (CETAC), sponsored by the U.S. Department of Education's (ED) Office of Safe and Drug-Free Schools (OSDFS). Character Education Teacher Resources.

Comer, J.P. (2001). *Schools that develop children*. Retrieved from http://www.prospect.org/cs/articles?article=schools_that_develop_children

Condition of Education 2010. National Center for Education Statistics. Retrieved from http://nces.ed.gov/programs/coe/

Council of Chief State School Officers (1996). *Interstate school leaders licensure consortium: Standards for school leaders*. Washington, D.D.: Author.

Covey, S. (2004). *Seven habits of highly effective people*. New York, NY: Free Press.

Danielson, C. (2006). *Teacher leadership that strengthens professional practice.* Alexandria, VA: ASCD.

Darling-Hammond, L. (2000). Teacher quality and student achievement. *Education policy analysis archives, 8*. Retrieved from http://epaa.asu.edu/ojs/article/view/392

Darling-Hammond, L. (2001). *The right to learn: A blueprint for creating schools that work*. Hoboken, NJ: Jossey-Bass.

Darling-Hammond, L. (2009). Teacher learning: What matters? *Educational leadership*, 66 (5), 46-53. Retrieved from HW Wilson database.

Darling-Hammond, L. (2010). *The flat world and education: How America's commitment to equity will determine our future*. New York, NY: Teachers College Press.

Deal, T.E., & Peterson, K.D. (2009). *Shaping school culture: Pitfalls, paradoxes, and promises (2nd.ed)*. Hoboken, NJ: John Wiley & Sons.

Deal, T.E. & Peterson, K.D. (1999). *Shaping school culture: The heart of leadership*. Hoboken, NJ: Jossey-Bass.

Dufour, R. (2004). Schools as Learning Communities, *Educational Leadership*, Vol 61, no. 8, p. 6-11.

Dweck, C. (2006). *Mindset: The new psychology of success*. New York, NY: Random House.

Harpaz, B. (2009, June 2). Preventing high school dropouts can start in 4th grade. *Education Week*. Retrieved from http://www.edweek.org/ew/articles/2009/06/01/278463usfeparentingteensdropouts _ap.html

Eggen, P.D., & Kauchak, D.P. (2001). *Strategies for teachers: Teaching content and thinking skills*. Boston, MA: Allyn & Bacon.

Elias, M.J., Parker, S.J., Kash, V.M., & Dunkeblau, E. (2007). Social-emotional learning and character and moral education in children: Synergy or fundamental divergence in our schools? *Journal of Character Education*, 5(2), 167-181. Retrieved from ProQuest Education Journals database.

Fenstermacher, G. (1990). In Goodlad, J.I., Soder, R., Sirotnik, K. A., *The moral dimensions of teaching*. San Francisco, CA: Jossey-Bass.

Fullan, M. (2001). *Leading in a culture of change*. San Francisco, CA: Jossey-Bass.

Gardner, H. (2006). *Multiple intelligences: New horizons*. New York, NY: Basic Books.

Gladwell, M. (2008). *Outliers: The story of success*. New York, NY: Little, Brown, and Company.

Goleman, D. (2007). *Social intelligence: The new science of human relationships*. New York, NY: Bantam Books.

Greenleaf, R.K. (2002). *Servant leadership: A journey into the nature of legitimate power and greatness*. Mahwah, NJ: Paulist Press.

Hanson, T. L., & Austin, G. A. (2002). *Health risks, resilience, and the Academic Performance Index. (California Healthy Kids Survey Factsheet 1)*. Los Alamitos, CA: WestEd.

Hargreaves, A. & Shirley, D. (2009). *The fourth way: The inspiring future for educational change*. Thousand Oaks, CA: Corwin Press.

Harmin, M. (1994). *Inspiring active learning: A handbook for teachers*. Alexandria, VA: ASCD.

Hattie, J. (2009). *Visible learning: A synthesis of over 800 meta-analyses relating to achievement.* New York, NY: Taylor & Francis, Inc.

James, Susan Donaldson. "Finds Two-Thirds of Students Admit Cheating." business.rutgers.edu Accessed 12/20/10. Retrieved from http://abcnews.go.com/US/story?id=4362510&page=1

Jensen, E. (2005). *Teaching with the brain in mind.* Alexandria, VA: ASCD.

Johnson, D.W., Johnson, R.T., & Johnson-Holubec, E. (1994). *Cooperative learning in the classroom.* Alexandria, VA: ASCD.

Johnson, D.W., & Johnson, R.T. (1994). *Learning together and alone: Cooperative, competitive, and individualistic learning* (4th ed.) Edina, MN: Interaction Book Company.

Joyce, B. & Showers, B. (2002). *Student achievement through staff development.* Alexandria, VA: ASCD.

Kouzes, J. and Posner, B. (2007) *The Leadership challenge, 4th edition.* San Francisco: John Wiley & Sons, Inc.

Lapsley, D., & Narvaez, D. (2004). *Moral development, self, and identity.* Mahwah, NJ: Lawrence Erlbaum Associates.

Learning Styles Inventory. (n.d). *Learning Styles Inventory.* Retrieved from http://www.personal.psu.edu/bxb11/LSI/LSI.htm

Lickona, T. (2004) *Character matters: How to help our children develop good judgment, integrity and other essential virtues.* New York: Touchstone.

Lickona, T & Davidson, M. (2008). *Smart and good high schools.* West Conshohocken, PA: Templeton Foundation.

Marzano, R.J. (2007). *The art and science of teaching: A comprehensive framework for effective teaching.* Alexandria, VA: ASCD.

Marzano, R.J. (2003). *What works in schools: Translating research into action.* Alexandria, VA: ASCD.

Marzano, R. J. ed. (2010). *On excellence in teaching.* Bloomington, IN: Solution Tree Press.

Marzano, R.J., Pickering, D.J., & Pollock, J.E. (2001). *Classroom instruction that works: Research-based strategies for increasing student achievement.* Alexandria, VA: ASCD.

Mayer, B. (2000). *The dynamics of conflict resolution: A practitioner's guide.* San Francisco, CA: Jossey-Bass.

National Center for Educational Statistics 2004. Indicators of School Crime and Safety: 2004 http://nces.ed.gov/pubs2005/crime_safe04/.

National Center for Educational Statistics 2009. Highlights from PISA 2009: Performance of U. S. 15-Year-Old Students in Reading, Mathematics, and Science

Literacy in an International Context. Retrieved on November 14, 2010 from
http://nces.ed.gov/pubsearch/pubsinfo.asp?pubid=2011004

National Council for Accreditation of Teacher Education (2007). *Professional standards for the accreditation of teacher preparation institutions.* Washington, D.C.: NCATE.

National Governors Association, the Council of Chief State Officers, and Achieve, Inc. (2008). *Benchmarking for Success: Ensuring U. S. Students Receive a World-Class Education.* Washington, D.C.: National Governors Association.

Newton's Laws: Third Law. 2000. Retrieved December 9, 2010.
http://www.schools.utah.gov/curr/science/sciber00/8th/forces/sciber/newton3.htm

Nieto, S. (2009). From surviving to thriving. *Educational Leadership*, 66(5), 8-13. Retrieved from HW Wilson database.

Nieto, S. (2005). Schools for a new majority: the role of teacher education in hard times. *The New Educator*, 1, (1), 27-43.

Nucci, L., Drill, K., Larson, C., & Brown, C. (2005). Preparing preservice teachers for character education in urban elementary schools: The UIC initiative. *Journal of Research in Character Education*, 3(2), 81-96. Retrieved from ProQuest Education Journals database

Office of Drug Free Schools, United States Department of Education. 2009. *Character Education Teacher Resource: An Online Guide.* CETAC.
http://www.guidetocareereducation.com/education?source=aff_cetacorg

Osguthorpe, R.D. (2008). On the reasons we want teachers of good disposition and moral character. *Journal of Teacher Education*, 59, 288-301. Retrieved from
http://jte.sagepub.com/cgi/content/abstract/59/4/288

Partnership for 21st Century Skills. (2008). *21st century skills, education, and competiveness.* Washington, DC: Author.

Partnership for 21st Century Skills. (2006). *Are they really ready to work? Employers'*

perspectives on the basic knowledge and applied skills of new entrants to the 21st century U.S. workforce. Retrieved March 2007 from
http://www.p21.org/documents/FINAL_REPORT_PDF09-29-06.pdf

Partnership for 21st Century Skills. (2009). *Framework for 21st century learning.* Retrieved on December 2, 2010 from
http://www.p21.org/documents/P21_Framework.pdf

Power, C.F., Nucci, R.J., Narvaez, D.F., Lapsley, D.K., & Hunt, T.C. (2007). *Moral education: A handbook.* Santa Barbara, CA: Greenwood Press.

Rebora, A. (2008). Making a Difference. *Education Week.* Vol. 2, Issue 01. Pages 26, 28-31. Retrieved from
http://www.edweek.org/tsb/articles/2008/09/10/01tomlinson.h02.html

Reeves, D. (2004). *Accountability for learning: How teachers and school leaders can take charge.* Alexandra, VA: ASCD.

Reeves, D. (n.d.). *High performance in high poverty schools: 90/90/90 and beyond.* Retrieved from http://www.sabine.k12.la.us/online/leadershipacademy/high%20performance%209 0%2090%2090%20and%20beyond.pdf

Reeves, D. (2003). *Making standards work: How to implement standards-based assessments in the classroom, school, and district.* Englewood, CO: Advanced Learning Press.

Reeves, D. (2007). *The daily disciplines of leadership: How to improve student achievement, staff motivation, and personal organization.* San Francisco, CA: Jossey-Bass.

Reeves, D. (2002). *The leader's guide to standards: A blueprint for education equity and excellence.* Hoboken, NJ: John Wiley and Sons.

Reeves, D. (2006). *The learning leader: How to focus school improvement for better results.* Alexandria, VA: ASCD.

Robertson, Pat. *The Secret Kingdom: Your Path to Peace, Love, and Financial Security* (Dallas: Word Publishing, 1992).

Schwartz, M.J. (2007). The modeling of moral character for teachers: Behaviors, characteristics, and dispositions that may be taught. *Journal of Research in Character Education*, 5(1), 1-28. Retrieved from ProQuest Education Journals database.

Shockley-Zalabak, P.S. (2008). *Fundamentals of organizational communication: Knowledge, sensitivity, skills, values (7th ed).* Upper Saddle River, NJ: Allyn & Bacon.

Smith, F. (2006, April). How to approach moral issues in the classroom. *Edutopia*, n.p.

Stiff-Williams, H.R. (1999). Unpacking the standards: Teaching the Virginia standards of learning. *VEA Journal.*

Stiff-Williams, H.R. (2010). Widening the lens to teach character education alongside standards curriculum. *Clearing House: Journal of Educational Strategies, Issues, and Ideas, 83(4), 115-120.*

Stiff-Williams, H. R. Systemic Character Education: Transforming K-12 Schools to Increase Student Learning. Presentation: CEP Conference, October 2007, Alexandria, VA.

Stiff-Williams, H. R. Systemic Character Education: Building Relationships to Increase Student Learning. Presentation: CEP Conference, October 2008, Alexandria, VA.

Stiff-Williams, H. R. Systemic Character Education: Using Character Education to Transform K-12 Schools and to Increase Student Learning. Presentation: ASCD Conference, March 2009, Orlando, FL

Thompson, R. A. (2006). *Nurturing future generations: Promoting resilience in children and adolescents through social, emotional and cognitive skills,* 2nd edition. New York: Routledge Taylor & Francis Group.

Tomlinson, C. A. (2006). Integrating Differentiated Instruction & Understanding by Design: Connecting Content and Kids" ISBN: 978-1416602842, Publisher: ASCD

Uten-O'Brien, M., Weissberg, R.P., Munro, S.B. (2005.). *Reimagining education: In our dream, social, and emotional learning – or "SEL" – is a household term.* Retrieved from ProQuest Education.

Viadero, D. "Study Probes Factors Fueling Achievement Gaps." *Education Week,* 11/26/2003.

Warren, Rick. *The Purpose Driven Life.* Grand Rapids, MI: Zondervan, 2002.

Zins, J., Bloodworth, M., Weissberg, R., & Walberg, H. (2004). *Building academic success on social and emotional learning: What does the research say?* New York, NY: Teachers College Press.

Zins, J. E, Walberg, H., & Weissberg, R. (2004). *Getting to the heart of school reform: social and emotional learning for academic success.* Retrieved on June 2002 from http://www.casel.org/sel_resources/SEL%20and%20Academics.php#articles

Appendices

APPENDIX A

THE BEATITUDE JOURNEY—
PERSONAL APPLICATIONS FOR CHRISTIAN EDUCATORS

William F. Cox, Jr., Ph.D.
Professor, Founder—Christian Education Programs
Regent University School of Education

*"The Beatitudes also show us a lot about the nature of
God, the one ruling the Kingdom. Complemented by
principles and virtues set forth throughout Scripture,
they provide the underpinning and framework for our lives,
even during a time of transition from the
old, discredited order into the emerging future."* [400]

PAT ROBERTSON, *THE SECRET KINGDOM*

Jesus' message to those He called out from the crowds begins with what is known as the Beatitudes (Matthew 5:3-12). We can think of the statements in these verses as comprising *eight attitudes* that are foundational principles for living spiritual lives on earth. The Beatitudes are the preamble to the Secret Kingdom Laws. Educators who practice these attitudes will tap into another realm and reap the benefits of increasing maturity in their Christian faith.

EIGHT KINGDOM ATTITUDES FROM THE BEATITUDES[401]

1. Blessed are the poor in spirit: for theirs is the Kingdom of heaven (verse 3).
2. Blessed are they that mourn: for they shall be comforted (verse 4).
3. Blessed are the meek: for they shall inherit the earth (verse 5).
4. Blessed are they which do hunger and thirst after righteousness: for they shall be filled (verse 6).
5. Blessed are the merciful: for they shall obtain mercy (verse 7).
6. Blessed are the pure in heart: for they shall see God (verse 8).
7. Blessed are the peacemakers: for they shall be called the children of God (verse 9).
8. Blessed are they which are persecuted for righteousness' sake: for theirs is the Kingdom of heaven. Blessed are ye, when men shall revile you, and persecute you,

---

[400] SK, 90.
[401] Matthew 5:3-12 KJV.

and shall say all manner of evil against you falsely, for my sake. Rejoice, and be exceeding glad: for great is your reward in heaven: for so persecuted they the prophets which were before you (verses 10-12).

The Beatitudes have the connotation of *spiritual* blessedness or prosperity, not necessarily a temporal or externally visible condition of being blessed. They tell us conceptually or generically what the journey to deeper Kingdom living looks like. They demonstrate true reality and give us the benefits of following the Beatitude journey into reality. The word "blessed" means more than "happy," as some writers have suggested. It means joyful as well as envied and worthy to be commended.

Every Beatitude takes you progressively deeper into the Kingdom and its commensurate blessings for attaining that deeper life. *(See Figure 1.)* It states the nature of that particular Beatitude and the positive outcome in your life if you fulfill it. However, it also infers that your lack of fulfillment will negate the intended outcome, which would have been a blessing. That is, *not* being merciful results in *not* receiving mercy.

The important thing to note for educators who are committed to growth in their Christian faith is that these attitudes can be demonstrated in any setting. One can practice meekness with the right motive without quoting the Beatitude line and verse. Practicing the Beatitudes coordinates the spiritual, mental, and physical actions that will result in blessings for all concerned.

PROGRESSIVE GROWTH TO MATURITY

If we study the Beatitudes systematically, we see what progressive growth or maturity in the Kingdom of God looks like. It is patently described there and throughout the remainder of the Sermon on the Mount (Matthew 5-7).

Figure 1

EMPTINESS	REPENTANCE	SATISFACTION	OUTPOURING	MATURITY
1. *Poor in Spirit* (theirs is the Kingdom). Awareness of spiritual lack and emptiness results in salvation (e.g., Peter in Luke 5:8).	2. *Mourn* (shall be comforted). Sorrow for own and perhaps others' sinfulness results in inward assurance (e.g., Pharisee contrasted with tax collector in Luke 18:10-13).	3. *Meek* (inherit the earth). Submission to God's ways and not your own ways gives you authority and power (e.g. Moses contrasted with Israelites in Exodus 17:2-4). 4. *Hunger and thirst for righteousness* (shall be filled) Continually wanting more of God results in receiving more of the Holy Spirit (e.g., Paul contrasted with Demas in Galatians 2:20, 2 Timothy 4:10).	5. *Merciful* (obtain mercy). Impartation of mercy to others based on Christ's heart, not natural compassion, results in receiving His mercy toward you (e.g., Good Samaritan in Luke 10:30-36 contrasted with Jonah) 6. *Pure in heart* (see God). Demonstrating the pure nature of our innocent Savior results in a new understanding of nature of God (e.g., disciples contrasted with Simon the sorcerer in Acts 8:18-23). 7. *Peacemakers* (children of God) Bringing God's peace to others results in your own sense of God's acceptance (e.g. Philip and Ethiopian in Acts 8:20-39 contrasted with Pharisees in Matthew 23:2-39)	8. *Persecuted* (theirs is the Kingdom). Suffering as a disciple results in citizenship in the Kingdom of God (e.g., John 21:19)

FIGURE 1. The first two Beatitudes constitute sequential phases of emptiness and repentance. Meekness or gentleness (the third Beatitude) and hunger and thirst for righteousness (the fourth Beatitude) occur simultaneously within the same category of infilling or satisfaction. These are the enhanced internal desires that come from growing intimacy with the Lord.

TAKING THE KINGDOM BY FORCE

The Bible says that Jesus came to earth "to destroy the devil's work" (1 John 3:8) and to replace the unsanctified Kingdoms of Satan and mankind with God's Kingdom here on earth (Matthew 12:28; John 18:37).

We know from personal experience that we are not currently living in a heavenly, utopian environment where Satan has been totally destroyed. In fact, a little later in 1 John the Bible says that Satan is still actively working in the world (1 John 4:4) to keep the world and all its people under his dominion. (See also 1 John 5:19 and 1 Peter 5:8.) So how can we have the victory that Jesus purchased?

Present Reality vs. Eternal Hope

God's Secret Kingdom is a present and powerful reality. Salvation brings a person into this Kingdom, which means that believers come into a right relationship with the Godhead. Reciprocally, the Kingdom enters the person, which means that believers progressively take on the nature of Christ.

When people become saved, they have won the battle for eternity but they have also entered into a subsequent battle to force their way progressively deeper into God's Kingdom on earth. Salvation does not automatically nullify all aspects of our sin nature. It still wars against us. The world and its evil forces work externally to derail us from Kingdom living while our sin nature works internally to the same destructive end.

Jesus put it bluntly. We must take the Kingdom by force (Matthew 11:12).

EDUCATIONAL APPLICATIONS OF THE BEATITUDES

In His earthly life, Jesus not only introduced but also literally embodied the Kingdom of God. One way to understand Kingdom living is to examine what the Scriptures say about Jesus' actions because they demonstrate Kingdom life and give us a clue as to how believers are to re-present Him to the world. Given that God desires that each person successfully travel the Beatitude journey into the full reality of His Kingdom and enjoy the respective blessings, a major role of Christian educators is to model for the students how to travel along the Kingdom road.

Sensitivity to Christian and Secular Environments

In a Christian school or homeschool setting, the educator can actively teach and facilitate this Beatitude journey. Educators in a secular setting can take the journey themselves and pray that their maturity will result in being a better model for their students. We will see later how actively teaching the Beatitudes in a Christian setting or modeling them in a secular setting can be done. In fact, it can reasonably be suggested that a teacher's motivation in this regard is likely the result of the Beatitudes working within that teacher.

It is important for educators in Christian settings, particularly, to understand that the ultimate responsibility rests not primarily with the teachers but with each individual and his/her relationship with the Holy Spirit. The Holy Spirit draws us along the path, so to speak, as we permit Him or desire Him to do so. Without going into deep theology regarding personal free will and the activity of the Holy Spirit, the point to be emphasized is that teachers can set an environment that either facilitates or inhibits a student's spiritual progression.

Educators in secular settings must pray for the Holy Spirit to use the environment they create in class to help them model behavior and attitudes consistent with the Beatitude principles. Teachers in public schools, for example, may not be able to directly teach the Beatitudes but they can live them without crossing over the "wall of church and state." In other words, all educators who are Christian can live out the Beatitudes and become more mature in their faith. In fact, the more mature we are as Christians, the better educators we will be in any setting. The major difference is that educators in a Christian setting can be more direct and purposeful in sharing their own Beatitude walk.

Creating an Environment of Edification

With this in mind, we look at what teachers can do to facilitate the students' journeys. The Bible says that God expects His disciples to have a loving, serving heart toward Him and others. Admonitions such as "Go the extra mile," "Love one another," "Prefer others over yourself" are representative of many others of a similar nature. There are logical and practical reasons for His expectations. He has configured human nature to thrive and flourish best in that kind of environment.

To put this in practice, let's look at each of the Beatitudes to discover what the teacher can do to facilitate student progress on the Beatitude journey.

BEATITUDE #1

**"Blessed Are the Poor in Spirit,
For Theirs Is the Kingdom of Heaven."**

"[Jesus'] words conveyed the meaning 'beggarly.'
Happy are the beggars in spirit, the spiritual beggars,
those who know they are needy and are not afraid to say so."[402]

PAT ROBERTSON, *THE SECRET KINGDOM*

Someone who is "poor in spirit" has personally recognized his spiritual emptiness and insufficiency and knows the emptiness of a figurative, heart-shaped vacuum that

---

[402] SK, 91.

desires to be filled by God. The essence of this first Beatitude is knowing and admitting that we need God. Augustine wrote that "our hearts are restless till they find rest in Thee."[403] God promises that people with this attitude will enter the Kingdom because they are hungry for Him.

Educational Applications: Secular Settings

Students often sense that they are not up to the task of being successful in a school setting—academically, behaviorally, or socially. God wants everyone to recognize their shortcomings but not to stay in that debilitating state. Educators and psychologists use terms such as "low self-esteem" to describe this condition. Many times educators blame themselves, the family, or the community if the child has low self-esteem.

Christian teachers in a secular setting can take a two-stage approach to helping students who are facing a challenge:

1. Admit that they have a problem they cannot handle alone.
2. Look for solutions and ask for help to overcome or solve the problem.

A teacher, for example, can model how she personally handles feelings and situations that are seemingly insurmountable. She can first verbally articulate the problem and her lack of ability to handle it on her own. But the teacher does not stop there.

Secondly, she can practice verbally walking through how to solve the problem, often by asking for help. For example, the teacher could relate an instance when she had a flat tire at night along a deserted road. The teacher could confess the initial fear and helplessness felt in that situation. However, the teacher would be quick to role play the processes used to get help and eventually fix the flat. A discussion ensues where students would be asked what they would do in that situation. The students could also give similar examples.

History, sports, and literature are filled with events where the eventual winner was filled with despair and doubt.

- George Washington kneeling in the snow at Valley Forge is one example. Washington actually lost several battles before he won the American Revolution.
- Tales of how people made it through the Great Depression
- Pro sports teams who overcame a dilemma through teamwork
- Inventions and advances in technology that came about through collaboration
- Stories about members of the students' cultural group or race who succeeded in spite of persecution or disadvantages
- Any other examples that teach how having a felt need could be the opportunity for a growth experience and not just one of several depressing experiences of low self-esteem

---

[403] *The Confessions of St. Augustine, Bishop of Hippo, Book I,* accessed 2010, http://www.leaderu.com/cyber/books/augconfessions/bk1.html.

Remember, the more you have experienced being "poor in sprit" yourself and allowed the Lord to bless you, the more you will think of ways to model this and the other Beatitudes.

Educational Applications: Christian Settings

Teachers in a Christian setting have a challenge to foster in students an awareness of their lack and a hunger for fulfillment. Following a general prescription of edification, the teacher can do two main things:

1. Make the Kingdom look attractive.
2. Help the student to want the Kingdom.

One approach to making something attractive involves linking both a pleasurable atmosphere and pleasurable outcomes to the learning event.

Pleasurable atmosphere. The thrust of this approach is to link something pleasurable to an understanding of the Kingdom. For example, early Hebrew education developed a love for the Bible by having young children taste honey while reading from or hearing the Bible read by adults. They connected the good, sweet taste to the Bible. Students thereafter associated sweetness and pleasantness with the Bible. Teachers in Christian schools can make certain kinds of pleasurable experiences (e.g., pleasant music, edible treats, physical activity, favorite settings) co-occur with visuals and teachings about heavenly things such as the members of the Trinity, angels, heaven itself, and so on. The method also works for an aged person, but the specific instances will obviously vary by age level. In public schools, the same type of pairing can occur but this time with moral teachings that are biblically compatible.

Pleasurable outcomes. The other method uses rewards and penalties as consequences for good and bad choices. However, care must be exercised to guard against developing a spirit of materialism in the students. This method includes distributing rewards (physical objects, verbal reinforcement, playtime) to affirm students' behavior that is expected in a Kingdom culture. This obviously applies to both public and Christian schools.

For both approaches, care must be taken to protect the dignity of students such that neither bribes nor threats are implied in the rewards and penalties, respectively. And certainly the particulars of these two approaches should be matched to the developmental level of the student.

The ultimate goal of such educational efforts is to help students appreciate the blessings of salvation, the Kingdom, a relationship with Jesus, external blessings, and Jesus' love. Developing awareness of a poor-in-spirit, beggarly, personal bankruptcy feeling helps students comprehend their "deficient" nature but without demoralizing or dishonoring them. You have to walk a tightrope. You give the students an initial motivation upon entering this Beatitude to realize that they are needy, but not to the point of feeling hopeless. While it often takes an "end of the rope" state to bring about surrender to God, hope in His benevolent existence makes the surrender both reasonable and desirable.

When helping a person see his/her imperfections, especially in the moral and spiritual realm, a teacher still treats that person with dignity as someone created in the image of God. When disciplining a child who is *guilty* of wrong actions, words, attitudes, etc., it is important for the child to know and experience how much he/she is loved and cherished and thus not *shamed*.

As Chapman's book *The Five Love Languages* (1995)[404] explains, love can be expressed in many different ways. Children best receive love when it is expressed in the mode they most desire. This does not necessarily require that you overlook a fault, although that is sometimes appropriate. Instead, you confront inappropriate actions while affirming the appropriateness of the child's very being. You may cumulatively add up infractions but not for the purpose of degrading the child, only to show that a habit or ingrained tendency needs to be adjusted.

Life after salvation. The other caution to exercise in giving students hope is to present a balanced view of the challenges of life after being saved. The newly saved student should know that while some of their problems will no longer exist, life will still have challenges. However, Jesus will guide them through from this point forward. As the saying goes, "God did not promise us a rose garden."

Ultimately, for this as well as the other Beatitudes, the Holy Spirit does the convicting and sanctifying work in each individual person. Additionally, just as Jesus overtly announced the pathway of sanctification to His early disciples, teachers need to overtly explain this journey to their students—not assume that they have figured it out on their own.

BEATITUDE #2

"Blessed Are Those Who Mourn, For They Shall Be Comforted."

"So the Lord's message in this second Beatitude was, in essence,
'If you want the comfort of God surrounding you, you must
come to a place where you mourn for your sins.' " [405]

PAT ROBERTSON, *THE SECRET KINGDOM*

This second Beatitude of the sanctification phase is essentially about repentance ("mourning") for sin and the sinful nature of yourself and others. This assumes that the individual has already entered into a personal relationship with the Lord, but that may not always be as evident as we would like. This assumption about salvation is founded in the

---

[404] Gary Chapman, *The Five Love Languages*. (Chicago: Northfield Publishing, 1995).
[405] SK, 92.

outcome of the previous Beatitude. Namely, those who admit to their spiritual emptiness will see/enter the Kingdom.

The end-promise of this Beatitude suggests a God-focus of prayer and intercession rather than a temporal substitute for mourning. After all, Jesus would not give an earthly answer to a spiritual need. This individual is motivated by godly sorrow. In other words, the individual in mourning is expressing God's heart for those outside of His will.

Educational Application: Secular Setting

The paradox of mourning and then being joyful is difficult to understand and apply even in a Christian setting, but Christians can live out this beatitude in a secular setting by first being in a constant state of repentance or mourning for their sins and also for the others' sins. A Christian teacher, for example, should not ask students whom she knows needs prayer to confess their sins in a public school setting. She can however pray for those students and their parents privately.

One public school teacher tells her students' parents at the first open house every year that she prays for them and their children. The students are not present so she does not break any rules. In her 30 plus years of teaching, not one parent has complained. Many parents mourn for their children's shortcomings and knowing that another significant adult is mourning with them is a blessing. That commitment brought joy to the teacher in this example. It also set a tone of respect and collaboration with the family for the rest of the year. You may not feel the freedom to do what this teacher did but you can pray privately and mourn for the condition of your students. The Lord promised eventual joy if you mourn for others.

One way that mourning can be modeled in the classroom is for the teacher to overtly show sadness at the misfortunes of others. A common example is the death of a family member of one of the students. Expressions of sympathy and compassion are allowed in secular settings as well as Christian ones. The teacher can discuss stages of grief that often occurs during this process in ways that students can understand according to their age and developmental levels. Cards and notes can be sent to the student and the family.

Another way that a teacher can model "mourning" could be related to current events. For example, if a disastrous storm hits a country and millions of people suffer, the teacher can express concern and sorrow for the victims. In a way appropriate to the age of the students, the teacher can discuss the problem, read the newspaper account, and discreetly show the effects of the tragedy in the form of film clips or pictures. The idea is not to be morbid but to let students know it is not only desirable but a mature thing to do to show empathy for those who need it. The teacher can then initiate a way to help the victims through writing letters, drawing pictures to send to children in the affected areas, or even participating in a fundraising effort conducted by a reputable agency. Older students could go on trips to help out in disasters close to home. The reports back from teachers and students are usually very positive. They feel the joy that comes from mourning for others, especially when action is involved.

Educational Applications: Christian Setting

So for teachers, the question is, "What does it take to facilitate this intercessory act of mourning in students?" As before, there are two main dimensions to the answer.

1. The first dimension is engaging the students in activities of personal mourning.
2. The second dimension is maintaining the students' intercessory activities for maximum benefit to themselves and others.

For issue number two, the teacher can help sensitize students to the worldwide need for intercessory prayer. That can be done, for instance, by exposing students to images, accounts, and testimonies of circumstances and living conditions significantly worse than their own. However, great caution needs to be exercised to guard against students personally assuming the weighty responsibility of the desperate plight of others and/or having students become anxious and hopeless about the negative aspects of world conditions.

In this regard, any presentation of dreadful circumstances needs to be accompanied by hope—"They shall be comforted." This comfort may come through direct impartation from God and/or by seeing answers to prayers of mourning. In this way, students will even be inspired to mourn and intercede since they will see and experience positive results of their intercessory efforts. Over time it can even be expected that intercession may become a habit with positive results. The Bible says that He will turn their mourning into dancing and their sorrow into joy (Jeremiah 31:13).

Going a bit deeper into this matter, the ultimate motive for mourning has to be spiritual or vertical in nature as opposed to the natural or horizontal dimension only. Jesus' heart for the plight of humanity is at the root of mourning and at the deepest level for the rescue of humans for all eternity, not just for the here and now.

Ultimately the student needs to have God's view of sin and sinful behavior. This can be done in Christian schools by presenting the eternal, damning consequences of people who are lost in sin. In other words, students can be taught in very graphic ways what spending eternity in hell is like but with the goal that they will be captivated by loving God instead of primarily being fearful of God's wrath. As has been said, "Lovers of God are more fruitful and blessed than servants of God." Or to use a different analogy, lovers will do anything (within moral boundaries of course) for one another and delight in doing it. So the main focus of teachers is to help students develop a love relationship with God. The sooner that students can transition from the first dimension of this Beatitude into the second dimension, the sooner that a love relationship with God is established and the better the Beatitude journey will be.

How do you foster a love relationship between students and God? One way is to model love and treat students as a loving God would treat His precious children. This divine remedy works for both dimensions of this Beatitude. The student both goes into mourning and stays lovingly diligent at intercessory activity. To be clear, treating students as God would does not mean overlooking improper behavior. The teacher always makes corrections and even gives chastisement that is redemptive and restorative. This is how God treats his children. He allows and even orchestrates corrective discipline but does it in such a way that it always works for our good. God's plans for us are for good and not evil (Jeremiah 29:11) and He causes circumstances to work for good for those who lovingly fit into His plans (Romans 8:28).

A teacher's personal mourning. Prior to addressing the remaining six Beatitudes, there is an additional aspect of this present Beatitude that is important to emphasize for teachers. Namely, it is just as important for the teacher to engage in mourning activity as it is for the students. The teacher can impart a prayer focus—mourning in intercessory prayer—for the students and those the students will reach.

BEATITUDE #3

"Blessed Are the Gentle [Meek], For They Shall Inherit the Earth."

"Biblical meekness does not call for the abject surrender of one's character or personal integrity. It calls for a total yielding of the reins of life from one's own hands to God's hands." [406]

PAT ROBERTSON, *THE SECRET KINGDOM*

The gentleness or meekness stated in this Beatitude refers to an outlook on life that can happen only with those who have made Jesus Lord and Savior of their lives. They have entrusted ownership and control of their lives to Jesus.

Jesus and His earthly mother (Mary) both said in so many words, "Be it done unto me accordingly to Thy will." Successful surrender requires a high degree of self-control. In other words, only those aspects of the self that are harnessed can be released to God. Without proficiency in self-control, the Holy Spirit will not reasonably be able to guide and direct the person. Absent the possibility of being guided and directed by the Holy Spirit, the person will not be able to govern for God and thus will not inherit the earth.

Educational Applications: Secular Settings

Meekness has been described as humility with strength. The Lord was not talking about being a doormat or being fearful about taking initiative. A person can be gentle while still being bold, vocal, and creative. Christians have the power to be under control in the most trying of circumstances. Paul reminds us, "For God did not give us a spirit of timidity, but a spirit of power, of love, and of self-discipline."[407]

The educator in a secular setting can model meekness. One typical example is in the area of discipline. Parent meetings and phone calls can be joyous events when the news is positive but potentially contentious if the teacher has "bad news." I worked with

---

[406] SK, 94.
[407] 2 Timothy1:7 NIV.

an assistant principle who was especially good at demonstrating meekness. Parents would angrily storm his office to demand mercy for their child and punishment for others involved in an incident. I watched as he used questioning skills to get at the core of the problem. He had an uncanny way of calmly addressing the issues despite barrages of anger and frustration coming from both the parents and students. He would listen to the answers with a kind demeanor.

Eventually, the administrator gave his recommendation on how to resolve the issue and what consequences should be meted out. Invariably, all parties would come out of the office relaxed and sometimes even joyful. When I asked him what was his "secret" he said, "It's simple. I am hard on the problem but easy on the people." I then realized that he demonstrated true meekness. His main goal was to solve the problem, not affix the blame. If rules were broken it usually became obvious after a logical, peaceful discussion. Consequences were accepted more readily and order was restored. He did not compromise his standards and he never attacked a person. The administrator modeled Christ-like meekness in a public school setting without violating the separation of church and state doctrine established by public schools.

Staying with the discipline theme, teachers can be challenged by students in the classroom. Confrontation, arguing, and obstinacy can often result from a simple directive by the teacher. The meek teacher can be under control and respond to even potentially dangerous situations with Christ-like peace and wisdom. When meekness is demonstrated by the teacher, not only the students in question are given another way to act but also the other students observing the situation can learn new behaviors and attitudes as well.

Educational Applications: Christian Setting

The implication for teachers of this third Beatitude relates to helping the student do two things.

1. Govern himself, particularly in right attitudes and living true to objective, right standards
2. Release herself to God's guidance in all aspects of life

This is a very important Beatitude from the perspective of eternity and obedience. Christians are to represent God, but without self-government they will misrepresent Him. Equally, students who want to have an impact for God have to do it God's way. The only way to do something God's way is to be guided by the Holy Spirit. Being guided by the Holy Spirit requires being moldable in His hands.

Students learn to obey God by becoming lovingly obedient to proper school-related expectations. That helps them to control themselves. Students who are open to the direction of earthly authorities can submit to and be governed by an unseen Authority, God. The teacher plays a very important role in representing physically and materially in the flesh the unseen God. In other words, the teacher incarnates Christ to the students.

Teachers can help students progress through the meek/gentle Beatitude if they are mature in the very same attitudes. They allow the Holy Spirit to guide their treatment of each student in their own uniqueness and surrender themselves to God's leading.

Figure 2

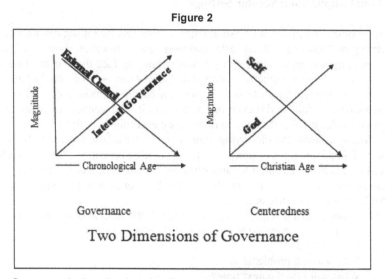

Governance   Centeredness

Two Dimensions of Governance

Someone who has developed self-governance can surrender to God's ways.

BEATITUDE #4

"Blessed Are Those Who Hunger and Thirst for Righteousness, For They Shall Be Satisfied [Filled]."

"With that cry of hunger and thirst for God, for more of His power, we in fact are crying out for an anointing of the Holy Spirit for service, which the Bible calls baptism in the Holy Spirit. This actually fulfills the next step in the progression of development revealed in the Beatitudes, providing an empowerment for serving God." [408]

PAT ROBERTSON, *THE SECRET KINGDOM*

This second aspect of the blessed infilling that comes with surrender to the Lord can be thought of as tasting the Lord's presence and goodness and wanting more. As with all the other Beatitudes, the hunger will be satisfied. In fact, this hungering will result in an anointing of the Holy Spirit.

An intriguing aspect of the Holy Spirit anointing is that there is no age limit. The young child and the elderly person can each receive the fullness of the Holy Spirit's empowerment. All people can possess some aspect of the supernatural nature of the Kingdom. "Blessed are they which do hunger and thirst after righteousness: for they shall be filled" means all that is personally needed (not necessarily what is wanted, but certainly what is needed) will come to the person, as Matthew 6:33 declares.

---

[408] SK, 95.

Educational Application: Secular Settings

As with the other Beatitudes, a Christian educator in a secular setting cannot teach the full meaning of "hunger and thirst" after righteousness." However, righteous living or doing what is right is appreciated in any school setting. In fact, the one standard most people hold to is "Do unto others as you would have others do unto you." I have known teachers to have the Golden Rule as their only rule because almost every school regulation would be followed if everyone adhered to it. The teacher can reiterate that following the rules is the right thing to do because everyone benefits.

Most of us know the old saying, however, "Every rule was made to be broken." Students will break the rules or otherwise act in unrighteous ways. What if a student tries as hard as he can to follow the rules and still fails? This is a prime opportunity for the Christian educator to model what the Holy Spirit does for us when we know we need to grow but hit a brick wall instead.

One strategy in a discipline situation is to ask the student three questions:

1. What did I do?
2. Why was it a problem?
3. What will I do the next time?

Often the student has an easy time answering the first two questions. The third question refers to changing behavior, and many students will confess that they have no idea what to do.

The Christian educator can use this time to instruct the student to act in right ways. He can offer ideas about how to avoid problems in the future. Most of all, the teacher can give assurances that she will be there for the student to support and guide him as he tries to do what is right. The Lord will use you to impart wisdom from above without mentioning a "religious" word.

Educational Applications: Christian Settings

Now what does all this mean to the teacher? As noted with other Beatitudes, the teacher should be Jesus-in-the-flesh for his or her students. As the Bible indicates, humans, as a general rule, first need to experience a representative of God in the flesh before they can trust Him whom they have not seen in the flesh (1 John 4:20). Obviously then, the teacher must be seen by the students as a loving, forgiving, encouraging person whom students enjoy being with. When students experience this kind of edifying interpersonal relationship, it is reasonable to expect that they will be open to God.

236

BEATITUDE #5

**"Blessed Are the Merciful,
For They Shall Receive Mercy."**

*"Having received mercy from One greater than we are,
we are to give mercy to those we are in a position to favor."* [409]

PAT ROBERTSON, *THE SECRET KINGDOM*

In contrast to the previous two Beatitudes that speak of the inward self and the upward orientation to God, the next three Beatitudes address the horizontal outflow to others that results from experiencing God.

The student who realizes that God has extended His mercy to make his or her personal salvation possible is in the natural frame of mind to extend that same mercy to others. Having progressed beyond the second Beatitude—mourning for the condition of others—individuals are pre-disposed to be merciful to others.

Educational Applications: Both Secular and Christian Settings

One way for a teacher to approach this matter with students is to tap into the Secret Kingdom Law of Reciprocity. Teachers who regularly extend mercy to students have a reasonable expectation that it will be reciprocated. Teachers can engage students in activities like visiting shut-ins, elderly people, and hospitals. They can view videos of destitute people groups and invite people to speak about personal experiences with such deprivations themselves. But even before venturing into the world outside the classroom, teachers can coach students how to demonstrate mercy to other teachers and classmates. These activities soften and sensitize the hearts of the students so they desire to extend mercy to those less fortunate. Activities could even include similar activities with animals, particularly those that are or could be pets.

Just as with certain other Beatitude categories, care should be exercised to avoid placing guilt and/or shame and anxiety on children as they experience activities that tug at their heart strings. Progression on the Beatitude journey is ultimately the work of the Holy Spirit guided by the individual's cooperation, or at least non-resistance. The teacher's role is to provide opportunities for the student to be receptive. Lest we forget, in all these Beatitudes teachers can model merciful behaviors for the students to naturally emulate.

---

[409] *SK*, 96.

BEATITUDE #6

"Blessed Are The Pure In Heart, For They Shall See God."

This Beatitude must surely constitute the highest order of reflection on the purity of God. This in many ways is the ultimate interior disposition. It likely is symbolized by the glow on Moses' face after he had spoken with God (Exodus 34:29-36). Those who have a pure heart will see God just as Moses did. And what we know of Moses is that even though he did wrong early in his life by murdering an Egyptian, God nonetheless loved him and purified his heart to the extent that he would do anything that God asked. Moses even had such favor with God that he was able to intercede for the Israelites and save them from God's wrath—talk about the second Beatitude of mourning and interceding for others!

Educational Applications: Both Settings

A teacher applying this Beatitude helps the student to develop a clear conscience, since that is what purity is all about. Focusing on the three functions or operations of conscience, teachers make sure that the following occur:

1. Rules and expectations are clearly understood.
2. Students are held accountable for compliance.
3. Restitution and redemption are always lovingly administered so that the student experiences full forgiveness.

In this way, neither guilt nor shame lodge within the student. The teacher is ministering to the student as God would. The teacher's unconditional acceptance and freedom from judgment help the student to build and maintain a pure heart. As the teacher maintains this kind of godly behavior, the student learns to prefer the freedom of being genuine and has less and less tendency to make sin and its cover-up the mode of operation.

BEATITUDE #7

"Blessed Are the Peacemakers, For They Shall Be Called Sons of God."

The Hebrew word for peace—*shalom*—refers to blessedness across all of life's dimensions, the ultimate exterior manifestation of inward righteousness. Jesus said that peacemakers are blessed. A peace *maker* is more than a peace *keeper*. "Keeping" implies maintaining something that is already in existence whereas "making" implies creating something new. The peacemaker is both peaceable and a maker of peace, not just a keeper of preexisting peace. Peacemaking implies more than negotiation and compromise. It suggests living true to a standard of peace in the midst of other perspectives that are not peaceable. After all, to be a son of God means to bring into circumstances that which Father God would bring into the Kingdom.

Educational Applications: Both Settings

As supremely exemplified by Jesus, the Kingdom involves sacrificing and serving others in such a way as to establish an environment of *peace*. Teachers who want to see this Beatitude quality of peacemaking demonstrated by the students must first and regularly demonstrate it themselves. A teacher whose actions and intentions conform to this Beatitude brings all the qualities of the Kingdom into interactions with students. As a peacemaker, the teacher brings peace, quietness, and rest. The teacher takes responsibility for setting a classroom atmosphere reflective of Jesus and in which the gentle Holy Spirit would feel comfortable, thereby displacing potential disorder with peace.

    The teacher reflecting the peace of Jesus responds only as Jesus would to disagreements, arguments, resistance, misbehavior, and so on. In other words, the teacher does not respond in kind to disruptive behavior but remains unperturbed, demonstrating all the fruit of the Holy Spirit. The teacher does not take responsibility for student misbehavior but holds the students responsible for their own misbehavior.

    Current psychological literature calls this the act of setting boundaries. The teacher moves quickly past personal hurt from students, carries no grudges, and forgets past infractions of every student. In this way a peaceful atmosphere can exist where the student is not held responsible for past infractions that have been dealt with, especially when there are no undercurrents of resentment. Even disruptive, failing students will attend a class where the teacher is a peace lover. There is an orderly predictability in the classroom where both students and teacher are treated with respect, where failure is an opportunity for future success, and all mistakes are eventually forgotten.

    Interestingly, this Beatitude has great significance for the eighth and final Beatitude. That is, being a peacemaker is the direct opposite and sometimes the provoker of the persecution that comes from a Beatitude lifestyle.

BEATITUDE #8

**"Blessed Are Those Who Have Been Persecuted
For the Sake of Righteousness,
For Theirs Is the Kingdom of Heaven."**

**"Blessed Are You When Men Cast Insults at You,
And Persecute You, and Say All Kinds of Evil
Against You Falsely, On Account of Me."**

Here we have, for the first time, two statements (not just one) to explain a single Beatitude. Also, for the first time the Beatitude is clearly a negative as opposed to a positive statement. However, in spite of the severity of the negatives, God promises that the persecuted are blessed and will be perpetually blessed. This Beatitude calls teachers to mind and heart control in order to believe it and keep their actions in accord with it. They have to be single-minded with a focus on Jesus' open, inviting, outstretched arms beckoning them as they remain blinder-oblivious to all negative circumstances.

Educational Applications: Secular Setting

Standing up for what is right in the face of strong opposition is always a difficult thing to do, but we can give many examples both in history and current events where people stood for what was right no matter what the consequences. History is replete with examples of religious persecution to the point of martyrdom. Patriots such as Nathan Hale died for what he believed to be right and true. African Americans marched and stood for Civil Rights. Students in China and Iran protested for democracy. In all of these cases people where persecuted for their beliefs.

Students face forms of persecution every day. We can openly discuss those instances of bullying, prejudice, and intolerance of differences in the classroom. Students should be acknowledged when they properly stand their ground in the face of ridicule and resistance. They should be especially recognized when they stand up for someone else who is being persecuted.

Educational Applications: Christian Settings

Teachers following this Beatitude can minister to students who are being persecuted. In fact, the groundwork should already be in place. The teacher can implant in the minds and hearts of students Scripture verses on persecution like James 1:2-15, 1 Peter 4:12-19, 1 Peter 5:10-11, 1 Thessalonians 5:18, and Philippians 3:10. Similarly, teachers can present testimonials and accounts of believers who have experienced great joy and peace in persecution. And finally, teachers can pray for students and model the lifestyle so that students observe them and even pray for their teachers who are undergoing persecution. The greatest preparation for this Beatitude comes from an intimate relationship with God. Then it is natural to rejoice in persecution (1 Thessalonians 5:16-18) just like Paul and Silas did after being beaten and imprisoned (Acts 16:23-26). Miraculous release may similarly occur!

CONCLUSION

Each Beatitude statement explains three things—the besetting condition, the result of experiencing that condition, and the commendable result.

These eight Beatitudes describe a progressive pathway of sanctification that believers can expect to travel as they live for Jesus Christ. Both the first and the last Beatitudes seem to indicate that once starting on a blessed path, first toward sanctification and lastly toward heaven, the Kingdom will be the reward.

The journey through the Beatitudes is primarily an inward one between the individual and the Holy Spirit. The results are the outcome of the work of the Holy Spirit within the person. The Beatitudes are not to be viewed as personally directed compliance efforts to meet external standards. Instead, they describe outward indicators of internal changes consistent with the nature of Jesus Christ.

Classroom teachers in Christian settings can serve as facilitators and encouragers for students throughout the Beatitude progression. Educators in secular settings can model the Beatitudes and discuss them through everyday events and curricular content.

However, of all the helps the teacher can provide, the most significant is the role the teacher plays as a direct function of having personally experienced the very same Beatitude that each student is experiencing. Whatever Beatitude qualities the teachers possess and demonstrate, they reveal even without overt explanations from Scripture an outlook on life that can happen only with those who have made Jesus Lord and Savior of their lives. They have entrusted ownership and control of their lives to Jesus.

APPENDIX B

MULTIPLE INTELLIGENCES AND LEARNING STYLES INVENTORIES

Standard 1: Maximize the use of talents and abilities.

Exercise 1: Learning Styles Inventory

Directions: Read each question and indicate your preference as "seldom," "sometimes," or "often." Based upon the items selected as "often" representative of the learner, the teacher can determine the learning style strengths of the learner. See the description that follows of the three learning styles that emerge as strengths on the basis of responses to this inventory.

EXERCISE 1. LEARNING STYLES INVENTORY			
QUESTIONS	**Seldom**	**Sometimes**	**Often**
1. Can remember more about a subject through the lecture method with information, explanations and discussion.			
2. Prefer information to be presented through the use of visual aids.			
3. Like to write things down or to take notes for visual review.			
4. Prefer to make posters, physical models, or actual practice and some activities in class.			
5. Require explanations of diagrams, graphs, or visual directions.			
6. Enjoy working with my hands or making things.			
7. Am skillful with and enjoy developing and making graphs and charts.			
8. Can tell if sounds match when presented with pairs of sounds.			
9. Remember best by writing things down several times.			
10. Can understand and follow directions on maps.			
11. Do better at academic subjects by listening to lectures and tapes as opposed to reading a textbook.			
12. Play with coins or keys in pockets.			
13. Learn to spell better by repeating the words out loud than by writing the word on papers.			
14. Can better understand a news article by reading about it in the paper than by listening to the radio.			
15. Chew gum, smoke, or snack during studies.			
16. Feel the best way to remember is to picture it in your head.			

17. Learn spelling by tracing the letters with my fingers.			
18. Would rather listen to a good lecture or speech than read about the same material in a textbook.			
19. Am good at working and solving jigsaw puzzles and mazes.			
20. Play with objects in hands during learning period.			
21. Remember more by listening to the news on the radio rather than reading about it in the newspaper.			
22. Obtain information on an interesting subject by reading relevant materials.			
23. Feel very comfortable touching others, hugging, handshaking, etc.			
24. Follow oral directions better than written ones.			

Exercise 2: Match Learner Intelligences with Subject Preferences

EXERCISE 2: MATCH LEARNER INTELLIGENCES WITH SUBJECT PREFERENCES

Directions: For each type of intelligence in the left column, identify a subject area or areas to correspond with the learning preference.

Subjects: Math, science, social studies, language arts/reading, health and physical education, art, music. (Assume that technology is integrated into all subjects.)

Intelligences (Learning Styles)	Subject Preferences
Linguistic intelligence ("word smart")	
Logical-mathematical intelligence ("number/reasoning smart")	
Spatial intelligence ("picture smart")	
Bodily-Kinesthetic intelligence ("body smart")	
Musical intelligence ("music smart")	
Interpersonal intelligence ("people smart")	
Intrapersonal intelligence ("self smart")	
Naturalist intelligence ("nature smart")	

ABOUT THE THREE LEARNING STYLES

If you are an AUDITORY learner, you may wish to use CDs. Recorded lectures help you to fill in the gaps in your notes but do listen and take notes, reviewing notes frequently. Sit in the lecture hall or classroom where you can hear well. After you have read something, summarize it and recite it aloud.

If you are a VISUAL learner, then by all means be sure that you look at all study materials. Use charts, maps, filmstrips, notes and flashcards. Practice visualizing or picturing words/concepts in your head. Write out everything for frequent and quick visual review.

If you are a TACTILE learner, trace words as you are saying them. Facts that must be learned should be written several times. Keep a supply of scratch paper for this purpose. Taking and keeping lecture notes will be very important. Make study sheets.[410]

---

[410] Designer unable to be identified.

APPENDIX C

UNDERSTANDING RECIPROCAL RELATIONSHIPS

Standard 2: Operate with full awareness of the powerful inherent effects of reciprocal relationships

Exercise 3: Engaging in Communication as a Reciprocal Relationship

---

EXERCISE 3: ENGAGING IN COMMUNICATION AS A RECIPROCAL RELATIONSHIP

Research Findings on Interpersonal Communications:

- 55 percent of communication is non-verbal. It is very important to be mindful of non-verbal communications, such as facial expressions, eye contact, hand gestures, position and movement of the body, etc.

- 7 percent of communication is determined by the words used by the speaker.

- 38 percent of communication is determined by the voice quality of the speaker.

Activity: Improving communications with a challenging or difficult student whom you teach

Purpose: Improve interpersonal communications

What to do: Complete at least a 10-minute exchange (conversation) with three different students that you teach or work with on a regular basis. The conversation should be aimed at becoming better acquainted, such as learning about the interests and talents of each student. You should participate in the exchange as a researcher by making mental notes of each student's and your own verbal and non-verbal communication. Take particular note of non-verbal and verbal communications initiatives that you initiate and any apparent reactions or replies from the respondent.

Summary: Reflect upon each of the three exchanges. Which kinds of verbal and non-verbal actions and reactions were apparent during each interchange? How could you improve your interaction with each student? What are the implications of this exercise for your practice as an educator? In conclusion, what is one important finding that you derived from completion of this exercise?

Exercise 4: Student Understanding of Reciprocal Relationship2

EXERCISE 4: STUDENT UNDERSTANDING OF RECIPROCAL RELATIONSHIPS

Activity for Students: Role Playing

Directions for Students: Invite two students to participate in a role playing exercise to simulate a 5 minute discussion of a topic of their choosing. Other student class members will participate as observers of the two students involved in the role playing exercise. The observers should record notes about aspects of verbal and non-verbal communications of the two conversationalists. The observers should consider the following aspects of interpersonal communications:

- Facial Expressions
- Hand Gestures
- Voice Quality
- Body Position
- Bodily Movement

Summary: Reflect upon the peer interchange. Which kinds of verbal and non-verbal actions and reactions were apparent during the interchange? How could any one of the participants improve his/her interaction with the other student? What are the implications of this exercise for your success as a learner? As a final consideration, what is one important conclusion that you derived from completion of this exercise?

APPENDIX D

QUALITIES OF INDUSTRIOUSNESS

Standard 3: Demonstrate industriousness through dedication, commitment, patience and self-discipline

Exercise 5: Assessment and Instruction of Student Industriousness

---

EXERCISE 5: ASSESSMENT AND INSTRUCTION OF STUDENT INDUSTRIOUSNESS

Directions: This assessment may be used to analyze the behaviors of one class of students or groups of students in a particular setting. Circle the one rating for each criterion that represents the extent to which your students demonstrate behaviors associated with being industrious. Choose a rating of "1" up to "5". A rating of "1" indicates poor performance/infrequent demonstration of the behavior. A rating of "5" indicates high performance/frequent demonstration of the behavior.

Part I: Assessment of Student Industriousness	Part II. Assessment of Instruction to Promote Student Industriousness
To what extent do your students demonstrate these behaviors? A rating of "1" indicates seldom. A rating of "5" indicates often.	To what extent have you taught and emphasized the demonstration of these values and behaviors within your classroom or educational setting? A rating of "1" indicates seldom. A rating of "5" indicates often.
1. Commitment 1 2 3 4 5 2. Determination 1 2 3 4 5 3. Patience 1 2 3 4 5 4. Self-Discipline 1 2 3 4 5	1. Commitment 1 2 3 4 5 2. Determination 1 2 3 4 5 3. Patience 1 2 3 4 5 4. Self-Discipline 1 2 3 4 5

Exercise 6: Educator's Self-Assessment of Industriousness

EXERCISE 6. EDUCATOR'S SELF-ASSESSMENT OF INDUSTRIOUSNESS.

Directions. Industriousness refers to dedication, commitment, patience and self-discipline. These behaviors and attitudes result in the fulfillment of responsibilities in an earnest and diligent manner resulting in high quality educational service to all learners. Consider each of the factors below identified as major responsibilities of educators, particularly instructional personnel. Rate your performance on each responsibility by using the scale of 1 to 7, with "one" being very low and "seven" being very high. After completing the numerical rating, complete the follow-up questions to address ways that you can increase your industriousness on any two areas of low performance.

Self-Assessment of Industriousness for Major Responsibilities of Educators

CRITERIA	RATING OF INDUSTRIOUSNESS						
	Low		Average			High	
Daily Lesson Planning	1	2	3	4	5	6	7
Delivery of Instruction	1	2	3	4	5	6	7
Assessment of Learning	1	2	3	4	5	6	7
Collaborative Work with Colleagues	1	2	3	4	5	6	7
Classroom Management	1	2	3	4	5	6	7
Professional Development	1	2	3	4	5	6	7
Long Range Planning	1	2	3	4	5	6	7
Communication with learners	1	2	3	4	5	6	7
Communication with parents	1	2	3	4	5	6	7

Two Areas of Low Performance:

Area #1: _____

Area #2: _____

Ways that you can improve your performance in the two areas identified above.

Area #1: _____

Area #2: _____

Summary: What could be the specific impact of your improved performance on the achievement of students within your classes?

APPENDIX E
A CULTURE OF UNITY

Standard 4: Maintain and work within a culture of unity, agreement, and harmony as these factors directly influence outcomes and the attainment of success.

Exercise 7: Assessment of Aspects of School/Classroom Culture

EXERCISE 7: ASSESSMENT OF ASPECTS OF SCHOOL/CLASSROOM CULTURE

Directions. Complete the assessment using the ratings of: (+) much evidence of strategic attention to this area; (√) some evidence of attention to this area; and, (-) little, if any, evidence of strategic attention in this area. In the space labeled "evidence," please include examples or explanations to support your rating for each item.

ASPECTS OF SCHOOL/CLASSROOM CULTURE	RATING		
	+	√	-
1. Is there evidence that the **school leadership** promotes unity, agreement, an harmony within the chool?			
Evidence:			
2. Are school/classroom **rules and procedures** designed and u ed to promote a civil and caring environment, engaging input from major stakeholders such as students, parents, and teachers within the school?			
Evidence:			
3. Do the **mission and vision** of the school support unity, agreement, and harmony among all constituencies, including students, parents, teachers, and community members?			
Evidence:			
4. Do the school/classroom **core values** include the promotion of unity, agreement, and harmony among all constituencies?			
Evidence:			
5. Are **teachers** organized in collaborative teams with established channels to promote unity, harmony, and agreement as well as facilitate shared decision making?			
Evidence:			
6. Are **students** prepared and routinely engaged in classroom and school-based experiences that promote unity, agreement, and harmony among diverse groups?			
Evidence:			

Designed by Dr. Helen Stiff-Williams. All Rights Reserved. Permission for Use Required.

APPENDIX F

FIDELITY SELF-ASSESSMENT

Standard 5: Demonstrate fidelity (trustworthiness and honesty) to the instructional process at all times.

Exercise 8: Self-Assessment of Fidelity of Instruction

EXERCISE 8. SELF-ASSESSMENT OF FIDELITY OF INSTRUCTION

Directions. As explained within the chapter reading, fidelity refers to the consistent demonstration of the highest quality of classroom instruction to support the highest level of learning for all students. This exercise challenges educators to assess their fidelity in the implementation of instruction.

Read each item and indicate the extent to which you agree with the statement. In the space below each item, record a personal reflective statement about your rating with particular attention to ways that you make increase your fidelity to instruction.

1. I maximize my use of instructional time by committing every day and every instructional period to planned teaching.

Consistently	Often		Occasionally		Seldom	Rarely	
5		4		3		2	1

Reflective Statement: _____
_____
_____

2. I strategically plan instruction to address the individual needs of all learners.

Consistently	Often		Occasionally		Seldom	Rarely	
5		4		3		2	1

Reflective Statement: _____
_____
_____

3. I plan and deliver instruction that is directly aligned to the mandated standards for my school and/or district.

Consistently	Often		Occasionally		Seldom	Rarely	
5		4		3		2	1

Reflective Statement: _____
_____

---

4. I plan and appropriately use formative assessments to get feedback on the extent to which learners are being successful and to plan for the next phase of instruction.

Consistently	Often	Occasionally	Seldom	Rarely
5	4	3	2	1

Reflective Statement: _____

_____

_____

_____

5. I provide constructive feedback to every student to guide his/her identification of personal learning goals.

Consistently	Often	Occasionally	Seldom	Rarely
5	4	3	2	1

Reflective Statement: _____

_____

_____

_____

6. I use data on student achievement to plan strategically for addressing the learning needs of all students.

Consistently	Often	Occasionally	Seldom	Rarely
5	4	3	2	1

Reflective Statement: _____

_____

_____

_____

7. I use evidence-based instructional strategies in the delivery of instruction to maximize learning opportunities for all students.

Consistently	Often	Occasionally	Seldom	Rarely
5	4	3	2	1

Reflective Statement: _____

_____

_____

_____

8. I plan academic experiences that engage all students in active learning that result in products and performances as representation of newly acquired skills and knowledge.

Consistently	Often	Occasionally	Seldom	Rarely
5	4	3	2	1

Reflective Statement: _____

_____

_____

_____

9. I intentionally plan instruction that supports preparation of students in the 21st century skills, including critical thinking, use of technology, working in teams, leadership and self-directed learning.

Consistently	Often	Occasionally	Seldom	Rarely
5	4	3	2	1

Reflective Statement: _____

_____

_____

_____

10. My words, voice quality, body language communicate respect and acceptance that must be accorded all students to maintain a positive, supportive culture for learning.

Consistently	Often	Occasionally	Seldom	Rarely
5	4	3	2	1

Reflective Statement: _____

_____

_____

_____

SUMMARY:

1.) Based upon your self-assessment of fidelity, which two areas did you identify as strengths? Explain why you consider the two identified areas as strengths.

Strength #1: _____

_____

Strength #2: _____

_____

2.) In reviewing your assessment results, which two areas did you recognize as areas of weakness? Explain what you might do to improve your performance

Weakness #1: _____

_____

Weakness #2: _____

_____

APPENDIX G

EMBRACING CHANGE INVENTORY

Standard 6: Embrace change with the understanding that new, evidenced-based practices result in advancements and the best outcomes.

Exercise 9: The Skillful Teacher—Use of Research-Based Instructional Strategies

Directions: Reflect upon your teaching and rate your use of each strategy by putting an X in the appropriate column to the right. Use the scale of 1 to 5, with "1" indicating little or no (low) use of the strategy up to a rating of "5" indicating extensive and very regular (high) use of the strategy. For evidence, describe what you do as a teacher that supports your numerical rating.

EXERCISE 9. THE SKILLFUL TEACHER—USE OF RESEARCH-BASED INSTRUCTIONAL STRATEGIES	1 Low	2	3 Avg	4	5 High
1.) Use of study circles where students engage in a democratic process for sharing thoughts and concerns on a particular issue.					
Evidence:					
2.) Use of cooperative learning					
Evidence:					
3.) Create lots of opportunities for creative expression through the arts -- art, music, drama, writing, storytelling					
Evidence:					
4.) Use of hands-on learning					
Evidence:					
5.) Use of project-based learning					
Evidence:					
6.) Use of varied instructional modalities, such as modeling and role-playing.					
Evidence:					
7.) Use of interactive teaching methods					
Evidence:					

8.) Provide a positive and supportive personal relationship between teacher and students								
Evidence:								
9.) *Minimize the use* of external control (such as the use of rewards, grades, points; the use or threats of punishment; pervasiveness of teacher's control over students)								
Evidence:								
10.) Elicitation of student thinking and active discussion								
Evidence:								
TOTAL	Low		Avg		High			

APPENDIX H

ASSESSMENT OF CARING TEACHER BEHAVIORS

Standard 7: Demonstrate being humble, open, and receptive to ideas and innovations to achieve success.

Exercise 10: Self-Assessment of Caring Teacher Behaviors

EXERCISE 10. SELF-ASSESSMENT OF CARING TEACHER BEHAVIORS

Directions: Read each item. Circle the number that corresponds with how you perceive your behaviors to be manifested for each item.

1.) **I maintain a classroom environment that is comfortable for students.**

Consistently	Often	Occasionally	Seldom	Rarely	
5	4	3	2	1

2.) **I allow my students to explore the possibilities of learning without being punitive when they do not get the correct answer.**

Consistently	Often	Occasionally	Seldom	Rarely	
5	4	3	2	1

3.) **I manage the classroom in ways that avoid being overbearing and authoritarian.**

Consistently	Often	Occasionally	Seldom	Rarely	
5	4	3	2	1

4.) **I initiate special events and activities for students, such as field trips and times to celebrate accomplishments.**

Consistently	Often	Occasionally	Seldom	Rarely	
5	4	3	2	1

5.) **I find appropriate ways to get to know the families of my students.**

Consistently	Often	Occasionally	Seldom	Rarely	
5	4	3	2	1

6.) **I provide extra support for my students who are struggling.**

Consistently	Often	Occasionally	Seldom	Rarely	
5	4	3	2	1

7.) I use culturally responsive teaching practices to enhance learning opportunities for the diversity of students that I teach.

Consistently	Often	Occasionally	Seldom	Rarely
5	4	3	2	1

8.) I engage all of my students in helping to define the rules of the classroom.

Consistently	Often	Occasionally	Seldom	Rarely
5	4	3	2	1

9.) I use a classroom management approach to establish that each student is first responsible for his/her conduct.

Consistently	Often	Occasionally	Seldom	Rarely
5	4	3	2	1

10.) I use praise with ALL learners.

Consistently	Often	Occasionally	Seldom	Rarely
5	4	3	2	1

APPENDIX I

RESPONSIBILITY FOR 21ST CENTURY INSTRUCTIONAL PROFICIENCY

Standard 8: Demonstrate the moral obligation to perform to your best ability.

Exercise 11: Gauging Readiness for 21st Century Instruction

Directions: This activity aims to help educators assess their proficiencies in the planning and delivery of instruction to learners for 21st century preparedness. To complete the tasks, the educator should select one common core standard from the examples listed below. You should complete the series of tasks by using the same standard, one that is relevant to the age and/or grade group of students you are most familiar.

NATIONAL COMMON CORE STANDARDS[411]

EXERCISE 11. GAUGING READINESS FOR 21ST CENTURY INSTRUCTION		
GRADE LEVEL	**MATHEMATICS STANDARDS**	**ENGLISH/LANGUAGE ARTS STANDARDS**
Grade 2	Recognize and draw shapes having specified attributes, such as a given number of angles or a given number of equal faces. Identify triangles, quadrilaterals, pentagons, hexagons, and cubes.	Recount or describe key ideas or details from a text read aloud or information presented orally or through other media.
Grade 4	Fluently add and subtract multi-digit whole numbers using the standard algorithm.	Write narratives to develop real or imagined experiences or events using effective technique, descriptive details, and clear event sequences.
Grade 7	Solve real-world and mathematical problems involving the four operations with rational numbers.	Demonstrate command of the conventions of standard English capitalization, punctuation, and spelling when writing.
Grade 10 (Algebra)	Derive the formula for the sum of a finite geometric series (when the common ratio is not 1), and use the formula to solve problems. *For example, calculate mortgage payments.*	Acquire and use accurately general academic and domain-specific words and phrases, sufficient for reading, writing, speaking, and listening at the college and career readiness level; demonstrate independence in gathering vocabulary knowledge when considering a word or phrase important to comprehension or expression.

---

[411] Source: "Common Core State Standards" (2010). Accessed June 10, 2010, http://www.corestandards.org/the-standards.

FOCUS AREA	TASK	YOUR RESPONSE
1. National Curriculum	1. Analyze or "unpack" a common core standard to determine: a.) WHAT to teach for attainment of the standard b.) HOW to teach for attainment of the standard.	1.
2. Instructional Planning	2. Use the common core standard to write one SMART objective.	2.
3. Instructional Strategy	3. Identify one research-based instructional strategy for teaching the selected common core standard. Explain how the identified strategy can be effective for teaching the learners.	3.
4. Student Engagement	4. Identify the strategies that will be used to engage all learners in the learning process.	4.
5. Assessment of Learning	5. Given your selected common core standard, identify one formative assessment and one summative assessment for measuring student learning.	5.
6. Student Use of Technology	6. Identify technology and describe how students can be engaged in the use of technology to reach proficiency on the common core standard?	6.
7. Teacher Use of Technology	7. Identify technology and describe how you, as the teacher, can use technology to deliver instruction on the common core standard.	7.
8. Feedback to Learners	8. Describe how you, as the teacher, will provide feedback on academic performance to the learner and his/her parents.	8.
9. Classroom Setting	9. Describe how your 21st century classroom is arranged and managed.	9.

Summary:

1. Were you successful in completing all the tasks?
2. Did you identify focus areas where professional training would improve your readiness for executing your professional duties?
3. To what extent are your colleagues prepared in these focus areas?
4. Have you provided input to your supervisors to arrange for professional training on any of these areas?

APPENDIX J

INNOVATIONS FOR SUCCESS

Standard 9: Be innovative to achieve exceptional outcomes.

Exercise 12: Conduct Action Research: Elicit Ideas to Design Innovations for Success

Introduction: Action research involves the systematic gathering of data to be analyzed in order to derive grounded conclusions. To conduct this action research project, you, in the role of the researcher, must first establish a mindset that allows you to display humbleness and openness. Further, an invitational manner must be used to elicit ideas and thoughts from the diverse stakeholders to be tapped within your educational setting.

IMPORTANT: The researcher's demeanor, communication style, and creative processing will directly impact the outcome of the investigation. The overall aim of the action research project is to collect ideas, changes, strategies, or innovations that could improve educational services and student learning within your school or classroom. You are encouraged to collect an adequate amount of data so that you can deduce at least three grounded changes and three viable innovations capable of improving educational services within your school or classroom.

Directions:

1. Plan and conduct a brief conversation, about 10 minutes in duration, with each of the stakeholder representatives on the matrix below.
2. Invite each representative to share at least one idea, change, strategy or innovation that could improve educational services for students within your school or classroom setting.
3. Use brief follow up questions to clarify ideas and to promote deep thinking about the topic. Invite respondents to stretch their thinking and offer innovative changes.
4. Record notes from responses in the right column of the matrix.
5. Analyze the data (stakeholder responses) to determine at least three changes (ideas, strategies, innovations) to increase student learning within the educational setting.
6. Record three ideas, changes, or innovations in the section below the matrix.
7. Conclude this exercise by completing the item involving your reflection on the activity.

	EXERCISE 12. CONDUCT ACTION RESEARCH: ELICIT IDEAS TO DESIGN INNOVATIONS FOR SUCCESS	
STAKEHOLDER	**ACTIVITY** **(Prompt For Data Collection)**	**RECORD OF DATA** **(Responses Of Stakeholders)**
Student #1	Inquire of a low achieving student how his/her school achievement could be improved by changes to what happens in the classroom.	
Student #2	Inquire of an average achieving student how his/her school achievement could be improved by changes to what happens in the classroom.	
Student #3	Inquire of a high achieving student how his/her school achievement could be increased by changes to what happens in the classroom.	
Peer or Colleague	Inquire of a peer or colleague about what changes might be undertaken to increase student learning within your professional setting.	
Supervisor	Inquire of a supervisor about what changes might be undertaken to increase student learning within your professional setting.	
Parent	Invite a parent to identify changes that might be undertaken to increase student learning within the educational setting.	

Summary of Findings (derived from the data):

1. _____

2. _____

3. _____

<u>Identify Three Innovations (Substantive changes to be made in your professional practice):</u>

1. _____

2. _____

3. _____

<u>Reflection:</u>

Assess the extent of your openness, communication style, and receptivity during each interview. Did your demeanor and communication style positively or negatively impact your collection of data? To what extent were you open-minded and genuinely engaged in the pursuit of innovations to improve your professional practice?

APPENDIX K

MORAL AUTHORITY CASE STUDY

Standard 10: Use authority in responsible ways and recognize the moral obligation to treat others with dignity and respect.

Exercise 13: Case Study Analysis: Moral Use of Authority and Respectful Treatment of Others

---

EXERCISE 13. CASE STUDY ANALYSIS: MORAL USE OF AUTHORITY AND RESPECTFUL TREATMENT OF OTHERS

Directions: Read the poignant case study that is the real life story of an adult who was at-risk during her K-12 education. Reflect upon expectations for moral and responsible use of authority and treatment of others as you respond to the questions that follow.

Now that I am an adult of forty-eight years and have been involved in education and educating myself for thirty years, I realize now more than ever that I was an at-risk student. I shudder to think what might have happened to me if I had not allowed God to enter my life. What defined me as an at-risk student included: divorce in my home, mother only had an eighth grade education, father was an alcoholic who physically abused my older siblings, and I was molested by a former family member. As a result of all that I experienced as a child, I was severely insecure and found it very difficult to concentrate in school and I had great difficulty making friends.

I remember nearly going into a panic if a teacher called on me to answer a question or questioned me about the very vivid scratch marks that went up and down my arms. At one point as a fourth grade student, my school sent me, with my mother's permission, to a psychologist. Many of these discussions were kept secret from my mother because I was afraid of making things worse or messing up someone's life. During my visits to the psychologist's office, I also remember drawing pictures (which I was not very good at) and receiving a piece of candy when my time was up. My time in school included failing a grade, having poor grades and dealing with "pathetic" teachers. For example, when I was in sixth grade I had a teacher that told the class that if I could get a C or above on my Friday spelling test, she would give the whole class candy bars. To say the least, I was humiliated over and over in her classroom. As a result of my life's circumstance, I became depressed and suicidal and, at age thirteen, I attempted to end my life. I am sure along the way, there were teachers in my younger years who were trying to reach out to me, but I only recall a very, very, few in my high school years that impacted me positively.

As I have stated in early writings, I became involved in education because I wanted to be a person that could take all the ugliness of my past and allow God to use it for His good. I want to be that tool that the Master can use to help restore hope in children of all ages. The word of God states in 2 Cor 4:9 ... we are struck down but not destroyed, and in the same chapter verses 16-18 it says (my words), do not give up, our affliction is producing for us an eternal weight of glory. Don't focus on what is seen and temporary but what is unseen and eternal.

I have since the age of seventeen made the decision to focus on what is eternal and grow from my past and use it for good. I am keenly aware in today's society what many children face every day and even more severely, just as I did so many years ago.

Questions for Analysis and Reflection:

1. After reading the case study, identify three examples of inappropriate use of authority and unacceptable treatment of the learner.
    a. _____
    b. _____
    c. _____

2. If educators are guided by moral principles and deep respect for others, what changes might have been evident in the life story of this writer?
    d. _____
    e. _____
    f. _____

3. Consider your use of authority and treatment of others as an educator. Which behaviors and practices do you use that are commendable? Which behaviors and practices as an educator should you consider changing?
    g. _____

    h. _____

    i. _____

APPENDIX L

POST-ASSESSMENT: TEN PROFESSIONAL STANDARDS FOR PRACTICING THE SECRET KINGDOM PRINCIPLES

Exercise 14: Post-Assessment of Secret Kingdom Professional Standards for Educators

EXERCISE 14. POST-ASSESSMENT OF SECRET KINGDOM PROFESSIONAL STANDARDS FOR EDUCATORS

Directions: Read each of the criteria in the first column. Rate yourself on a scale from 1 to 5 as to the extent that you meet each criterion. Put an X in the column to indicate your numerical rating on each factor. Include a statement in the evidence area to support your rating.

EVALUATION CRITERIA	1 Low	2	3 Average	4	5 High
Standard 1: Use the talents and abilities of everyone involved.					
Evidence:					
Standard 2: Function with the full understanding that teaching and learning are reciprocal relationships.					
Evidence:					
Standard 3: Demonstrate industry as represented by dedication, commitment, patience, self-discipline.					
Evidence:					
Standard 4: Maintain a culture of unity, agreement, and harmony, knowing that these factors directly influence outcomes and success.					
Evidence:					
Standard 5: Demonstrate trustworthiness and honesty at all times.					
Evidence:					
Standard 6: Embrace change with the full understanding that new, evidenced-based practices will result in advancements and the best outcomes.					
Evidence:					
Standard 7: Demonstrate humbleness, openness, and receptivity to other's ideas and suggestions as contributions to success.					
Evidence:					
Standard 8: Demonstrate a moral commitment to the highest quality of professional performance.					
Evidence:					
Standard 9: Serve as an innovator to achieve exceptional outcomes.					
Evidence:					
Standard 10: Use authority in responsible ways and recognize the moral obligation to treat others with dignity and respect.					
Evidence:					
TOTALS					

Summary:
Standards with a rating of 5: _____
Standards with a rating of 4: _____
Standards with a rating of 3: _____
Standards with a rating of 2: _____
Standards with a rating of 1: _____

Review sections of chapter 14 that correspond with standards where you desire to make additional improvements.

Identify specific activities that you might use to improve your performance on the targeted standards.

Personal Reflections on the Assessment: